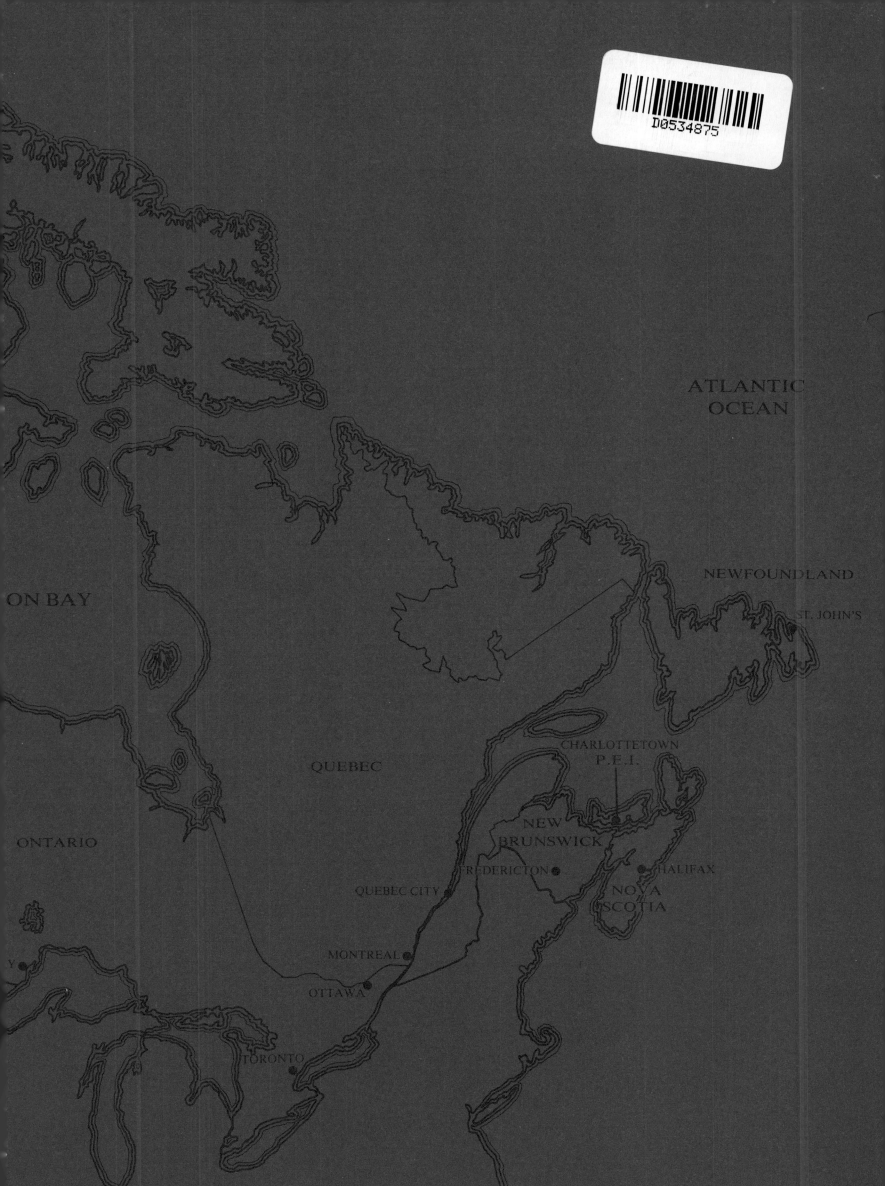

ATLANTIC
OCEAN

NEWFOUNDLAND

ST. JOHN'S

ON BAY

QUEBEC

CHARLOTTETOWN
P.E.I.

NEW
BRUNSWICK

ONTARIO

FREDERICTON

HALIFAX

NOVA
SCOTIA

QUEBEC CITY

MONTREAL

OTTAWA

TORONTO

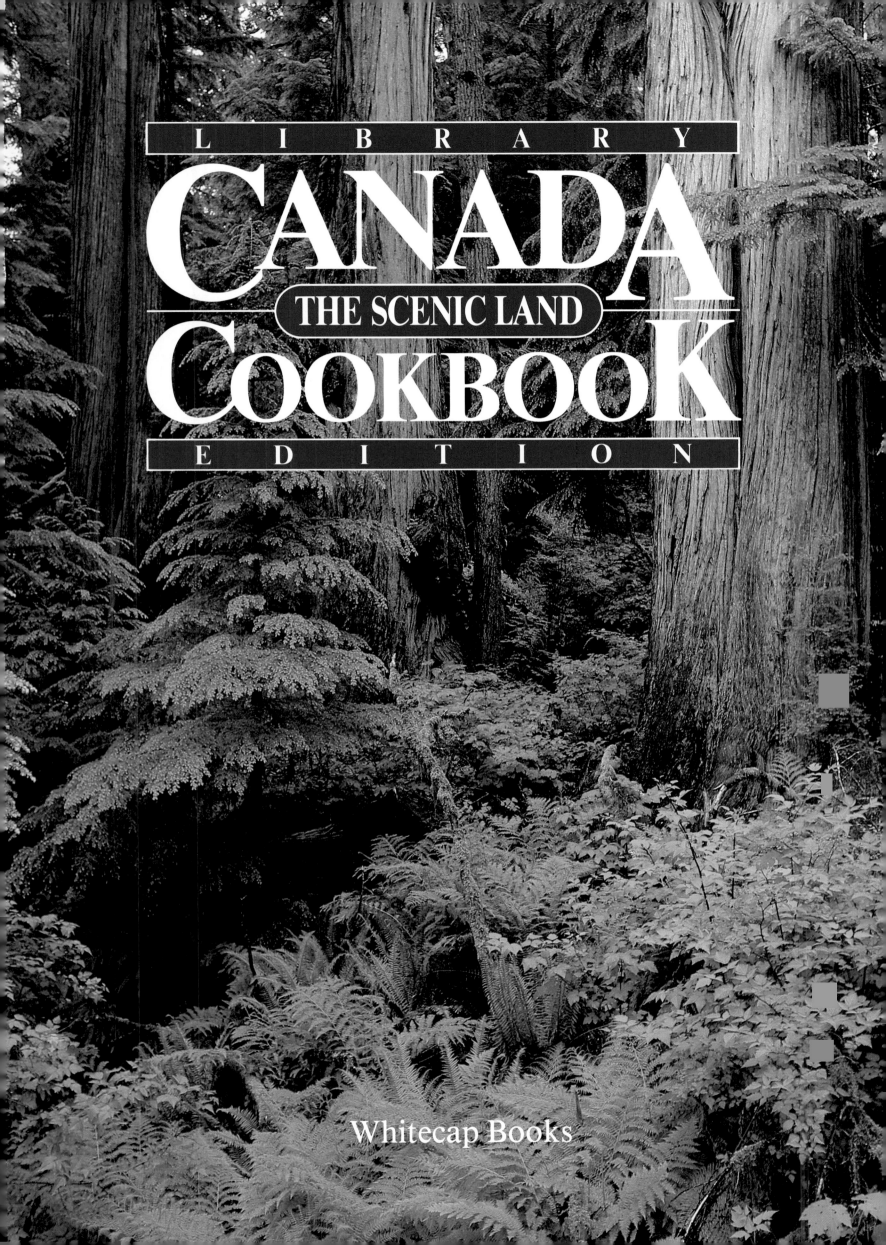

LIBRARY
CANADA
THE SCENIC LAND
COOKBOOK
EDITION

Whitecap Books

Published by
Whitecap Books Ltd.
1086 West 3rd Street
North Vancouver,
British Columbia,
Canada

© Whitecap Books Ltd.

Designed by Steve Penner

Printed and bound by
Friesen Printers

Food photography by
Pol Martin (Ont.) Ltd.

Printed in Canada

ISBN 0–920620–54–X

LIBRARY

CANADA

THE SCENIC LAND

COOKBOOK

EDITION

Compiled and edited by

POL MARTIN

Whitecap Books

North Vancouver, British Columbia, Canada

The Keltic Lodge, Ingonish, Nova Scotia

The Point Atkinson Lighthouse, West Vancouver, British Columbia.

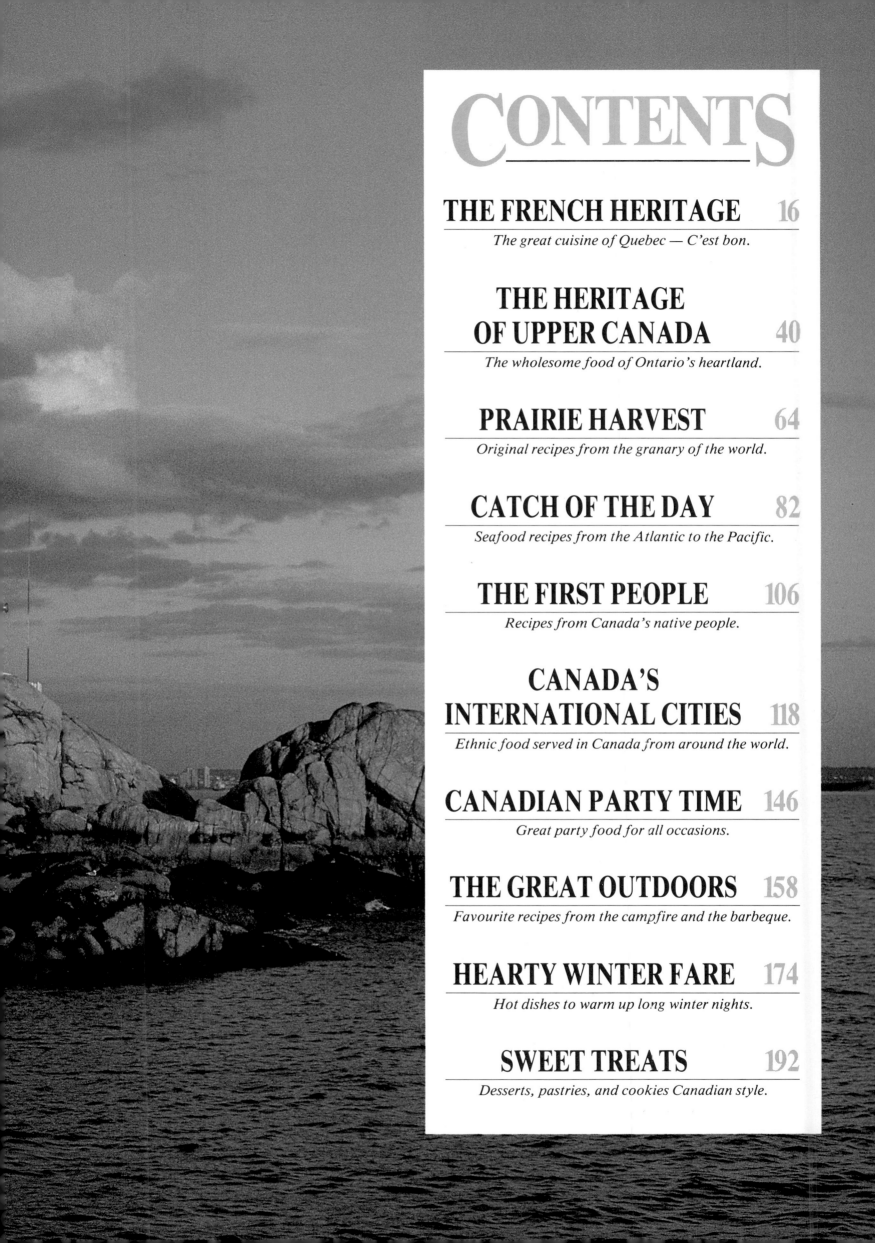

CONTENTS

THE FRENCH HERITAGE · 16
The great cuisine of Quebec — C'est bon.

THE HERITAGE OF UPPER CANADA · 40
The wholesome food of Ontario's heartland.

PRAIRIE HARVEST · 64
Original recipes from the granary of the world.

CATCH OF THE DAY · 82
Seafood recipes from the Atlantic to the Pacific.

THE FIRST PEOPLE · 106
Recipes from Canada's native people.

CANADA'S INTERNATIONAL CITIES · 118
Ethnic food served in Canada from around the world.

CANADIAN PARTY TIME · 146
Great party food for all occasions.

THE GREAT OUTDOORS · 158
Favourite recipes from the campfire and the barbeque.

HEARTY WINTER FARE · 174
Hot dishes to warm up long winter nights.

SWEET TREATS · 192
Desserts, pastries, and cookies Canadian style.

Moraine Lake, Banff National Park, Alberta.

Writing-on-Stone Provincial Park, Alberta.

HISTORY

Imagine a vast land of equal opportunity for all who wish to call it home. Imagine lush, green rolling hills beneath towering mountain tops, majestic thick forests housing only nature's wonder, miles and miles of prosperous plains, glistening streams and lakes nestled between villages, towns, and cities. Imagine a people with lasting traditions and strong beliefs — imagine Canada.

Canada is an active and enthusiastic country surrounded by three oceans: the Atlantic, the Pacific, and the Arctic. Being the second largest country in the world, Canada has always been very independent and proud. Inhabited by many who came to discover the mystery and fortune of the western world, Canada's population has remained an advantageous mix of different cultures. Undoubtedly, life in this huge country was very difficult and its people have proved their durability by overcoming hardships time and time again. Their persistence is seen in today's society as the people of Canada continue to prove that they belong to a hearty, strong-willed nation.

Canada's geographical diversity is among the most interesting in the world. From the fertile plains of the Prairies to the powerful mountain landscapes of British Columbia, this country provides beautiful attractions for both visitors and fortunate residents.

This book is a celebration of this scenic land and is dedicated to Canadians and friends near and far. It is a portrait of Canada's natural charm, its people and their diverse cuisine. We invite you to explore Canada, perhaps for the first time, or to remember and reminisce with us about the beauty you have seen and felt in this country.

We will be guiding you on a cross-country tour through the regional cuisines. After sampling just a few of these recipes, it will become obvious to newcomers that Canadians love to eat! And what better way to share Canada with old and new friends than to unite in enjoying this fabulous multicultural cuisine.

Sunrise Valley, Cape Breton, Nova Scotia.

Laval Avenue, Montreal, Quebec

THE
FRENCH HERITAGE

Though Canada's French heritage is scattered across the country, Quebec is the seat of French culture in Canada, and this province boasts a cuisine which is known world wide. French-Canadian cuisine has always been a special blend of wholesomeness, flair, and, of course, finesse.

Among countless specialties, perhaps the technique of making maple syrup is the best known. Even now, with other provinces sharing in the creation of maple syrup, Quebec proudly continues to provide 75 to 90% of Canada's supply. The unique goodness of maple is best savoured in traditional maple syrup pie garnished with a meringue topping.

For meat lovers, pork has been used in French-Canadian cooking for over 300 years and pork dishes such as Ragoût de Boulettes have long provided satisfaction for hearty appetites. Another unique creation using pork is French-Canadian Cretons, which becomes a tasty spread after several hours of stove-top simmering. Not surprising, this all-time favourite has remained so popular that it can be purchased in Quebec supermarkets.

Our selection of cuisine from Quebec would not be complete without including the famous Tourtière. A delicious mix of meats nestling in a rich pastry crust, this dinnertime pie is as popular today as it was years ago. Traditionally served on Christmas Eve after Midnight Mass, Tourtière is both wholesome and tasty.

With creativity and extreme pride, Canada's French people continue to lend the concept and secrets of their cuisine to those across the land. And so they should, for if a French-Canadian is asked to reveal the ultimate pleasure in life, the answer is not surprising. French-Canadians love to eat well!

Pot Roast

Serves 4 to 6

1.8 kg (4 pound) beef chuck in one piece
45 ml (3 tablespoons) melted butter
1 Spanish onion, thinly sliced
250 ml (1 cup) ketchup
125 ml (½ cup) chili sauce
30 ml (2 tablespoons) wine vinegar
salt and pepper

Preheat oven to 180°C (350°F).
Place chuck roast in roasting pan and brush with melted butter. Season well and cover with sliced onions.

In small bowl, mix ketchup, chili sauce and vinegar. Pour mixture over meat, cover and cook in oven for 2½ to 3 hours.

Serve with pickles and potatoes.

Veal Marengo

Serves 4

1.8 kg (4 pound) veal shoulder, cut into
2.5 cm (1 inch) cubes
45 ml (3 tablespoons) flour
30 ml (2 tablespoons) vegetable oil
2 onions, thinly sliced
6 tomatoes, peeled, seeded and diced
2 garlic cloves, smashed and chopped
250 ml (1 cup) hot chicken stock
1 bay leaf
1 ml (¼ teaspoon) basil
250 ml (1 cup) dry white wine
zest of 1 lemon
chopped parsley
salt and pepper from mill

Preheat oven to 180°C (350°F).
Pepper meat well and dredge with flour.
Heat vegetable oil in ovenproof casserole. Add meat; cook 3 to 4 minutes.

Add onions; continue cooking 3 to 4 minutes.

Add tomatoes, garlic, chicken stock, spices and lemon zest. Stir and bring to boil.

Pour wine into small saucepan and cook 3 to 4 minutes over high heat. Pour wine over meat mixture; cover and cook in oven for 1½ hours.

Serve with sautéed mushrooms and chopped parsley.

Sweet Chicken Legs

Serves 4

4 large chicken legs
45 ml (3 tablespoons) molasses
60 ml (4 tablespoons) chili sauce
1 onion, finely chopped
½ green pepper finely diced
5 ml (1 teaspoon) Worcestershire sauce
5 ml (1 teaspoon) prepared mustard
pinch cloves
salt and pepper

Preheat oven to 180°C (350°F).
Season chicken legs well and place in roasting pan.

In mixing bowl, combine remaining ingredients and pour over chicken legs. Cook 40 minutes in oven.

Baste chicken legs with sauce during cooking process. Serve with rice.

Raspberry Jam

1.5 L (6 cups) fresh raspberries
15 ml (1 tablespoon) wine vinegar
1.3 L (5½ cups) granulated sugar

Preheat oven to 130°C (270°F).
Wash raspberries and remove stems. Place in large saucepan and add vinegar; cover and cook 5 to 6 minutes over medium heat.

Pour sugar into large roasting pan. Place in oven and cook for 17 minutes. Then sprinkle sugar over raspberries and continue to cook 3 to 4 minutes.

Cool and pour jam into sterilized jars, wax and seal tight.

Remove saucepan from stove and cool 3 to 4 minutes under cold water. Drain well.

In small bowl, combine mustard, shallots, vinegar, salt and pepper. Add oil in thin stream mixing constantly with whisk. Add parsley and sprinkle with lemon juice.

Arrange leeks on service platter. Pour vinaigrette over leeks and let marinate 7 to 8 minutes. Serve.

Meat Pie

Serves 6

Dough:
500 ml (2 cups) all purpose flour
2 ml (¹/₂ teaspoon) salt
250 ml (1 cup) shortening
75 ml (5 tablespoons) cold water

Sift flour and salt in a mixing bowl.

With a pastry cutter, incorporate shortening into flour until mixture resembles coarse cornmeal.

Quickly add water and form into a ball. Lightly dust with flour and wrap in cloth. Refrigerate 3 to 4 hours.

30 ml (2 tablespoons) chopped onions
750 g (1¹/₂ pound) lean minced pork
5 ml (1 teaspoon) ground cloves
2 ml (¹/₂ teaspoon) savory
1 bay leaf
60 ml (4 tablespoons) cold water
1 uncooked potato, peeled and grated
pinch ground allspice
salt and pepper

Preheat oven to 180°C (350°F).

Mix onions, pork and spices in saucepan. Add bay leaf and water. Season with salt and pepper; cook for 10 minutes.

Add grated potato and continue to cook for 15 minutes. Remove saucepan from stove and let mixture cool for few minutes.

Remove bay leaf and skim off fat.

Line 22 cm (9–inch) pie plate with pastry and fill with meat mixture. Cover with pastry, seal edges and cut small steam vents in top of pie. Bake in oven for 40 to 45 minutes.

Serve with tomato ketchup.

Leeks Vinaigrette

Serves 4

8 leeks
15 ml (1 tablespoon) Dijon mustard
15 ml (1 tablespoon) chopped dry shallots
50 ml (¹/₄ cup) wine vinegar
175 ml (³/₄ cup) vegetable oil
15 ml (1 tablespoon) chopped parsley
juice ¹/₂ lemon
salt and pepper

Trim leeks: Cut off root ends and green stems. Cut each in four lengthwise being careful not to cut all the way through the root end. Wash thoroughly.

Place leeks in saucepan containing 1.5 L (6 cups) salted water. Add lemon juice and bring to boil. Cook 15 minutes at medium heat.

Pâté

Serves 6 to 8

Spiced salt:
> 5 ml (1 teaspoon) thyme
> 5 ml (1 teaspoon) basil
> 30 ml (2 tablespoons) salt
> 25 ml (1½ tablespoons) pepper
> 5 ml (1 teaspoon) sage

Mix all ingredients and set aside.

Pâté:
> 12 thin slices lard
> 45 ml (3 tablespoons) chopped parsley
> 500 g (1 pound) lean minced pork
> 375 g (¾ pound) minced pork
> 375 g (¾ pound) minced chicken liver
> 45 ml (3 tablespoons) cognac
> 40 ml (2½ tablespoons) spiced salt

> 15 ml (1 tablespoon) flour
> 3 garlic cloves, smashed and chopped
> 2 whole eggs
> 1 medium chopped onion
> 2 bay leaves

Preheat oven to 180°C (350°F).

Line pâté mould with slices of lard.

In food processor or bowl, mix parsley, meat, cognac, spiced salt, flour and garlic.

Add eggs and onions; mix well.

Pour mixture in pâté mould and cover with remaining slices of lard. Place 2 bay leaves on top of lard, cover and place mould in roasting pan containing 2.5 cm (1 inch) hot water.

Cook in oven for 1 hour 45 minutes.

Once pâté is cooked, remove from oven. Remove cover and place plate on top of pâté. Put a weight on plate to press pâté. Leave pâté on kitchen counter for 2 hours.

Remove weight and plate from pâté and replace cover.

Refrigerate for 12 hours.

The Chateau Frontenac, Quebec City.

Rabbit With Maple Syrup

Serves 4

1 — 2.3 to 2.7 kg (5 to 6 pound) rabbit
30 ml (2 tablespoons) melted butter
45 ml (3 tablespoons) maple syrup
15 ml (1 tablespoon) chopped parsley
2 shallots, finely chopped
125 ml (½ cup) dry white wine
250 ml (1 cup) light chicken stock, hot
15 ml (1 tablespoon) cornstarch
30 ml (2 tablespoons) cold water
pinch thyme
salt and pepper

Preheat oven to 220°C (425°F).

Cooking time: 12 minutes per pound.

Season rabbit well.

Mix together butter and maple syrup. Brush rabbit generously with mixture.

Place rabbit in roasting pan and sear at 220°C (425°F) for 15 minutes. Reduce heat to 200°C (400°F) and continue cooking for 1 hour.

Baste meat 2 to 3 times during cooking.

Remove rabbit from roasting pan and keep warm on service platter.

Place roasting pan on stove top over high heat. Add thyme, parsley and shallots; cook 2 minutes.

Add wine and cook 3 minutes.

Add chicken stock; stir well.

Mix cornstarch with cold water. Incorporate mixture into sauce.

Cut rabbit into pieces and serve with sauce, Parisienne potatoes and steamed broccoli.

Grand-pères

Serves 4

500 ml (2 cups) all-purpose flour
30 ml (2 tablespoons) baking powder
2 ml (¹/₂ teaspoon) salt
2 large eggs, beaten
250 ml (1 cup) milk
15 ml (1 tablespoon) melted butter
1 L (4 cups) fresh maple syrup
icing sugar

Sift flour, baking powder and salt into bowl. Add eggs and milk; mix well and pass through a sieve. Add melted butter and mix well. Refrigerate 1 hour.

Pour maple syrup into large saucepan and bring to boil. Drop 15 ml (1 tablespoon) dough into syrup and cook 4 to 6 minutes.

Sprinkle with icing sugar. Serve.

Ketchup, French Style

15 ml (1 tablespoon) oil
60 ml (4 tablespoons) chopped onions
1 garlic clove, smashed and chopped
12 large tomatoes, peeled and chopped
2 celery, washed and diced
1¹/₂ red peppers, diced
¹/₂ green pepper, diced
2 ml (¹/₂ teaspoon) dry mustard
2 ml (¹/₂ teaspoon) allspice
2 ml (¹/₂ teaspoon) cloves
250 ml (1 cup) white vinegar
salt and pepper

Heat oil in large saucepan. Add onions, garlic and tomatoes. Season well; cover and cook for 30 minutes. Pour mixture into blender and purée.

Pour purée into saucepan and add remaining ingredients. Season well. Bring to boil and cook 1 hour 15 minutes over low heat.

Cool and pour into sterilized jars, wax and seal tight.

Maple-Glazed Baked Ham

Serves 6 to 8

1 — 3.6 to 4.5 kg (8 to 10 pound) fully cooked bone-in ham
15 whole cloves
50 ml (¹/₄ cup) maple syrup
15 ml (1 tablespoon) soya sauce
15 ml (1 tablespoon) brown sugar
375 ml (1¹/₂ cups) hot chicken stock
15 ml (1 tablespoon) cornstarch
30 ml (2 tablespoons) cold water
¹/₂ green pepper, thinly sliced
¹/₂ red pepper, thinly sliced
pinch cinnamon

Preheat oven to 180°C (350°F).

Remove excess fat from ham. Stud ham with cloves.

Mix together maple syrup, soya sauce and brown sugar. Brush ham with mixture and sprinkle with cinnamon.

Place ham, fat side up, in a roasting pan and cook in oven for 1 hour. Baste often during cooking.

Remove ham and set aside.

Place roasting pan on stove top and pour in chicken stock; stir and cook 3 minutes.

Mix cornstarch with cold water. Incorporate mixture into sauce. Add peppers and cook 3 minutes over low heat.

Serve ham with sauce, mashed potatoes and cherry tomatoes.

Fall colours near St. Augustine, Quebec.

Potato Salad

Serves 4

*5 large potatoes, cooked, peeled and
sliced
1 cucumber, peeled, seeded and thinly
sliced
60 ml (4 tablespoons) wine vinegar
75 ml (5 tablespoons) vegetable oil
50 ml ($^{1}/_{4}$ cup) yogurt
50 ml ($^{1}/_{4}$ cup) mayonnaise
15 ml (1 tablespoon) fresh basil
15 ml (1 tablespoon) chopped fresh
chives
lemon juice
salt and pepper*

In bowl, place potatoes and cucumber; season well. Add vinegar and oil.

Mix yogurt with mayonnaise and incorporate to potatoes.

Add remaining ingredients; mix well. Serve.

Baked Beans,
French Canadian Style

Serves 4 to 6

*500 g (1 pound) dry white beans
1.5 L (6 cups) cold water
250 g ($^{1}/_{2}$ pound) salted pork fat
15 ml (1 tablespoon) dry mustard
1 onion, chopped
125 ml ($^{1}/_{2}$ cup) tomato ketchup
50 ml ($^{1}/_{4}$ cup) molasses
1 garlic clove, smashed and chopped
1.3 L (5 cups) hot water
salt and pepper*

Preheat oven to 150°C (300°F).

Place beans in bowl. Add cold water and let soak for 12 hours.

Pour beans and liquid in large saucepan and bring to boil. Cook for 30 minutes.

Drain beans and place them in bean pot. Add remaining ingredients and hot water; mix well. Cover and cook 3 hours in oven.

Remove cover and continue to cook 1 hour in oven.

Serve with bacon and fresh bread.

Beef à la Mode

Serves 4

*250 g ($^{1}/_{2}$ pound) salted pork, cubed
1.6 kg (3$^{1}/_{2}$ pound) beef round, cubed
3 onions, sliced
5 ml (1 teaspoon) allspice
50 ml ($^{1}/_{4}$ cup) flour
salt and pepper from mill
water*

Preheat oven to 150°C (300°F).

In ovenproof casserole, place salted pork. Add one layer of beef and one layer of onions. Season with salt and pepper. Sprinkle with flour.

Repeat to use all remaining meat and onions. Sprinkle with flour and allspice. Cover completely with water; bring to boil. Cover and cook in oven for 3 hours. Serve.

Beef and Barley Soup

Serves 4

375 ml (1½ cups) hulled barley
1.2 kg (2½ pound) beef brisket
4 L (16 cups) water
4 parsley sprigs
2 ml (½ teaspoon) thyme
2 ml (½ teaspoon) savory
1 bay leaf
1 large celery stalk, diced
2 large carrots, peeled and diced
1 Spanish onion cut into small cubes
salt and pepper

Place barley into bowl and cover with lukewarm water. Soak for 2 hours. Drain.

Place beef brisket in large saucepan. Add 4 L (16 cups) water. Bring to boil and remove scum.

Add barley, parsley, thyme, savory and bay leaf. Cook for 2 hours over low heat.

Add vegetables and cook a further 30 minutes.

Remove meat and dice. Return diced meat to soup. Mix and serve.

Brome Lake Duck

Serves 2

1 – 2.3 kg (5 pound) Brome Lake Duck
1 bay leaf
1 stalk celery, chopped
1 small onion, chopped
10 mushrooms, washed and cut in 2
1 L (4 cups) water
30 ml (2 tablespoons) melted butter
3 dry shallots, chopped
125 ml (½ cup) white wine
25 ml (1½ tablespoons) cornstarch
30 ml (2 tablespoons) cold water
30 ml (2 tablespoons) yogurt
pinch thyme
pinch rosemary
salt and pepper

Preheat oven to 190°C (375°F).

Cut legs from duck, remove skin and discard.

Place legs in saucepan. Add spices, bay leaf, celery, onions and mushrooms. Season to taste. Add water and bring to boil. Cook for 1 hour over medium heat.

Strain liquid and set aside 375 ml (1½ cups).

Cut breast from duck, remove skin and discard.

Melt butter in skillet. Add duck breast and cook 3 to 4 minutes on each side.

Add shallots and white wine.

Place skillet in oven and continue cooking for 15 to 18 minutes.

Remove breast from skillet and transfer to service platter.

Place skillet on stove top and add 375 ml (1½ cups) duck stock. Bring to boil.

Mix cornstarch with cold water and incorporate into sauce. Simmer for 3 minutes.

Place legs and breast in sauce. Add yogurt and cook 2 minutes over low heat.

Serve with steamed broccoli.

French–Canadian Crêtons

1.4 kg (3 pound) pork loin, deboned and diced into cubes
3 pork kidneys, cleaned and minced
2 large onions, diced
250 g (½ pound) kidney fat
2 ml (½ teaspoon) allspice
1 ml (¼ teaspoon) cloves
pinch nutmeg
salt and pepper

Rinse meat under cold water and place in bowl. Add onions and refrigerate for 8 hours.

Place kidney fat in large saucepan. Add meat and all remaining ingredients. Season well with salt and pepper. Cover with water and bring to boil; cook for 1½ hours over medium heat stirring once or twice during cooking. Add water if necessary.

When mixture is cooked, remove from stove and cool. Pour into small soufflé dishes. Refrigerate.

Serve cold with French bread.

Montreal Vegetable Soup

Serves 4

15 ml (1 tablespoon) butter
1 chopped onion
1 stalk celery cut into julienne style
3 branches chinese cabbage cut into julienne style
1 green pepper cut into julienne style
1 red pepper cut into julienne style
1.5 L (6 cups) light chicken stock, hot
1 ml (¼ teaspoon) oregano
1 bay leaf
pinch thyme
few sprigs parsley
salt and pepper

Melt butter in large saucepan. Add vegetables and season well. Cover and cook 8 to 10 minutes over low heat stirring twice during cooking.

Pour in chicken stock and spices; stir and bring to boil. Serve.

Fricassée, Grandmother Style

Serves 4

50 ml (¼ cup) bacon or chicken fat
1 Spanish onion, diced
750 ml (3 cups) cooked beef, diced
3 potatoes, diced
1 ml (¼ teaspoon) ground cloves
pinch savory
salt and pepper

Melt bacon fat in ovenproof casserole. Add onions; cook 2 to 3 minutes.

Add meat and potatoes. Season well with salt and pepper. Add spices. Cover with water. Place lid on casserole and cook on stove top 1 hour over low heat.

Serve with marinated beets.

Pea Soup

Serves 4 to 6

300 ml (1¼ cups) yellow split peas
45 ml (3 tablespoons) butter
1 chopped onion
1 carrot, finely chopped
1 bay leaf
1.8 L (7 cups) water
125 g (¼ pound) precooked ham, diced
pinch thyme
pinch basil
salt and pepper

Place peas in bowl, cover with water and let soak for 8 hours. Drain well.

Melt 15 ml (1 tablespoon) butter in large saucepan. Add onions and carrots; cover and cook 3 to 4 minutes.

Add peas and spices. Season with salt and pepper. Add water and bring to boil. Cover saucepan partially and cook 30 minutes over medium heat.

Add ham. Season to taste. Cover saucepan partially and continue to cook for 1 hour.

Just before serving, add remaining butter.

Onion Soup au Gratin

Serves 4

30 ml (2 tablespoons) butter
3 medium size onions, thinly sliced
45 ml (3 tablespoons) cognac
30 ml (2 tablespoons) flour
1.5 L (6 cups) hot beef stock
1 bay leaf
375 ml (1¹/₂ cups) grated Gruyère cheese
4 slices toasted french bread
freshly ground pepper
few drops Tabasco sauce
salt
4 ovenproof earthenware onion soup bowls

In medium size saucepan, melt butter over high heat. Add onions; simmer, uncovered, for 20 minutes over low heat, stirring occasionally.

Pour cognac over onions and reduce liquid by ²/₃ over high heat. Sprinkle with flour; cook 1 minute.

Gradually mix in beef stock. Add bay leaf and season with salt and pepper. Bring liquid to boil over high heat. Cook, uncovered, for 30 minutes over low heat, stirring occasionally.

Add few drops Tabasco sauce. Correct seasoning.

Preheat oven to broil.

Place 15 ml (1 tablespoon) grated cheese in the bottom of each bowl. Remove bay leaf and pour into soup bowl. Cover with slice of toasted bread and sprinkle with grated cheese.

Broil soup, in middle of oven, for 10 minutes. Serve.

Fiddlehead Soup

Serves 4

60 ml (4 tablespoons) butter
500 g (1 pound) fiddleheads, washed and drained
65 ml (4¹/₂ tablespoons) flour
1.2 L (5 cups) hot chicken stock
50 ml (¹/₄ cup) light cream
pinch nutmeg
juice ¹/₄ lemon
few drops Tabasco sauce
salt and pepper

Melt butter in large saucepan. Add fiddleheads; season with salt and pepper. Cover and cook 3 to 4 minutes.

Add flour; mix well and cook 1 minute.

Add chicken stock and spices. Season to taste. Bring to boil and cook 30 minutes over medium heat.

Pass soup through food mill. Incorporate cream and sprinkle with lemon juice. Serve.

Tomato Soup

Serves 4

45 ml (3 tablespoons) butter
1 large onion, diced
1 celery stalk, diced
12 large tomatoes, peeled
5 ml (1 teaspoon) sugar
1 celery heart, diced
1 bay leaf
125 ml (¹/₂ cup) heavy cream
fresh basil
salt and pepper

Melt butter in saucepan. Add onions and celery; cover and cook 5 to 6 minutes over low heat.

Add remaining ingredients (except cream) and season well. Stir, cover and bring to boil. Cook 30 minutes over low heat.

Pass soup through food mill. Add cream, stir and pour in saucepan; simmer 2 minutes to heat cream. Serve.

Roquefort Salad

Serves 4

Roquefort dressing:
    15 ml (1 tablespoon) Dijon mustard
    45 ml (3 tablespoons) wine vinegar
    120 ml (8 tablespoons) olive oil
50 ml (¹/₄ cup) mashed Roquefort cheese
    30 ml (2 tablespoons) yogurt
        paprika
        salt and pepper

In small bowl, combine mustard, salt, pepper and vinegar. Add olive oil, in steady stream, mixing constantly with whisk.

Add cheese and paprika; mix well. Incorporate yogurt. Set aside.

Salad:
    2 Boston lettuce, washed and dried
    2 large tomatoes cut in sections
        4 sliced radishes
1 cucumber peeled, seeded and sliced
    2 hard boiled eggs, sliced
125 ml (¹/₂ cup) Roquefort dressing
        lemon juice
        bacon bits
        salt and pepper

In large salad bowl, place lettuce, tomatoes, radishes, cucumbers and eggs. Mix well. Season to taste and sprinkle with lemon juice.

Add Roquefort dressing, mix and top with bacon bits. Serve.

Ham Casserole

Serves 4

50 ml (¹/₄ cup) salted pork, cut into
    small cubes
1 onion, cut into small cubes
2 green onions, cut into small pieces
4 potatoes peeled and thinly sliced
500 ml (2 cups) diced cooked ham
30 ml (2 tablespoons) flour
625 ml (2¹/₂ cups) milk
1 ml (¹/₄ teaspoon) thyme
    pinch nutmeg
salt and pepper

Preheat oven to 160°C (325°F).
Cook salted pork in saucepan for 2 minutes. Add onions; cook 3 minutes.

In ovenproof casserole, place one potato layer and sprinkle with cooked onions and salted pork.

Add ham. Repeat layers. Season well with salt and pepper. Sprinkle with spices.

Mix flour and milk. Pour mixture over ham; cover and cook in oven for 40 minutes. Then remove cover and continue to cook for 10 minutes. Serve.

Roast Leg of Lamb with Garlic

Serves 4 to 6

1 leg of lamb 2.7 kg (6 pound)
2 garlic cloves cut in three
45 ml (3 tablespoons) melted butter
1 onion, chopped
1 carrot peeled and chopped
1 small celery branch, chopped
1 bay leaf
500 ml (2 cups) light beef stock, hot
25 ml (1½ tablespoons) cornstarch
45 ml (3 tablespoons) cold water
pinch thyme
pinch oregano
salt and pepper

Preheat oven to 220°C (425°F).

Remove skin and excess fat from lamb. Stud meat with garlic and place in roasting pan. Season well with salt and pepper. Baste meat generously with melted butter.

Cook in oven at 220°C (425°F) for 30 minutes. Baste and reduce heat to 190°C (375°F) and continue to cook for 35 to 40 minutes.

20 minutes before end of cooking: Add remaining butter, onions, carrots, celery and spices to roasting pan.

When meat is done, remove from roasting pan and let stand 7 minutes.

Place roasting pan on stove top. Pour in beef stock and season well. Cook 5 to 6 minutes over high heat.

Mix cornstarch with cold water and incorporate into sauce. Pass sauce through sieve. Serve with lamb and garnish with green vegetables.

Caesar Salad

Serves 4

15 ml (1 tablespoon) Dijon mustard
2 garlic cloves, smashed and chopped
5 anchovy filets, chopped
15 ml (1 tablespoon) chopped parsley
45 ml (3 tablespoons) wine vinegar
125 ml (½ cup) olive oil
1 romaine lettuce, washed and dried
1 egg cooked 1½ minutes in boiling water, chopped
125 ml (½ cup) parmesan cheese
375 ml (1½ cups) garlic croûtons
5 slices bacon cooked crisp and cut into pieces
juice of 1 lemon
salt and pepper

Rising 86 metres Percé Rock in the Gaspé Peninsula is now a tourist destination. In 1534 Jacques Cartier anchored nearby to claim the region for France.

Place mustard into large wooden bowl. Add garlic, anchovies and parsley. Mix well with back of spoon.

Add lemon juice and vinegar. Season with salt and pepper; mix well.

Incorporate oil mixing constantly with a whisk.

Break lettuce leaves into large pieces and add to vinaigrette. Add egg; mix well.

Sprinkle with parmesan cheese, croûtons and bacon. Mix and serve.

Braised Pork Chops with Apples
Serves 4

8 pork chops, 2 cm (³/₄ inch) thick
15 ml (1 tablespoon) vegetable oil
1 garlic clove, cut in 3
30 ml (2 tablespoons) butter
3 large apples, cored, peeled and sliced
15 ml (1 tablespoon) maple syrup
30 ml (2 tablespoons) plain yogurt
pinch cinnamon
salt and pepper

Trim off most fat from pork chops. Season chops well with salt and pepper.

Heat oil in sauté pan. Add garlic; cook 2 minutes. Remove garlic.

Place pork chops in hot oil; cook 5 minutes or more on each side, depending on thickness. Remove pork chops and transfer to service platter. Keep warm in oven at 70°C (150°F).

Melt butter in sauté pan. Add apples and maple syrup; cover and cook 7 to 8 minutes.

Add cinnamon, mix and continue cooking for 2 minutes. Incorporate yogurt and simmer few seconds.

Serve with pork chops.

Beef Bourguignon
Serves 4

1.6 kg (3¹/₂ pound) beef chuck, cut into
2.5 cm (1 inch) pieces
250 ml (1 cup) flour
45 ml (3 tablespoons) melted butter

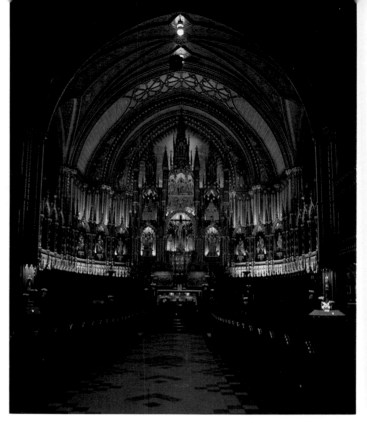

Notre-Dame Church in Montreal was built in 1829 and resembles Notre-Dame Cathedral in Paris.

1 onion, chopped
2 garlic cloves, smashed and chopped
15 ml (1 tablespoon) parsley
500 ml (2 cups) dry red wine
500 ml (2 cups) brown sauce
1 bay leaf
30 ml (2 tablespoons) oil
250 g (¹/₂ pound) fresh mushrooms,
washed and cut in two
250 ml (1 cup) cooked small onions
garlic croûtons
salt and pepper

Preheat oven to 180°C (350°F).

Dredge meat with flour. Season with pepper.

Heat half of butter in sauté pan. Add half of meat and cook 3 minutes on each side. Repeat for remaining meat.

Return all meat to sauté pan. Add chopped onions, garlic and parsley; mix and cook for 2 minutes.

Incorporate red wine and cook 3 to 4 minutes over high heat to evaporate alcohol.

Add brown sauce and bay leaf; cover and cook 2 hours in oven.

10 minutes before end of cooking: Heat oil in frying pan. Add mushrooms. Season with salt and pepper; cook 3 minutes.

Add small onions; cook 1 minute. Place with meat.

Serve with garlic croûtons.

Lac St-Jean Tourtière

Serves 4 to 6

*1 – 1.4 kg (3 pound) chicken, deboned,
skinned and diced*
500 g (1 pound) pork, diced
500 g (1 pound) veal, diced
1 small rabbit, deboned and diced
1 large onion, chopped
1 ml (¼ teaspoon) cloves
2 ml (½ teaspoon) cinnamon
1 garlic clove, smashed and chopped
3 potatoes, peeled and diced
salt and pepper from mill
*pastry dough, enough to cover bottom,
sides and top of roasting pan*

Place chicken, pork, veal and rabbit in bowl. Add onions and spices. Season with salt and pepper. Refrigerate for 12 hours.

Preheat oven to 190°C (375°F).

Cover bottom and sides of roasting pan with pastry dough. Spread one meat layer in roasting pan. Add one potato layer and season well with salt and pepper. Repeat layers. Cover with water. Cover with dough and seal edges.

Place roasting pan in oven and cook 40 minutes at 190°C (375°F). Reduce heat to 120°C (250°F) and continue to cook for 2½ hours. Serve.

Ragoût de Boulettes

Serves 4

2 pork hocks, washed
1 large Spanish onion, sliced
500 g (1 pound) lean ground pork
45 ml (3 tablespoons) chopped onions
1 ml (¼ teaspoon) allspice
15 ml (1 tablespoon) bacon fat
*125 ml (½ cup) flour, grilled under
broiler*
1 ml (¼ teaspoon) cinnamon
1 ml (¼ teaspoon) cloves
salt and pepper
all-purpose flour

In large saucepan, place pork hocks and sliced onions; cover with water and bring to boil. Cook 2 hours over medium heat or until meat separates from bone.

Remove fat from pork hocks. Discard fat and bone. Set aside meat. Pass cooking liquid through sieve and reserve.

In large mixing bowl, mix meat, chopped onions and allspice. Season well with salt and pepper. Form mixture into small balls.

Roll meat balls lightly into all-purpose flour. Remove excess flour.

Melt bacon fat in frying pan over high heat. Add meat balls and sear 2 to 3 minutes on each side.

Pour strained cooking liquid into large saucepan. Add pork hock meat and meat balls; cook for 10 minutes.

Meanwhile, mix grilled flour with 375 ml (1½ cups) water. Incorporate mixture into cooking liquid. Add spices and correct seasoning. Cook until sauce is thick. Serve.

Chicken Sautéed in Red Wine

Serves 4

2 chickens, 1.5 kg (3 pounds) each
250 ml (1 cup) flour
6 slices bacon
2 shallots, chopped
45 ml (3 tablespoons) chopped onions
2 garlic cloves, smashed and chopped
500 ml (2 cups) dry red wine
50 ml (¼ cup) brandy
1 bay leaf
1 ml (¼ teaspoon) thyme
250 ml (1 cup) brown sauce
45 ml (3 tablespoons) butter
*500 g (1 pound) fresh mushrooms,
washed and cut in two*
*250 ml (1 cup) small white onions,
cooked*
chopped parsley
salt and pepper

Preheat oven to 180°C (350°F).

Cut chicken in 8 pieces and remove skin.

Season pieces with salt and pepper. Dredge with flour.

Cook bacon in sauté pan for 3 minutes on each side. Remove bacon and set aside.

Discard half of bacon fat.

Place chicken in remaining bacon fat and brown over high heat, 4 minutes on each side.

Add shallots, chopped onions and garlic; cook 2 to 3 minutes.

Add brandy and flambé. Add red wine, bay leaf and thyme; cook 2 to 3 minutes over high heat.

Incorporate brown sauce. Season well; cover and cook in oven for 25 minutes. Remove from stove. Set aside.

Melt butter in frying pan. Add mushrooms and season well; cook 4 minutes. Add small onions and continue to cook for 1 minute.

Remove chicken from sauté pan. Set aside. Return sauté pan to stove top and bring sauce to boil for 3 to 4 minutes.

Add mushrooms, small onions and bacon; stir. Add chicken pieces and parsley; simmer 3 to 4 minutes. Serve.

Bouillabaisse Port–Cartier Style

Serves 4

45 ml (3 tablespoons) vegetable oil
1 onion, chopped
2 garlic cloves, smashed and chopped
15 ml (1 tablespoon) lemon zest
3 large tomatoes, peeled and chopped
3 parsley sprigs
1 ml (¼ teaspoon) fennel
1 bay leaf
125 ml (½ cup) dry white wine
2 cooked lobsters, 500 g (1 pound) each, cut into cubes
500 g (1 pound) sole fillet, cut into large pieces
250 g (½ pound) raw baby shrimp, shelled
pinch thyme
salt and pepper

Heat oil in large saucepan. Add onions and cook 3 minutes.

Add garlic, lemon zest, tomatoes and spices. Season well with salt and pepper; cover and cook 4 to 5 minutes.

Add white wine, stir and cook uncovered for 3 to 4 minutes.

Add lobster flesh and sole; cook 3 minutes.

Add shrimp and continue to cook for 1 minute.

Remove immediately from stove. Let stand 2 minutes.

Serve with garlic bread.

Broiled Halibut Steak with Oysters and Mussels

Serves 4

4 halibut steaks
30 ml (2 tablespoons) melted butter
250 ml (1 cup) shucked oysters
250 ml (1 cup) cooked mussels
juice 1 lemon
salt, pepper, paprika
oil

Preheat oven to 200°C (400°F).

Place halibut steaks in oiled baking dish.

In small bowl, combine melted butter, lemon juice and paprika. Brush fish steaks with mixture.

Place in oven, 15 cm (6 inches) from top element and broil 4 to 5 minutes. Turn fish steaks over and cover with oysters and mussels. Sprinkle with lemon juice and continue to broil for 4 minutes.

Serve with tartar sauce.

Tartar sauce:
150 ml (⅔ cup) mayonnaise
15 ml (1 tablespoon) lemon juice
30 ml (2 tablespoons) relish
30 ml (2 tablespoons) chopped olives
2 ml (½ teaspoon) dry mustard
chopped parsley
salt and white pepper

Combine all ingredients in small bowl. Correct seasoning and serve with fish.

Broiled Lobster
Serves 4

4 L (16 cups) water
15 ml (1 tablespoon) salt
4 live lobsters, 750 g (1½ pounds) each
125 ml (½ cup) melted butter
juice ½ lemon
pepper from mill
chopped parsley

Preheat oven to 200°C (400°F).

Pour water into large saucepan. Add salt and bring to boil. Immerse lobsters, cover and cook only 10 minutes. Remove and cool 10 minutes.

Cut lobster in half and place in large roasting pan.

Mix melted butter with lemon juice and season with pepper. Brush lobster flesh with mixture.

Place lobster in oven, 15 cm (6 inches) from broiler. Broil for 10 minutes basting flesh with melted butter.

Serve broiled lobster with chopped parsley and butter and lemon mixture.

Broiled Halibut Steak
Serves 4

4 halibut steaks
30 ml (2 tablespoons) melted butter
45 ml (3 tablespoons) dry white wine
15 ml (1 tablespoon) chopped chives
juice of 1 lemon
salt and pepper
paprika

Preheat oven to 200°C (400°F).

Season halibut steaks well with salt, pepper and paprika. Place fish in shallow pan.

In small bowl, combine melted butter, lemon juice, wine and chives. Pour mixture over fish steaks.

Place in oven, 15 cm (6 inches) from top element. Broil 4 minutes on each side basting with cooking juice.

Serve with green vegetables.

Gaspé Salmon
Serves 4

1.5 L (6 cups) water
1 small onion, thinly sliced
1 carrot, peeled and thinly sliced
1 leek (white part), thinly sliced
3 parsley sprigs
1 bay leaf
4 salmon steaks, 2.5 cm (1 inch) thick
juice of ½ lemon
few celery leaves, washed and dried
salt and pepper from mill

Place all ingredients, except salmon, in large sauté pan. Bring liquid to boil and simmer 10 minutes over low heat.

Pass liquid through sieve and pour back in sauté pan.

Place salmon steaks into strained liquid and bring to boil over medium heat. As soon as liquid reaches boiling point, reduce heat to very low and cook 8 minutes depending on thickness.

Serve with melted butter or hollandaise sauce.

Cod Tongue Delight
Serves 4

900 g (2 pounds) cod tongues, rinsed
375 ml (1½ cups) flour
3 eggs
5 ml (1 teaspoon) vegetable oil
500 ml (2 cups) soda cracker crumbs
salt and pepper
lemon

Heat peanut oil in deep fryer to 180°C (350°F).

Pour 750 ml (3 cups) water in saucepan. Add salt and bring to boil. Add tongues and cook 3 minutes. Drain well.

Place eggs in mixing bowl. Add vegetable oil; mix well.

Dredge tongues with flour, dip in egg mixture and roll in cracker crumbs.

Deep fry 2 to 3 minutes.

Serve with lemon.

One of the many restaurants in Old Montreal's Place Jacques-Cartier.

Mussels with Tomatoes

Serves 4

1.5 kg (3 pound) mussels
250 ml (1 cup) dry white wine
45 ml (3 tablespoons) butter
3 dry shallots, chopped
1 garlic clove, smashed and chopped
2 ml (½ teaspoon) tarragon
3 tomatoes, peeled, seeded and chopped
15 ml (1 tablespoon) chopped parsley
juice of ½ lemon
salt and pepper

Wash mussels under cold water. Remove beard with small paring knife and scrub well with brush.

Rinse mussels again and place in large saucepan. Add lemon juice and white wine. Cover and bring liquid to boil; cook 4 to 5 minutes stirring during process to cook mussels evenly.

Mussels are cooked when they open. Discard closed mussels.

Remove mussels from saucepan and set aside. Strain cooking liquid through a cheese cloth to remove any sand. Set aside.

Melt butter in saucepan. Add shallots, garlic and spices; cover and cook 2 minutes.

Add tomatoes. Season to taste; cook, uncovered, 8 to 10 minutes.

Add parsley and cooking liquid. Pepper well and cook 2 minutes over high heat. Pass through food mill.

Return mussels to sauce; cover and let stand 2 minutes in hot sauce. Serve.

Trout à l'Estrie

Serves 4

4 large trout filets
125 ml (¹/₂ cup) flour
45 ml (3 tablespoons) butter
2 dry shallots, chopped
250 ml (1 cup) hot fish stock
1 bunch watercress leaves, washed and
dried
125 ml (¹/₂ cup) heavy cream
juice ¹/₂ lemon
salt and pepper

Season trout filets well and dredge with flour.

Melt 30 ml (2 tablespoons) butter in frying pan. Add trout filets and cook, over high heat, 2 to 3 minutes on each side depending on size.

Remove from frying pan and transfer to hot service platter. Keep hot.

Add remaining butter to frying pan. Add shallots; cook 2 minutes.

Add fish stock and watercress leaves; cover and cook 3 to 4 minutes.

Incorporate cream into sauce and continue to cook for 2 minutes.

Pass mixture through food mill or blender. Sprinkle with lemon juice. Correct seasoning. Serve with fish.

Baked Cod

Serves 4

30 ml (2 tablespoons) butter
1 onion, finely chopped
4 slices cooked bacon, chopped
2 pickles, finely chopped
250 ml (1 cup) salted cracker crumbs
1.8 kg (4 pound) cod, in one piece
4 slices salted pork
juice of 1 lemon
salt and pepper

Preheat oven to 180°C (350°F).
Melt butter in saucepan. Add onions; cook 3 minutes.

Add bacon and pickles; mix well and cook 3 minutes.

Add cracker crumbs, mix and stuff fish. Tie well and place in roasting pan. Cover fish with salted pork and bake in oven for 50 minutes.

Serve with a green salad and lemon juice.

Maple Syrup Pie

Serves 4 to 6

250 ml (1 cup) fresh maple syrup
125 ml (¹/₂ cup) milk
125 ml (¹/₂ cup) light cream
15 ml (1 tablespoon) butter
15 ml (1 tablespoon) vanilla
3 egg yolks, beaten
1 – 22 cm (9 inch) baked pie shell

Pour maple syrup in small saucepan and bring to boiling point. Add milk and cream; stir and cook over low heat. Do not boil.

Add butter, vanilla and eggs; mix and cook over low heat to thicken mixture.

Pour mixture into cooked pie shell. Set aside.

Preheat oven to 180°C (350°F).

Meringue:

3 egg whites
125 ml (¹/₂ cup) sugar

Place egg whites and sugar in double boiler. Mix with electric beater at low heat until mixture forms peaks.

Spread mixture over pie and cook in oven until meringue is brown.

Butter Tarts

Dessert

175 ml (³/₄ cup) sweet butter
425 ml (1³/₄ cups) brown sugar
2 large eggs, beaten (or 3 small)
175 ml (³/₄ cup) currants
15 ml (1 tablespoon) vanilla
24 unbaked small tart shells

Preheat oven to 190°C (375°F).

Cream butter and sugar. Add 1 egg at a time mixing with electric beater until smooth.

Add currants and vanilla. Incorporate well.

Fill tart shells ²/₃ full. Bake 17 minutes in oven.

Delicious Doughnuts
Serves 4

4 large eggs
500 ml (2 cups) sugar
125 ml (¹/₂ cup) shortening
5 ml (1 teaspoon) baking soda
5 ml (1 teaspoon) white vinegar
1.7 L (6¹/₂ cups) all-purpose flour
5 ml (1 teaspoon) salt
45 ml (3 tablespoons) baking powder
750 ml (3 cups) milk
1 can evaporated milk

Heat peanut oil in deep fryer to 180°C (350°F).

Beat eggs thoroughly in bowl. Add sugar and shortening; mix well with an electric beater.

Mix soda and vinegar; incorporate to egg mixture.

Sift flour, salt and baking powder in bowl. Incorporate ¹/₃ flour to egg mixture. Combine milk and evaporated milk. Then add ¹/₂ liquid to egg and flour mixture; mix well.

Add half of remaining flour; incorporate.

Add remaining liquid; mix well. Then incorporate remaining flour.

Refrigerate dough for 1 hour.

Deep fry doughnuts in hot oil. Enjoy!

Lemon Pie
Serves 4 to 6

4 egg yolks, beaten
125 ml (¹/₂ cup) lemon juice
45 ml (3 tablespoons) lemon zest
150 ml (²/₃ cup) sugar
125 ml (¹/₂ cup) 35% cream
4 egg whites
1 - 25 cm (10 inch) baked graham cracker pie crust

Place egg yolks, lemon juice, lemon zest and (¹/₂ cup) sugar in double boiler. Mix and cook over medium heat, stirring constantly, until mixture becomes thick.

Remove from stove and cool.

Beat cream until very firm and incorporate to egg mixture.

Beat egg whites until stiff. Add remaining sugar and beat for 1 minute. Fold into egg yolk mixture.

Pour mixture into cooked pie crust and cover with plastic wrap paper. Freeze for 1 hour.

Remove pie from freezer and let stand at room temperature until pie becomes soft. Serve.

Autumn in the Muskoka Lakes, Ontario

THE HERITAGE OF UPPER CANADA

The culinary roots of Upper Canada are a strong mix of Scottish, Irish, and English. Early settlers in the 1800s were a rugged, determined lot, undiscouraged by continuous hardship in their new land. Due to the location of Upper Canada, settlers were forced to rely on local produce and their own ingenuity to create healthy, appealing food. Before the convenience of a cooking stove, a hearth was used which required more skill than you might imagine. Not only was the cook required to estimate appropriate temperatures and approximate cooking times, she had to stir and continually shift logs, ashes, and embers to accommodate her cooking vessels. Considering these elements, Upper Canada cuisine was quite remarkable.

Soups were common on a daily basis, and in trying times they constituted the major portion of a meal. Perhaps this is why Upper Canada soups are known for their substance. Sauces were served with almost every meat dish, as they were often needed to hide the flavour of stale meat. From backyard gardens, an abundance of vegetables were grown and served either boiled or stewed. Rarely eaten raw, vegetables were thought to be dangerous for a person's health unless cooked.

The most enthusiastic part of Upper Canada meals were the desserts. This trait remains, as the British are known for their sweet tooth. Puddings, pies, and, of course, sweet biscuits were served in most homes and are now a trademark of authentic Upper Canada fare.

As you will observe, a great many culinary techniques and concepts remain from the early days. Sauces are still very common and have become even more delicious over the years. Soups, such as Cream of Pumpkin, are classic reminders of Upper Canada's heritage. Join in our salute to this royal cuisine and you will be introduced to the determined people who created it.

Grilled Arctic Char
Serves 4

4 Arctic char steaks, 2.5 cm (1 inch)
thick
salt and pepper
Marinade:
50 ml ($^{1}/_{4}$ cup) olive oil
45 ml (3 tablespoons) dry white wine
1 garlic clove, smashed and chopped
1 ml ($^{1}/_{4}$ teaspoon) tarragon
1 ml ($^{1}/_{4}$ teaspoon) dry mustard
juice $^{1}/_{2}$ lemon
pepper from mill

In bowl, combine all ingredients for marinade.

Place Arctic char steaks in roasting pan. Pour marinade over and let stand for 1 hour.

Remove fish from marinade. Set aside.

Oil barbecue grill and heat. Place fish on hot grill and cook 5 minutes on each side basting with marinade.

Serve with Greek salad.

Baked Cabbage
Serves 4

1 large green cabbage, cored and
quartered
250 ml (1 cup) 35% cream
30 ml (2 tablespoons) butter
1 onion, chopped
pinch nutmeg
salt and pepper

Preheat oven to 180°C (350°F).

Place cabbage in large saucepan containing 2.5 L (10 cups) boiling salted water; cook for 25 minutes over medium heat. Remove cabbage from saucepan and drain well.

Chop cabbage finely and place in ovenproof casserole. Add cream. Set aside.

Melt butter in frying pan. Add onions and cook for 3 minutes. Pour onion mixture over cabbage and sprinkle with nutmeg. Mix and cook 45 minutes in oven. Serve.

Hot air balloons soar over the Houses of Parliament, Ottawa.

Roast Loin of Pork
Serves 4 to 6

1 - 2.3 kg (5 pound) pork loin
45 ml (3 tablespoons) melted butter
1 large chopped onion
30 to 45 ml (2 to 3 tablespoons) chopped
fresh sage
juice $^{1}/_{2}$ lemon
salt and pepper

Preheat oven to 190°C (375°F).

Remove part of fat and brush meat with melted butter. Season well.

Cook in oven at 190°C (375°F) for 30 minutes. Reduce oven temperature to 180°C (350°F) and continue to cook for 1½ hours.

15 minutes before end of cooking: Heat remaining butter in small saucepan. Add onions; cover and cook 3 minutes.

Add sage; cook 1 minute. Spread mixture over roast. Sprinkle with lemon juice. Finish cooking process.

Serve roast with apple sauce.

Deep Fried Ontario Smelts

Serves 4

1.2 kg (2¹/₂ pounds) smelts
250 ml (1 cup) flour
1 ml (¹/₄ teaspoon) salt
3 beaten eggs
5 ml (1 teaspoon) vegetable oil
375 ml (1¹/₂ cups) soda cracker crumbs
lemon wedges.

Heat olive oil in deep fryer to 180°C (350°F).

Clean smelts and season well with salt. Dredge with flour.

Place beaten eggs in bowl. Add oil and mix well. Dip smelts in egg mixture and roll in cracker crumbs.

Deep fry for 3 to 4 minutes.

Serve with lemon.

Tomato and Dill Soup

Serves 4

30 ml (2 tablespoons) butter
1 garlic clove, smashed and chopped
1 small onion, chopped
12 tomatoes, skinned and chopped
250 ml (1 cup) hot chicken stock
3 branches fresh dill
30 ml (2 tablespoons) tomato paste
1 bay leaf
45 ml (3 tablespoons) 35% cream
pinch sugar
few drops lemon juice
salt and pepper

Melt butter in large saucepan. Add garlic and onions; cover and cook 5 to 6 minutes.

Add tomatoes, sugar and chicken stock; stir. Add dill and tomato paste; mix and bring to boiling point.

Add spices, bay leaf and lemon juice; mix and cook 20 minutes over medium heat. Pass through food mill or blender.

Incorporate cream. Serve.

Pot Roast

Serves 4 to 6

*1 - 2.3 kg (5 pound) fresh boneless beef
brisket
3 carrots, peeled
2 large onions studded with 2 cloves
each
2 celery stalks, washed and cut in 3
1 bay leaf
3 parsley sprigs
30 ml (2 tablespoons) butter
pinch thyme
salt and pepper*

Remove excess fat from brisket.

Place meat in large saucepan and barely
cover it with water. Cover and bring to boil.
Cook for 1 hour over very low heat.

Season with salt and pepper and continue to
cook, covered for 30 minutes.

Important: Do not add water during cooking process.

Add vegetables and spices. Cover and continue to cook for 1½ hours over low heat or
until meat is tender.

Once meat is cooked, remove from saucepan and transfer to service platter.

Pass liquid and vegetables through a food
mill or in a blender. Incorporate butter. Serve
with meat.

Accompany with fresh vegetables.

Famous Scotch Broth

Serves 4

*250 ml (1 cup) barley
3 L (12 cups) water
500 g (1 pound) lamb shoulder, cut into
pieces
2.5 cm (1 inch) thick
3 carrots, peeled and diced
1 large onion, chopped
1 small cabbage head, sliced
1 celery stalk, sliced
30 ml (2 tablespoons) chopped parsley
salt and pepper*

Pour barley into large saucepan. Add water
and bring to boil; skim.

Add lamb and cook for 30 minutes; skim.

Add remaining ingredients and bring to
boil. Simmer for 2 hours.

Broiled Whiting

Serves 4

*3 - 500 g (1 pound) whiting
125 ml (½ cup) flour
45 ml (3 tablespoons) melted butter
15 (1 tablespoon) chopped chives
30 ml (2 tablespoons) capers
juice of 1 lemon
salt and pepper*

Preheat oven to 180°C (350°F).

Wash and pat dry fish. Season well and
dredge with flour. Place in roasting pan and
baste with melted butter and lemon juice. Season well.

Cook in oven for 10 to 12 minutes.

2 minutes before end of cooking: Sprinkle
chives and capers over fish. Serve.

Beef Stewed with Apples

Serves 4

*30 ml (2 tablespoons) butter
900 g (2 pound) chuck beef, thinly sliced
1 large onion, thinly sliced
4 large cooking apples, peeled, cored
and thinly sliced
250 ml (1 cup) hot beef stock
1 sprig parsley
salt and pepper*

Preheat oven to 180°C (350°F).

Butter large ovenproof casserole and place
one layer of beef in the bottom. Add one layer
of onions and one layer of apples. Season well.

Repeat to use remaining meat, onions and
apples.

Add beef stock and parsley; cover and cook
2½ hours in oven or until meat is tender.

Rice Croquettes
Serves 4

*75 ml (¹/₃ cup) long grain rice, washed
and drained
375 ml (1¹/₂ cups) milk
5 ml (1 teaspoon) vanilla
50 ml (¹/₄ cup) sugar
3 egg yolks
1 beaten egg
250 ml (1 cup) white bread crumbs*

Heat peanut oil in deep fryer to 180°C (350°F).

Place rice in saucepan. Add 500 ml (2 cups) water and bring to boil; cook 3 minutes.

Drain rice and pour back into saucepan. Add milk, vanilla and sugar; mix and bring to boil. Cook over medium heat until milk is absorbed.

Remove saucepan from stove. Incorporate egg yolks; mix well. Return saucepan to stove and cook 2 minutes stirring constantly.

Pour mixture on a tray and cover with wax paper. Refrigerate 3 to 4 hours.

Shape mixture into small croquettes and brush with beaten egg. Coat with bread crumbs.

Deep fry, few at a time, for 2 minutes.
Serve with jam.

Baked Acorn Squash
Serves 4

*2 medium acorn squash
60 ml (4 tablespoons) butter
60 ml (4 tablespoons) brown sugar
1 ml (¹/₄ teaspoon) cinnamon
1 ml (¹/₄ teaspoon) allspice
pinch nutmeg
few drops lemon juice*

Cut each squash in half and remove seeds.

Cut one slice from base to allow squash to sit firmly.

In the center of each squash, place the combined remaining ingredients. Bake in oven for 45 minutes basting during cooking. Serve.

Corn Oysters
Serves 4

*500 ml (2 cups) grated corn
3 eggs well beaten
30 ml (2 tablespoons) 35% cream
30 ml (2 tablespoons) melted butter
175 ml (³/₄ cup) flour
50 ml (¹/₄ cup) melted butter
pinch nutmeg
salt and pepper*

In bowl, combine corn, eggs, cream and 30 ml (2 tablespoons) melted butter. Add flour; season well and mix to obtain batter.

Sprinkle with nutmeg; mix again.

Heat half of melted butter in frying pan. Spoon large tablespoon of batter and cook in hot butter until brown on both sides.

Repeat to cook remaining batter. Serve.

Salted Boiled Cod Fish with Egg Sauce
Serves 4

*900 g (2 pound) salted cod fish
45 ml (3 tablespoons) butter
60 ml (4 tablespoons) flour
500 ml (2 cups) hot milk
1 ml (¹/₄ teaspoon) nutmeg
2 hard boiled eggs, chopped
salt and pepper*

Place salted cod in small pan and cover with lukewarm water. Refrigerate overnight. NOTE: YOU MUST CHANGE WATER 2 OR 3 TIMES DURING THAT TIME.

Drain cod and transfer to roasting pan; cover with fresh cold water and bring to boil. Cook 15 minutes over very low heat. DO NOT BOIL.

Melt butter in saucepan. Add flour; mix and cook 2 minutes over low heat.

Add milk and mix well with whisk. Season to taste and sprinkle with nutmeg. Cook 12 minutes over low heat.

Add eggs; mix delicately. Serve with fish.

Potted Shrimp

Serves 4

125 g (¹/₄ pound) unsalted butter
1 garlic clove, smashed and chopped
375 g (³/₄ pound) raw shrimp, peeled
1 small tin crab meat, well drained
few drops lemon juice
Tabasco sauce
paprika
salt and pepper

Melt butter in saucepan. Add garlic; cook 2 minutes over low heat. Add shrimp. Season well with pepper. DO NOT SALT. Cook 2 minutes mixing during process.

Add crab meat and continue cooking for a minute.

Place mixture in blender; purée. Season with lemon juice, Tabasco sauce and paprika. Mix well.

Refrigerate and let cool.

Serve with toasted French bread or on crackers.

Broiled Oysters

Serves 4

30 ml (2 tablespoons) butter
2 shallots, chopped
45 (3 tablespoons) flour
40 ml (2¹/₂ tablespoons) light cream
750 ml (3 cups) shucked oysters with
their juice
few drops lemon
paprika
pepper from mill

Melt butter in saucepan. Add shallots; cook 2 minutes over low heat.

Add flour; mix and cook 1 minute.

Add cream; stir and cook 3 to 4 minutes over low heat.

Add oysters and juice. Sprinkle with lemon juice and paprika; simmer 4 minutes over low heat.

Serve on toast.

Rural scene near Stratford, Ontario.

The Toronto skyline from Toronto Island Park.

Stewed Oysters
Serves 4

500 ml (2 cups) oysters with their juice
250 ml (1 cup) water
30 ml (2 tablespoons) butter
30 ml (2 tablespoons) flour
250 ml (1 cup) light cream or milk
15 ml (1 tablespoon) ketchup
15 ml (1 tablespoon) parsley
15 ml (1 tablespoon) grated lemon
paprika
pepper from mill

Place oysters, juice and water into saucepan; cover and bring to boil. Reduce heat to very low and simmer 2 minutes.

Drain oysters and set aside. Reserve liquid.

Melt butter in saucepan. Add flour; mix and cook 1 minute. Add cooking liquid from oysters; stir well and bring to boil. Reduce heat to very low and add cream or milk. Stir, add ketchup, parsley and grated lemon. Pepper well.

Incorporate oysters; simmer 3 minutes over very low heat.

Sprinkle with paprika. Serve with soda crackers.

Terrine of Sole
Serves 4

375 g (³/₄ pound) spinach leaves, washed and dried
6 sole filets
500 g (1 pound) salmon, boned and skinned
250 ml (¹/₂ pound) shrimp
3 egg whites
15 ml (1 tablespoon) parsley
125 ml (¹/₂ cup) heavy cream
2 ml (¹/₂ teaspoon) Worcestershire sauce
few drops Tabasco sauce
lemon juice
butter
salt and pepper

Preheat oven to 190°C (375°F).

Line loaf pan with well buttered wax paper. Set aside.

Steam spinach leaves for few minutes, drain well and chop.

Place one layer of fish in pan bottom. Add one layer of chopped spinach. Season well.

Purée salmon in blender. Add shrimp and purée.

Add half egg mixture, parsley, Tabasco and Worcestershire sauce. Sprinkle with lemon juice and purée.

Add remaining egg whites. Incorporate cream, little by little. Purée.

Spread one layer of mixture over spinach. Repeat one layer of fish and spinach. Cover with remaining mixture. Top with one layer of sole. Dot with butter and season well with pepper.

Place loaf pan in roasting pan containing 2.5 cm (1 inch) water. Bake in oven for 50 minutes.

Cool and remove liquid. Serve with mustard mayonnaise.

Baked Stuffed Pike
Serves 4

1 – 1.4 kg (3 pound) pike
15 ml (1 tablespoon) butter
¹/₂ cucumber, seeded, peeled and finely chopped
1 small onion, chopped
250 ml (1 cup) cooked rice
1 hard boiled egg, chopped
15 ml (1 tablespoon) parsley
1 beaten egg
30 ml (2 tablespoons) melted butter
50 ml (¹/₄ cup) coarse bread crumbs
salt and pepper
lemon slices for garnish

Preheat oven to 180°C (350°F).

Scale fish and remove gills. Wash and pat dry fish. Season well outside and inside.

Heat 15 ml (1 tablespoon) butter in saucepan. Add cucumbers and onions; cover and cook 3 minutes. Add cooked rice, chopped egg and parsley; mix well and cook 2 minutes.

Stuff pike and sew it up. Place in roasting pan. Season well. Pour melted butter over fish and brush with beaten egg. Sprinkle with bread crumbs.

Bake in oven for 40 minutes.

Note: If pike becomes too brown, cover with foil.

Serve with lemon.

Chicken and Oyster Pot Pie
Serves 4

1 – 2.2 kg (5 pound) chicken, deboned, skinned and cut in 8 pieces
2 carrots, peeled and sliced
2 celery stalks, sliced
2 onions, diced
750 ml (3 cups) water
500 ml (2 cups) shucked oysters
60 ml (4 tablespoons) butter
60 ml (4 tablespoons) flour
125 ml (1/2 cup) heavy cream
50 ml (1/4 cup) milk
1 recipe of pie dough
juice of 1/4 lemon
salt, pepper, paprika

Preheat oven to 180°C (350°F).

Season chicken pieces well and place in large saucepan.

Add carrots, celery and onions. Season well and add 750 ml (3 cups) water. Bring to boil. Cook 15 minutes over medium heat.

Remove chicken from saucepan. Set aside. Pass liquid through sieve and reserve.

Preheat oven to 190°C (375°F).

Place oysters in small saucepan. Add 250 ml (1 cup) water, 5 ml (1 teaspoon) butter and lemon juice; cook 3 minutes over low heat. Set aside.

Melt remaining butter in saucepan. Add flour, mix and cook 2 minutes.

Add cooking liquid from chicken; stir and cook 8 minutes over low heat. Add cream and paprika; stir and simmer 1 minute.

Place chicken pieces in baking dish and cover with sauce. Cover with loose pie crust. Brush dough with milk and bake in oven for 15 minutes.

Then, carefully remove pastry top and add drained oysters. Replace pastry top and continue baking for 5 minutes. Serve.

Cream of Pumpkin Soup
Serves 4 to 6

900 g (2 pound) pumpkin, peeled, seeded and cut into chunks
45 ml (3 tablespoons) butter
1 small onion, chopped
30 ml (2 tablespoons) flour
750 ml (3 cups) hot milk
125 ml (1/2 cup) hot chicken stock
croûtons
salt and pepper

Place pumpkin into large saucepan and cover with salted water. Bring to boil and cook for 20 minutes. Drain and purée. Set aside.

Melt butter in saucepan. Add onions; cook 2 minutes. Add flour; mix and cook 1 minute.

Add milk; stir and cook 3 to 4 minutes. Season well and incorporate pumpkin purée and chicken stock; stir and cook 20 minutes over low heat.

Serve with croûtons.

Upper Canada Village at Morrisburg, Ontario displays buildings and the lifestyle of 19th century Upper Canada.

Steak and Kidney Pie
Serves 4

30 ml (2 tablespoons) butter
250 g (¹/₂ pound) beef kidney, cleaned and thinly sliced
1 chopped shallot
1 onion, chopped
15 ml (1 tablespoon) chopped parsley
900 g (2 pound) rump steak, thinly sliced
125 ml (¹/₂ cup) flour
750 ml (3 cups) brown stock
1 recipe of pie dough
salt and pepper

Preheat oven to 180°C (350°F).

Melt butter in frying pan. Add kidney, shallots, onions and parsley. Season well. Cook 2 to 3 minutes. Remove and set aside.

Place beef in plastic bag. Add flour; season well and shake.

In well buttered ovenproof casserole, place one beef layer, then one kidney layer. Season with salt and pepper; cover with brown stock.

Roll pie dough. Wet edge of casserole with water and cover with dough. Press down to seal the dish. With paring knife, make small opening on dough.

Cook in oven for ¹/₂ hour. Serve.

Clam Chowder
Serves 4

36 clams, scrubbed and washed
500 ml (2 cups) light fish stock, hot
90 g (3 ounces) salted pork, thinly sliced
3 potatoes, peeled and thinly sliced
1 leek (white part only), thinly sliced
45 ml (3 tablespoons) flour
1 bay leaf
1 green onion, chopped
¹/₂ green pepper, chopped
15 ml (1 tablespoon) chopped parsley
125 ml (¹/₂ cup) heavy cream
few drops lemon juice
salt and pepper

Place clams in large saucepan. Add 250 ml (1 cup) fish stock; cover and cook 4 to 5 minutes to open clams.

Remove clams from shell and set aside.

Pass cooking liquid through cheese cloth and reserve.

Cook salted pork in saucepan for 3 minutes. Add potatoes and leeks; cook 2 minutes.

Add flour and cook 2 minutes. Add cooking liquid, remaining fish stock and bay leaf. Bring to boil and cook 8 to 10 minutes.

Add green onions, peppers and parsley. Season to taste. Cook 2 minutes.

Add clams and incorporate cream. Simmer 3 to 4 minutes. Sprinkle with lemon juice. Serve.

Chicken Liver Pâté

Serves 4 to 6

500 g (1 pound) chicken liver
250 g (¹/₂ pound) duck liver
30 ml (2 tablespoons) butter
1 onion, finely chopped
2 garlic cloves, smashed and chopped
15 ml (1 tablespoon) chopped parsley
25 ml (1 ounce) cognac or brandy
25 ml (1 ounce) port wine
175 ml (³/₄ cup) whipped cream
pinch thyme
Tabasco sauce
salt and pepper

Remove fat from liver.

Melt butter in frying pan. Add onions and garlic; cover and cook over low heat 2 to 3 minutes.

Add liver and spices. Season well with salt and pepper. Cook 8 to 10 minutes over low heat. Remove liver from frying pan and set aside.

Return frying pan to stove top and reduce cooking liquid by ²/₃ over high heat.

Add liver and cognac; flambé. Purée in blender.

Pour purée into double boiler. Add port wine and whipped cream; stir and season with salt and pepper. Cook 10 minutes over low heat.

Remove from stove, cool and serve with toasted French bread.

Pastry Dough for Quiche and Pie

375 ml (1¹/₂ cups) all-purpose flour
60 ml (4 tablespoons) butter cut into pieces
30 ml (2 tablespoons) shortening
30 to 45 ml (2 to 3 tablespoons) cold water
pinch salt

Sift flour and salt in large mixing bowl. Place butter and shortening in center of flour and incorporate with a pastry cutter.

Add cold water and form a ball.

Cover dough and refrigerate 1 hour.

Bacon and Corn Quiche

Serves 4 to 6

1 can 198 g (7 ounce) kernel corn
6 slices bacon, cooked crisp and diced
15 ml (1 tablespoon) chopped parsley
50 ml (¹/₄ cup) grated cheddar cheese
3 eggs
300 ml (1¹/₄ cup) light cream
pinch nutmeg
salt and pepper
1 – 22 cm (9 inch) fluted quiche plate lined with pastry dough

Preheat oven to 200°C (400°F).

Drain corn and place in quiche plate. Add bacon and parsley. Sprinkle with grated cheese.

Beat eggs and cream. Season with salt and pepper. Sprinkle with nutmeg. Pour mixture over corn.

Bake in oven at 200°C (400°F) for 15 minutes. Reduce heat to 180°C (350°F) and continue cooking for 20 minutes.

Serve.

Scalloped Potatoes

Serves 4

6 cooked potatoes, peeled and sliced
250 ml (1 cup) rolled crackers
60 ml (4 tablespoons) butter
375 ml (1¹/₂ cups) light cream
salt and white pepper

Preheat oven to 190°C (375°F).

Place one layer of potatoes in baking dish. Sprinkle with rolled crackers and dot with butter. Season well.

Repeat to use all potatoes.

Pour cream over potatoes. Season with salt and pepper. Cook in oven for 30 minutes. Serve.

Spinach Salad
Serves 4

Lemon vinaigrette:
  60 ml (4 tablespoons) wine vinegar
  2 ml (½ teaspoon) salt
  175 ml (¾ cup) olive oil
  juice ½ lemon
  pepper from mill

Pour vinegar into mixing bowl. Season with salt and pepper. Sprinkle with lemon juice.

Add oil in thin stream mixing constantly with whisk. Serve.

375 g (¾ pound) fresh spinach leaves,
  washed and dried
2 hard boiled eggs, chopped
250 ml (1 cup) lemon vinaigrette
1 scallion, chopped
250 ml (1 cup) fresh mushrooms,
  washed and sliced
125 ml (½ cup) bacon bits
30 ml (2 tablespoons) grated parmesan
  cheese
salt and pepper

In large salad bowl, place spinach leaves and season well.

Add eggs and lemon vinaigrette; mix well.

Add remaining ingredients. Toss and serve.

Baked Ham with Cumberland Sauce
Serves 4 to 6

1.8 kg (4 pound) fresh country ham
1 onion, cubed
1 carrot, peeled and sliced
1 celery stalk, diced
bouquet garni
peppercorns

Cooking time: 30 minutes per pound.

Place ham in saucepan. Add remaining ingredients; cover with water and bring to boil. Cook 30 minutes per pound.

Remove ham from saucepan. Peel away skin and remove part of fat.

Place ham in roasting pan and sprinkle with brown sugar and orange juice. Cook 30 minutes in oven preheated to 190°C (375°F).

Serve with Cumberland sauce.

Cumberland Sauce:
  250 ml (1 cup) red currant jelly
  60 ml (4 tablespoons) port wine
    juice of 2 oranges
    juice of ½ lemon

Bring red currant jelly to boil in small saucepan. Add remaining ingredients; cook 3 minutes. Mix well.

Serve with ham.

Romaine Salad, with Blue Cheese Dressing
Serves 4

300 ml (1¼ cups) blue cheese
15 ml (1 tablespoon) chopped parsley
5 ml (1 teaspoon) Dijon mustard
50 ml (¼ cup) wine vinegar
175 ml (¾ cup) olive oil
2 small heads romaine lettuce, washed
  and dried
250 ml (1 cup) garlic croûtons
125 ml (½ cup) cooked crisp bacon,
  chopped
salt and pepper
lemon juice

Mash blue cheese in small mixing bowl. Add parsley and mustard; mix well.

Add vinegar. Season with salt and pepper.

Add oil in thin stream mixing constantly with whisk to incorporate well into vinegar and cheese. Correct seasoning.

Break lettuce leaves into salad bowl. Add half of dressing; mix well. Sprinkle with lemon juice.

Add croûtons and remaining dressing; mix. Sprinkle with bacon bits. Serve.

Roast Beef, Horseradish Sauce

Serves 6 to 8

1 ml (¹/₄ teaspoon) basil
1 ml (¹/₄ teaspoon) thyme
2 ml (¹/₂ teaspoon) chervil
*30 ml (2 tablespoons) oil or melted
butter*
*1.8 kg (4 pound) beef sirloin tip roast
salt and pepper*

Preheat oven to 220°C (425°F).
Cooking time: 18 minutes per pound
Mix basil, thyme and chervil in bowl. Add oil; mix well. Brush top of roast with mixture. Pepper well. Do not salt.

Place meat in roasting pan and sear, at 220°C (425°F), for 30 to 35 minutes. Reduce heat to 180°C (350°F) and continue cooking process. Baste and season meat with salt and pepper during cooking.

To prepare beef juice:
1 large onion, diced
1 celery stalk, diced
15 ml (1 tablespoon) chopped parsley

30 ml (2 tablespoons) flour
*750 ml (3 cups) hot beef stock
salt and pepper*

30 minutes before the end of roast cooking time: Place all vegetables and parsley beside roast beef.

When roast beef is done, remove from roasting pan and let stand for 5 minutes. Keep warm.

Place roasting pan on stove top and add flour; mix well. Cook 3 minutes over medium heat.

Add beef stock and continue to cook for 5 to 6 minutes. Strain sauce and serve with roast beef.

Horseradish sauce:
*60 ml (4 tablespoons) prepared
horseradish*
2 ml (¹/₂ teaspoon) sugar
5 ml (1 teaspoon) white vinegar
5 ml (1 teaspoon) dry mustard
*45 ml (3 tablespoons) 35% cream or
yogurt*

Mix all ingredients together in small saucepan and cook 4 to 5 minutes over low heat. Do not boil.

Serve with roast.

Apple Sauce

Serves 4

750 g (1¹/₂ pounds) cooking apples
30 ml (2 tablespoons) butter
*45 ml (3 tablespoons) chopped lemon
zest*
50 ml (¹/₄ cup) brown sugar
15 ml (1 tablespoon) cinnamon
30 ml (2 tablespoons) water

Peel, core and slice apples.
Melt butter in saucepan. Add apples; cook 4 to 5 minutes.

Add remaining ingredients; cover and cook 16 to 18 minutes.

Purée mixture in blender. Serve.

Chicken Fricassée

Serves 4

*1 – 1.8 kg (4 pound) chicken, cut in 8
pieces*
750 ml (3 cups) water
2 large onions, diced
1 celery stalk, sliced
1 large green pepper, cubed
125 g (¹/₄ pound) salted pork, diced
60 ml (4 tablespoons) flour
15 ml (1 tablespoon) parsley
Worcestershire sauce
salt and pepper

Season chicken pieces well and place in sauté pan. Cover with water and bring to boil. Partially cover the pan and cook 15 minutes over low heat.

Add onions and celery; partially cover the pan and continue to cook for 14 minutes.

Add green peppers; partially cover and cook for 6 minutes. Remove chicken and vegetables from sauté pan. Set aside.

Pour liquid into bowl and reserve.

Cook salted pork 3 minutes in saucepan over low heat. Add flour, mix and cook 2 minutes.

Add cooking liquid and parsley; mix with whisk. Sprinkle with Worcestershire sauce. Correct seasoning. Cook 8 to 10 minutes over low heat.

Add chicken and vegetables; simmer 5 to 6 minutes. Serve.

Chicken with Sweet Pepper

Serves 4

1 – 2 kg (4¹/₂ pound) chicken, skinned and cut into 6 pieces
250 ml (1 cup) flour
30 ml (2 tablespoons) vegetable oil
1 sweet red pepper, cubed
1 sweet green pepper, cubed
1 garlic clove, smashed and chopped
375 ml (1¹/₂ cups) hot chicken stock
15 ml (1 tablespoon) cornstarch
30 ml (2 tablespoons) cold water
15 ml (1 tablespoon) chopped parsley
salt and pepper

Preheat oven to 190°C (375°F).

Season chicken pieces well and dust with flour.

Heat oil in skillet. Add chicken and cook 3 to 4 minutes on each side. Then continue to cook in oven, without cover, for 15 minutes.

Remove skillet from oven and transfer chicken to service platter. Keep hot.

Return skillet to stove top. Add peppers and garlic; cook 3 minutes. Add chicken stock, stir and cook 2 minutes. Season well.

Mix cornstarch with cold water. Incorporate mixture into sauce. Pour sauce over chicken. Sprinkle with parsley. Serve.

Scalloped Tomatoes
Serves 4

6 large tomatoes, sliced
5 ml (1 teaspoon) sugar
50 ml (¼ cup) butter
375 ml (1½ cups) soda cracker crumbs
50 ml (¼ cup) chicken stock
15 ml (1 tablespoon) chopped parsley
salt and pepper

Preheat oven to 180°C (350°F).
In well buttered ovenproof casserole, spread one layer of tomatoes. Season well with salt and pepper; sprinkle with sugar. Add dots of butter. Sprinkle with part of cracker crumbs.
Repeat and finish with layer of soda cracker crumbs and dots of butter.
Pour chicken stock over scalloped tomatoes. Cook in oven for 20 minutes. Sprinkle with parsley. Serve.

Roast Stuffed Turkey with Cranberry Sauce
Serves 6 to 8

Cranberry Sauce:
750 g (1½ pounds) fresh cranberries
250 g (½ pound) sugar
50 ml (¼ cup) water

Bring all ingredients to boil in stainless steel pan. Cook for 1 hour over very low heat.
Serve hot or cold.

Stuffing:
250 g (½ pound) white coarse bread crumbs
125 g (¼ pound) chopped suet
45 ml (3 tablespoons) parsley
15 ml (1 tablespoon) thyme
15 ml (1 tablespoon) chopped lemon zest
1 ml (¼ teaspoon) nutmeg

30 ml (2 tablespoons) milk
salt and pepper

Incorporate all ingredients in large bowl. If mixture is too dry, add a little more milk.

Roast stuffed turkey:
1 – 4.5 kg (10 pound) turkey
125 ml (½ cup) melted drippings
thyme and parsley stuffing
salt and pepper

Preheat oven to 200°C (400°F).
Cooking time: 20 minutes per pound
Remove neck and giblets. Rinse turkey with water; drain well. Season inside and outside with salt and pepper.
Stuff neck cavity of turkey lightly with stuffing. Fold neck skin over stuffing.
Stuff body cavity loosely with stuffing. Tie with thin string.
Place turkey in roasting pan and brush generously with melted drippings. Cook at 200°C (400°F) until turkey is golden brown. Then, reduce heat to 160°C (325°F) and continue to cook basting every 15 minutes.
Once turkey is done, remove from oven.
Carve and serve with cranberry sauce.

Yorkshire Pudding
Serves 4

250 ml (1 cup) water
175 ml (¾ cup) milk
375 ml (1½ cups) all-purpose flour
2 ml (½ teaspoon) salt
3 eggs
45 ml (3 tablespoons) beef drippings

Preheat oven to 220°C (425°F).
Mix water and milk together. Set aside.
Sift flour and salt into bowl. Add eggs and half liquid; mix well to obtain a smooth batter.
Add remaining liquid, mix and refrigerate 1 hour.
Pour beef drippings into a 12 muffin pan and place in oven to heat drippings. Add batter and cook in oven for 20 minutes.
Serve with roast.

Poached Chicken Breast

Serves 4

*2 chicken breasts, skinned and cut in
half
1 celery stalk, diced
1 onion, diced
750 ml (3 cups) light chicken stock, hot
1 bay leaf
45 ml (3 tablespoons) butter
50 ml (¼ cup) flour
250 g (½ pound) mushrooms, washed
and sliced
½ green pepper, thinly sliced
½ red pepper, thinly sliced
30 ml (2 tablespoons) light cream
15 ml (1 tablespoon) chopped parsley
salt and pepper*

Place chicken breasts in saucepan. Add celery, onions, chicken stock and bay leaf; bring to boil. Cook 15 minutes over low heat.

Melt butter in small saucepan. Add flour; mix and cook 2 minutes over medium heat.

Strain cooking liquid and incorporate into flour mixture mixing with a whisk.

Add mushrooms and peppers; cook 8 minutes over low heat. Season well. Add cream; continue to cook for 2 minutes.

Add chicken breasts and simmer 3 to 4 minutes. Sprinkle with parsley. Serve.

Boston Lettuce, with Thousand Island Dressing

Serves 4

*2 heads Boston lettuce, washed and
dried
375 ml (1½ cups) mayonnaise
3 cherry tomatoes, finely chopped
30 ml (2 tablespoons) chili sauce
30 ml (2 tablespoons) canned pimiento,
chopped
15 ml (1 tablespoon) chopped parsley
juice of ½ lemon
few drops Worcestershire sauce
salt and pepper*

Place lettuce leaves in large salad bowl. Season with salt and pepper. Sprinkle with lemon juice.

Combine all remaining ingredients into bowl. Mix well and pour over lettuce; toss.

Sprinkle with lemon juice. Garnish with sliced boiled eggs. Serve.

Ox Tail Soup

Serves 4

2 onions
2 whole cloves
1.4 kg (3 pound) ox tail cut into pieces
2 large carrots peeled
1 turnip peeled and cut in 2
1 bay leaf
2 L (8 cups) water
30 ml (2 tablespoons) butter
pinch thyme
salt and pepper

Stud each onion with 1 clove.

Place all ingredients (except butter) in large saucepan. Season well. Bring to boil and cook over low heat for 1½ hours.

Remove all vegetables from saucepan and set aside. Continue cooking ox tail for 1 hour.

Remove meat and set aside.

Pass cooking liquid and vegetables through food mill or in blender. Pour mixture into saucepan and add meat. Continue to cook for 1 hour.

Add butter and serve.

Chocolate Mousse

Serves 6

6 squares semi-sweet chocolate
175 ml (³/₄ cup) granulated sugar
50 ml (¹/₄ cup) espresso coffee
6 egg yolks
6 egg whites, beaten very stiff
250 ml (1 cup) whipped cream
30 ml (2 tablespoons) rum

Place chocolate, sugar and coffee in double-boiler; mix and add egg yolks. Mix well and cook until mixture becomes creamy. Remove and cool 4 to 5 minutes.

Fold egg whites, then whipped cream into mixture. Add rum.

Pour chocolate mousse into small glass cups and refrigerate 1 hour.

Garnish with a cherry. Serve.

Bread and Butter Pudding

Serves 4

625 ml (2¹/₂ cups) light cream
2 eggs
2 egg yolks
50 ml (¹/₄ cup) granulated sugar
15 ml (1 tablespoon) lemon zest
30 ml (2 tablespoons) maple syrup
5 slices white bread, well buttered
125 ml (¹/₂ cup) currants
50 ml (¹/₄ cup) raisins
45 ml (3 tablespoons) brown sugar

Preheat oven to 180°C (350°F).

Scald cream; set aside.

Place eggs and egg yolks in bowl. Add granulated sugar and beat together. Incorporate cream, lemon zest and maple syrup. Set aside.

Place sliced bread in ovenproof baking dish. Scatter raisins and currants. Pour custard over. Sprinkle with brown sugar.

Place baking dish in roasting pan containing 2.5 cm (1 inch) hot water. Cook in oven for 30 to 35 minutes.

Cool and serve.

Roast Duck with Honey
Serves 4

Stuffing:
30 ml (2 tablespoons) butter
1 onion, chopped
30 ml (2 tablespoons) chopped parsley
1 celery stalk, chopped
175 ml (³/₄ cup) chopped walnuts
1 ml (¹/₄ teaspoon) allspice
2 ml (¹/₂ teaspoon) coarse bread crumbs
1 beaten egg
pinch thyme
salt and pepper

Melt butter in saucepan. Add onions, parsley and celery; cook 4 to 5 minutes.

Add walnuts, spices and bread crumbs; mix and season with salt and pepper.

Add enough egg to bind mixture.

Roast Duck:
1 – 2.2 to 2.7 kg (5 to 6 pound) duck
1 small onion, diced
1 carrot, peeled and sliced
500 ml (2 cups) water
30 ml (2 tablespoons) melted butter
50 ml (¹/₄ cup) honey

30 ml (2 tablespoons) cornstarch
45 ml (3 tablespoons) cold water
juice ¹/₄ lemon
salt and pepper

Preheat oven to 200°C (400°F).

Remove neck and giblets from duck and place in saucepan. Add onions and carrots. Season well. Add 500 ml (2 cups) water and bring to boil. Cook 1 hour over low heat. Strain and set aside.

Stuff duck and place in roasting pan. Prick skin with paring knife. Baste with melted butter.

Spread honey over duck and cook in oven at 200°C (400°F) for 1 hour. Reduce oven to 190°C (375°F) and continue cooking for 40 minutes.

Remove duck from roasting pan and transfer to service platter.

Remove fat from roasting pan. Return roasting pan to stove top. Add stock from giblets and neck. Bring to boil.

Mix cornstarch with cold water. Incorporate mixture into sauce. Correct seasoning and cook 4 to 5 minutes.

Serve with stuffed duck.

The Trent–Severn Waterway at Fenelon Falls, Ontario. The 380–kilometre Waterway links Lake Ontario with Lake Huron and traces a centuries–old canoe route through the Kawatha Lakes.

Apple Pie

Serves 6

*5 large apples, peeled, cored and thinly
sliced
15 ml (1 tablespoon) cornstarch
15 ml (1 tablespoon) cinnamon
125 ml (1/2 cup) brown sugar
15 ml (1 tablespoon) butter
pinch salt
pinch nutmeg
few drops lemon juice
milk
pie dough*

Preheat oven to 220°C (425°F).

Line 22 cm (9 inch) pie plate with dough.
Set aside.

Place apples in large bowl. Add salt, cornstarch, cinnamon and nutmeg; mix well.

Add half brown sugar; mix again.

Transfer apple mixture into pie plate. Add
remaining brown sugar and dot with butter.
Sprinkle with lemon juice. Cover with upper
crust.

Brush crust with milk. Bake in oven at
200°C (425°F) for 8 minutes. Reduce oven
temperature to 190°C (375°F) and continue
cooking 30 to 35 minutes.

4 minutes before end of cooking: Sprinkle
pie crust with mixture of sugar and cinnamon.

Lemon Chiffon Pie

Serves 4 to 6

*1 envelope gelatine
45 ml (3 tablespoons) water
2 eggs, separated
75 ml (1/3 cup) sugar
30 ml (2 tablespoons) chopped lemon
zest
125 ml (1/2 cup) 35% cream, whipped
juice of 1 1/2 lemons
1 graham cracker pie crust, cooked*

Pour gelatine in small bowl. Add water and
let stand 3 minutes.

Place egg yolks, sugar, lemon juice and zest
in double-boiler. Mix with an electric beater
and cook over low heat until thick. Remove
from stove.

Pour gelatine mixture into small saucepan
and dissolve over low heat. Incorporate to egg
mixture. Let cool mixing occasionally.

Beat egg whites until very stiff and fold in
egg yolk mixture.

Fold in whipped cream.

Pour mixture over cooked pie crust.
Refrigerate for 1 hour. Serve.

Cheese Cake with Pastry

Serves 6

Pastry dough:
*375 ml (1 1/2 cups) flour
125 ml (1/2 cup) butter
45 ml (3 tablespoons) sugar
2 egg yolks
pinch salt*

Sift flour and salt into bowl. Add butter,
sugar and eggs; work ingredients together to
obtain a smooth dough. Chill for 1 hour.

Filling:
*90 ml (6 tablespoons) butter
125 ml (1/2 cup) sugar
3 large eggs, separated
550 ml (2 1/4 cups) cottage cheese
15 ml (1 tablespoon) lemon zest*

Preheat oven to 190°C (375°F).

Roll dough and line a 22 cm (9 inch) springform mould. Prick bottom with a fork and
cook in oven, at 190°C (375°F), for 15 minutes.
Set aside.

Mix butter in bowl for 30 seconds. Add
sugar; mix well. Add egg yolks; mix again.
Incorporate cottage cheese and lemon zest.

In stainless steel bowl, beat egg whites until
very stiff. Fold into egg yolk mixture.

Pour mixture into springform mould and
cook in oven, at 180°C (350°F), for 50 minutes.

Serve cool with strawberry sauce.

Golden ears of Saskatchewan wheat.

PRAIRIE HARVEST

Prairie food is much like the people who create it: down to earth, healthy, and generous. Samplings of this unique cuisine will surely leave a desire that leads to another bite, and then perhaps just one bite more.

With miles and miles of fertile plains that gave these provinces their name, crops grow quickly and well, furnishing the major ingredients that dominate Prairie food. Unfortunately nature has not always been so kind and throughout many difficult seasons, the people of the west struggled to retain their successful harvest. With unforgiving, long and often cruel winters, the Prairie people were molded into a group of strong-willed, ambitious Canadians.

Today's Prairies has overcome many difficulties and is an area of growing wealth and importance to the rest of the country. The provinces' chief products, wheat and other grains, are perhaps the most important element in their cuisine. From homes to restaurants, breads and biscuits are daily fare.

With Ukrainian and Scandinavian settlements scattered among the provinces, Prairie cookery retains a European style, which is evident in recipes using tender Alberta beef. Visitors can enjoy this succulent meat in many ways, such as Rib Roast or in a steaming pot roast. When serving one of these specialties why not include Kartoshnich as an accompaniment? Made from potatoes, eggs, and cream, this mixture is then baked and becomes a tasty potato pancake. Kartoshnich is great for brunch too. And for dessert? A generous slice of Saskatoon Berry Pie with perhaps a dollop of whipped cream — a perfect ending to an already perfect meal.

We are sure that everybody on your dinner list will be delighted with your presentation of Prairie food, but do not count on having any leftovers!

Crêpe Loaf

Serves 4

Crêpes:

250 ml (1 cup) flour
3 eggs
375 ml (1½ cups) milk
45 ml (3 tablespoons) melted butter
pinch salt

Sift flour and salt together into bowl. Add eggs and half of milk; whisk well.

Add remaining milk and butter; whisk until smooth. Pass batter through sieve and let stand 30 minutes.

Proceed to prepare crêpes.

Filling:

4 egg yolks
45 ml (3 tablespoons) sugar
250 ml (1 cup) 35% cream, lightly beaten
15 ml (1 tablespoon) chopped lemon zest

Preheat oven to 180°C (350°F).

Place egg yolks and sugar in bowl. Combine with electric beater for 2 minutes. Add cream and lemon zest; mix again.

Place 2 crêpes flat on ovenproof platter. Spread a layer of egg mixture over top. Continue to layer with crêpes and filling. Cook in oven 15 to 18 minutes.

Serve.

St. Basil's Bread

675 ml (2³/₄ cups) sifted flour
15 ml (1 tablespoon) active dry yeast
2 ml (½ teaspoon) powdered anise
15 ml (1 tablespoon) chopped lemon zest
175 ml (³/₄ cup) milk
75 ml (5 tablespoons) butter
30 ml (2 tablespoons) sugar
2 whole eggs
1 egg yolk

15 ml (1 tablespoon) water
pinch salt
mixed candied fruits

Combine 250 ml (1 cup) flour, yeast, powdered anise, and lemon zest in electric mixer.

Heat milk, butter, sugar, and salt in saucepan. Cook until hot. Do not boil!

Add milk mixture to dry ingredients in electric mixer. Mix very well.

Blend in eggs and remaining flour; mix to form soft dough.

Knead dough on lightly floured counter top for 5 minutes. Form ball, set in buttered bowl and turn until completely coated. Cover with clean towel and set in warm place for 1½ hours to rise.

Preheat oven to 190°C (375°F).

Punch dough down. Place half of dough flat in buttered 20 cm (8 inch) round cake pan. Shape remaining dough into 2 'rope like' rolls, 40 to 46 cm (16 to 18 inches) in length. Fold rolls in half and twist. Join rolls to form 18 cm (7 inch) circle. Place over dough in cake pan.

Beat egg yolk with water. Brush dough with glaze and sprinkle with mixed candied fruits. Set in warm place for 25 minutes to rise.

Bake 20 minutes then reduce heat to 180°C (350°F); continue baking 15 minutes.

Cool on wire rack.

Famous Western Chuck Stew

Serves 4

250 ml (1 cup) flour
5 ml (1 teaspoon) salt
2 ml (1/2 teaspoon) pepper
1.8 kg (4 pound) beef chuck
45 ml (3 tablespoons) beef drippings
2 onions, peeled and largely diced
1 celery stalk, largely diced
1 L (4 cups) hot beef stock
30 ml (2 tablespoons) tomato paste
1 bay leaf
salt and pepper

Preheat oven to 180°C (350°F).

Combine flour, salt, and pepper in bowl. Dredge beef with seasoned flour; set aside.

Heat half of beef drippings in cast iron casserole. When very hot, add half of beef. Brown on all sides 5 to 6 minutes.

Remove beef and set aside. Add remaining drippings and beef to casserole; repeat searing process.

Replace browned beef in casserole and add all remaining ingredients. Season well and bring to boil.

Cover and cook 2 1/2 hours in oven.

Serve with kartoshnich.

Wild Rice with Vegetables

Serves 4

250 ml (1 cup) wild rice
1 L (4 cups) water
5 ml (1 teaspoon) oil
30 ml (2 tablespoons) butter
1/2 celery stalk, diced
1 garlic bud, smashed and chopped
250 g (1/2 pound) mushrooms, washed and cut in two
1/2 green pepper, diced
salt and pepper

Place rice in large saucepan on stove top. Cover with water and add salt; mix well. Bring to boil, cover, and cook 40 minutes over low heat.

Drain rice and keep warm in oven.

Heat oil and butter in saucepan. Add celery and garlic; cook 3 minutes.

Stir in mushrooms and green peppers. Season and cook 4 minutes.

Mix vegetables with rice and serve.

Roast Duck with Apples

Serves 4

125 ml (1/2 cup) raisins
50 ml (1/4 cup) Canadian whisky
2.3 kg (5 pound) duck
1 onion, finely chopped
500 ml (2 cups) hot beef stock
15 ml (1 tablespoon) cornstarch
45 ml (3 tablespoons) water
45 ml (3 tablespoons) butter
3 apples, cored, peeled, and sliced
30 ml (2 tablespoons) brown sugar
5 ml (1 teaspoon) cinnamon
salt and pepper

Preheat oven to 220°C (425°F).

Marinate raisins in small bowl with whisky. Meanwhile, remove insides from duck. Clean duck, dry, and trim extra skin.

Season duck cavity and secure with kitchen string. Set in roasting pan and prick skin with paring knife. Cook 1 hour.

Remove roasting pan from oven and lower heat to 190°C (375°F). Discard fat from pan and continue cooking duck 1 1/2 hours. Season well during cooking. 20 minutes before cooking end, add onions.

Remove roasting pan and place on stove top. Add whisky (without raisins) and flambé. Transfer duck to ovenproof platter; keep hot.

Stir in beef stock to roasting pan; continue cooking 6 minutes. Mix cornstarch with water; add to sauce. Strain sauce, add raisins, and keep hot.

Heat butter in frying pan. Add apples, cover, and cook 5 minutes over medium heat. Stir in brown sugar and cinnamon. Continue cooking 5 minutes.

Serve sautéed apples with duck and sauce.

Soufflé Czecho–Slovak Style

Serves 4

6 eggs, separated
60 ml (4 tablespoons) sugar
250 ml (1 cup) dried fruits, chopped
15 ml (1 tablespoon) cornstarch
zest of 1 lemon

Preheat oven to 200°C (400°F)

Place egg yolks in bowl. Add sugar and beat with electric mixer for few seconds.

Mix dried fruits with cornstarch and add to egg yolk mixture. Incorporate lemon zest.

Beat egg whites until they form stiff peaks. Incorporate to egg yolk mixture.

Pour mixture into soufflé mould. Cook for 25 minutes in oven.

Serve immediately.

Beef Pot Roast

Serves 4

45 ml (3 tablespoons) beef drippings
1.8 kg (4 pound) beef brisket
2 onions, peeled and cut in 4
2 celery stalks, largely diced
3 cloves
1 to 1.2 L (4 to 5 cups) hot beef stock
1 large turnip, peeled and cut in 6
5 carrots, peeled
2 leeks, washed
45 ml (3 tablespoons) cornstarch
60 ml (4 tablespoons) water
salt and pepper

Preheat oven to 150°C (300°F).

Heat beef drippings in cast iron casserole on stove top. Add beef brisket and sear 10 to 12 minutes over high heat.

Season well and add onions. Continue cooking 3 to 4 minutes over medium heat.

Mix in celery, cloves, and cover with beef stock. Season well, bring to boil, and cover.

Cook in oven 3 hours.

1 hour before cooking end, add vegetables to casserole.

When cooked, remove 750 ml (3 cups) cooking liquid and pour into saucepan. Mix cornstarch with water; add to pan. Stir and cook 2 minutes to thicken sauce.

Serve sauce with beef and vegetables.

Kartoshnich (Potato Cake)

Serves 4

6 large potatoes, washed and unpeeled
5 large eggs
125 ml (¹/₂ cup) heavy cream
45 ml (3 tablespoons) melted butter
pinch nutmeg
salt and pepper

Preheat oven to 220°C (425°F).

Set potatoes in large saucepan and cover with water. Salt well and bring to boil.

When cooked, cool and peel. Mash potatoes into large bowl; season well.

Blend in eggs and cream. Add nutmeg and season well.

Brush rectangular 30 cm (12 inch) ovenproof mold with melted butter. Fill with potato mixture and cook 25 to 30 minutes.

Serve with beef.

Barbecued T–Bone Steaks Western Style

Serves 6

30 ml (2 tablespoons) oil
125 ml (¹/₂ cup) chopped onions
2 garlic buds, smashed and chopped
500 ml (2 cups) chili sauce
15 ml (1 tablespoon) Worcestershire
sauce
30 ml (2 tablespoons) dry red wine or
cider vinegar
50 ml (¹/₄ cup) brown sugar
6 T-bone steaks, 4 cm (1¹/₂ inches) thick
barbecue sauce to taste
juice 1 lemon
few drops Tabasco sauce
pinch paprika
salt and pepper

Heat oil in saucepan. Add onions and garlic; cook 4 to 5 minutes over medium heat.

Add remaining ingredients except steaks. Bring to boil, then continue cooking 20 minutes.

Generously brush steaks with mixture. Cook on barbecue 6 to 7 minutes each side. Baste frequently during cooking.

Serve with green salad.

Stuffed Pike

Serves 4

2.3 to 2.8 kg (5 to 6 pound) pike
10 slices white bread, soaked in milk
2 onions, finely chopped
2 eggs
3 carrots, thinly sliced
2 beets, peeled and thinly sliced
125 ml (¹/₂ cup) water
pinch thyme
juice ¹/₂ lemon
salt and pepper

Preheat oven to 180°C (350°F).

Cut fish into 4 equal pieces. Carefully remove flesh without damaging skin. Set skin aside.

Debone flesh and place in blender. Squeeze excess milk from bread and place bread in blender.

Add onions, eggs, thyme, and season. Blend for 30 seconds.

Stuff skins with mixture. Arrange layer of vegetables in baking dish. Set fish on top and cover with remaining vegetables.

Pour in water and lemon juice. Season, cover, and cook 2½ hours.

Pass vegetables through sieve and serve with stuffed pike.

Calgary Stampede Chili

Serves 4

250 g (½ pound) dried red kidney beans, presoaked for 6 hours
15 ml (1 tablespoon) oil
15 ml (1 tablespoon) butter
1 red onion, chopped
2 garlic cloves, smashed and chopped
500 g (1 pound) round steak, diced
2 ml (½ teaspoon) chili powder
2 ml (½ teaspoon) paprika
2 ml (½ teaspoon) crushed red pepper
375 ml (1½ cups) tomatoes, peeled and chopped
several drops Tabasco sauce
salt and pepper

Drain beans and place them into saucepan containing sufficient boiling salted water to cover them.

Cover saucepan and cook beans over low heat for ½ hour.

Meanwhile, heat oil and butter in frying pan over medium heat. Add onions and meat. Cook for 2 minutes.

Add garlic and spices; mix and cook for 3 to 4 minutes.

Combine meat mixture with beans. Continue cooking over low heat for ½ hour.

Finally, add tomatoes. Correct seasoning and cook slowly for ½ hour.

Serve on toasted bread.

Prairie Rabbit Stew

Serves 4

125 ml (½ cup) flour
1.8 kg (4 pound) rabbit or hare, cut in pieces
45 ml (3 tablespoons) oil
1 garlic bud, smashed and chopped
1 onion, peeled and chopped
250 ml (1 cup) beef stock
4 tomatoes, seeded and cut in 4
1 bay leaf
2 ml (½ teaspoon) thyme
1 turnip, peeled and cut in 4
salt and pepper

Preheat oven to 180°C (350°F).

Season flour generously with salt and pepper. Dredge rabbit pieces with flour.

Heat oil in large deep frying pan. Add rabbit and sear 6 to 7 minutes.

Stir in garlic and onions; continue cooking 3 minutes. Mix in beef stock, tomatoes, and spices. Season well.

Bring to boil and cover. Cook in oven 1 hour and 15 minutes.

40 minutes before cooking end, add turnip. Serve.

Cabbage Salad

Serves 4

1 small cabbage
2 carrots
1 onion
125 ml (½ cup) sugar
175 ml (¾ cup) vegetable oil
175 ml (¾ cup) white vinegar
15 ml (1 tablespoon) prepared mustard
juice ½ lemon
salt and pepper

Shred all vegetables in blender.

Place remaining ingredients in saucepan. Cook 3 to 4 minutes; stir well.

Pour over vegetables and marinate for 24 hours. Serve.

Canola field near Rosenfeld, Manitoba.

Roast Leg of Lamb with Rosemary

Serves 4

2.3 kg (5 pound) leg of lamb, prepared
for roasting by butcher
3 garlic buds, smashed and chopped
15 ml (1 tablespoon) rosemary
60 ml (4 tablespoons) oil
2 onions, peeled and diced
500 ml (2 cups) light beef stock
5 ml (1 teaspoon) chopped parsley
30 ml (2 tablespoons) cornstarch
45 ml (3 tablespoons) water
salt and pepper

Preheat oven to 240°C (450°F).

Using small paring knife, remove most fat and skin from lamb. Make small incisions in flesh and fat. Mix 2 garlic buds with rosemary and rub over lamb. Brush with oil.

Cook lamb in roasting pan, 15 minutes per 500 g (1 pound). Increase cooking time by 5 minutes for well done. Season and baste with oil during cooking.

20 minutes before cooking end, add onions and remaining chopped garlic to pan.

When lamb is cooked, remove and set aside. Place roasting pan on stove top and remove ⅔ of fat.

Add beef stock and parsley; boil 5 minutes.

Mix cornstarch with water; stir into pan. Simmer several minutes.

Pass sauce through sieve, season and serve with lamb.

Meat and Cucumber Soup

Serves 4 to 6

750 g (1½ pound) beef round,
diced 2.5cm (1 inch)
500 g (1 pound) ham,
diced 2.5 cm (1 inch)
45 ml (3 tablespoons) butter
2 onions, peeled and sliced
3 sausages, sliced
1 cucumber, seeded and sliced
125 g (¼ pound) mushrooms, washed
and sliced
2 tomatoes, peeled, seeded, and cut in 6
salt and pepper
lemon slices for garnish

Set beef and ham in saucepan; cover with water. Bring to boil and cook 3 minutes. Skim, reduce heat and continue cooking 1½ hours.

Heat butter in frying pan. Add onions and sausages; cover and cook 3 minutes.

Stir in cucumbers, mushrooms, and tomatoes. Season and cook 3 to 4 minutes over high heat.

15 minutes before cooking end, add vegetables to saucepan.

Serve with lemon slices.

Saskatoon Berry Pie

Serves 4 to 6

1.2 L (5 cups) Saskatoon berries,
washed
60 ml (4 tablespoons) water
250 ml (1 cup) sugar
45 ml (3 tablespoons) flour
30 ml (2 tablespoons) chopped
lemon zest
pastry dough for bottom and top of
pie plate
juice 1 lemon

Preheat oven to 200°C (400°F).

Place berries in medium size saucepan. Add water, lemon juice, and sugar. Stir in flour and lemon zest.

Mix well and bring to boil. Cover and cook 8 minutes over low heat.

Roll dough. Line bottom of pie plate with dough. Fill with berry mixture. Cover pie with upper crust and seal edges. Prick dough and brush with eggwash.

Cook pie in oven for 12 minutes. Reduce heat to 190°C (375°F); continue cooking 25 to 30 minutes.

Serve pie cold with whipped cream.

Kulich

175 ml (³/₄ cup) dark rum
2 ml (¹/₂ teaspoon) saffron
250 ml (1 cup) mixed candied fruits
1.2 L (5 cups) sifted flour
45 ml (3 tablespoons) lukewarm water
45 ml (3 tablespoons) active dry yeast
300 ml (1¹/₄ cups) brown sugar
300 ml (1¹/₄ cups) 10% cream
175 ml (³/₄ cup) soft butter
4 eggs, separated
175 ml (³/₄ cup) toasted almonds,
ground

Mix rum with saffron; set aside.

In separate bowl, combine fruits and 250 ml (1 cup) flour; set aside.

Place water, yeast, and 45 ml (3 tablespoons) sugar in small bowl. Mix and let stand until surface bubbles.

In electric mixer, combine cream, butter, and remaining sugar. Mix in egg yolks. Add almonds, yeast mixture, and remaining flour. Mix well with pastry hook until thoroughly blended.

Remove dough and knead on lightly floured counter top. Form ball, set in buttered bowl and turn until completely coated. Using sharp knife slash a cross on top. Cover with clean towel and set in warm place for 1¹/₂ hours to rise.

Punch dough down and place in electric mixer. Blend in rum and fruit mixtures. Beat egg whites until stiff then incorporate to dough.

Place dough in buttered bowl, turn to coat, and cover. Let rise in warm place 1 hour.

Butter 4 small 23 cm (9 inch) cylinder bread molds. Place dough in molds, cover, and let rise 2 hours.

Preheat oven to 190°C (375°F).

Bake 30 minutes then reduce heat to 160°C (320°F); continue baking 50 minutes.

Cool on wire rack.

Grain elevators can be seen throughout Canada, but are predominant in the Prairie provinces of Alberta, Saskatchewan, and Manitoba.

Lamb and White Bean Stew

Serves 4 to 6

250 ml (1 cup) dry white beans
1 L (4 cups) water
30 ml (2 tablespoons) oil
1.8 (4 pound) lamb shoulder, fat removed and cut into 2.5 cm (1 inch) squares
1 garlic bud, smashed and chopped
2 onions, peeled and diced
796 ml (28 ounce) can tomatoes and juice
1 L (4 cups) beef stock
2 ml (1/2 teaspoon) chili powder
2 apples, cored and chopped
salt and pepper

Preheat oven to 180°C (350°F).

Place beans in bowl and cover with water. Soak 12 hours then drain.

Place oil in large ovenproof casserole. Heat and brown lamb 6 to 7 minutes. Add garlic and onions; season well. Cook 3 to 4 minutes.

Stir in tomatoes and beef stock. Add beans, season, and bring to boil.

Mix in chili powder, cover and cook in oven 2½ hours. 30 minutes before cooking end, add apples.

Serve.

Ukrainian Braised Pork

Serves 4

30 ml (2 tablespoons) pork drippings
1.4 kg (3 pound) boneless pork loin, fat trimmed
3 garlic buds, smashed and chopped
5 ml (1 teaspoon) caraway seeds
1 carrot, cut in 0.60 cm (1/4 inch) slices
1 onion, thinly sliced
250 ml (1 cup) hot beef stock
15 ml (1 tablespoon) tomato paste
15 ml (1 tablespoon) cornstarch

30 ml (2 tablespoons) water
250 ml (1 cup) sour cream
dash paprika
chives to taste
salt and pepper

Heat pork drippings in dutch oven. Add pork and brown on all sides. Season well.

Add garlic, caraway seeds, carrots and onions. Mix well, cover and cook on stove top 2½ hours over low heat.

1 hour before cooking end, add beef stock and tomato paste.

When meat is cooked, remove and place on service platter. Set dutch oven on stove top. Mix cornstarch with water; incorporate to liquid.

Cook over high heat 3 to 4 minutes. Remove from heat and add cream, chives, and paprika. Season well.

Slice pork and serve with sauce.

Buffalo Ribs

Serves 4

30 ml (2 tablespoons) soya sauce
50 ml (1/4 cup) cider vinegar
250 ml (1 cup) chili sauce
2 garlic buds, smashed and chopped
170 ml (6 ounce) can tomato juice
15 ml (1 tablespoon) brown sugar
4 to 5 buffalo ribs, cut in 13 cm (5 inch) pieces
juice 1 lemon
few drops Tabasco sauce
salt and pepper

Preheat oven to 220°C (425°F).

Mix soya sauce, cider vinegar, chili sauce, lemon juice, garlic, and tomato juice in bowl. Season and add Tabasco sauce. Stir in brown sugar.

Place ribs in roasting pan. Pour sauce over top and cover with aluminum foil. Cook 2 hours.

Remove foil and continue cooking 1 hour. Mix ribs 2 to 3 times during cooking.

Serve with wild rice.

Seasoned Potatoes with Cream

Serves 4

60 ml (4 tablespoons) oil
30 small round potatoes, washed
90 ml (6 tablespoons) 35% cream
30 ml (2 tablespoons) fresh chopped fennel
salt and pepper

Heat oil in cast iron casserole. Add whole potatoes and season well.

Cook 20 minutes over medium heat, partly covered.

When cooked, add cream and fennel. Season again and cook 2 minutes.

Toss and serve.

Saskatoon Berry Torte

Serves 4 to 6

Cake batter:

6 eggs, separated
250 ml (1 cup) sugar
5 ml (1 teaspoon) vanilla
125 ml (½ cup) sifted cake flour
5 ml (1 teaspoon) baking soda
50 ml (¼ cup) powdered almonds
pinch salt

Preheat oven to 180°C (350°F).

Butter 2 - 23 cm (9 inch) springform cake molds.

Set egg yolks in bowl and beat 1 minute with electric beater. Add sugar and continue beating 2 to 3 minutes. Stir in vanilla.

In separate bowl, sift flour, baking soda, almonds, and salt. Incorporate to egg yolks.

Beat egg whites until stiff and fold into batter.

Divide batter between molds. Cook 25 to 30 minutes. Cool on cake rack.

Filling:

750 ml (3 cups) Saskatoon berries, washed

500 ml (2 cups) sugar
30 ml (2 tablespoons) lemon juice
500 ml (2 cups) whipped 35% cream

Place berries, sugar, and lemon juice in saucepan. Cook 6 to 7 minutes. Cool.

Cut each cake into 2 layers. Spread bottom cake layer with berries and whipped cream. Replace cake layer.

Repeat filling and top with remaining cake layer. Decorate with any remaining whipped cream.

Honey Candies

50 ml (¼ cup) honey
250 g (½ pound) chopped nuts
250 g (½ pound) chopped almonds
2 ml (½ teaspoon) cinnamon
15 ml (1 tablespoon) chopped lemon zest

Place all ingredients in saucepan. Bring to boil and cook 3 to 4 minutes, mixing constantly.

Lightly oil marble pastry board or cookie sheet. Spread candy mixture over board and let cool 2 minutes.

Break into small pieces.

Baked Buffalo Steak

Serves 4 to 6

15 ml (1 tablespoon) oil
1.4 kg (3 pound) buffalo steak, 5 cm (2 inches) thick
30 ml (2 tablespoons) melted butter
salt and pepper

Preheat oven to 220°C (425°F).

Rub inside of cast iron frying pan with oil. Place in oven 3 to 4 minutes.

Meanwhile, pepper steak well and brush with melted butter.

Set steak in pan and cook in oven, 8 minutes each side. Increase cooking by 2 minutes each side for well done steak.

Serve.

Chicken with Sour Cream

Serves 4

30 ml (2 tablespoons) butter
1.8 kg (4 pound) chicken, washed and cut into 6
2 leeks, white section only, washed and sliced
1 large carrot, sliced
75 ml (⅓ cup) hot chicken stock
250 ml (1 cup) sour cream
15 ml (1 tablespoon) chopped chives
dash paprika
salt and pepper

Preheat oven to 180°C (350°F).

Heat butter in sauté pan. Add chicken pieces and vegetables; season well. Cook 6 to 7 minutes on stove top, stirring only once.

Cover and cook in oven 35 to 40 minutes.

When cooked, remove chicken and set aside. Place pan on stove top. Stir in chicken stock and cook over high heat 2 to 3 minutes.

Remove from heat, replace chicken and add sour cream. Mix well and season.

Stir in chives and paprika. Serve.

Manitoba Borsch

Serves 6

Beet fermentation:
6 to 7 beets

Wash and clean beets thoroughly. Slice in half and place in large jar. Cover with lukewarm water and secure top.

Keep at room temperature for several days.

6 to 7 fermented beets
900 g (2 pound) blade steak, fat trimmed
1 medium onion
2 carrots, chopped
796 ml (28 ounce) can tomatoes, drained and chopped
4 small potatoes
liquid from beets
chopped garlic to taste
pinch sugar
salt and pepper

Place all ingredients, except potatoes, in large saucepan. Season well and cook over low heat 2 to 2½ hours or until well cooked.

40 minutes before cooking end, add potatoes.

Before serving, slice vegetables and garnish with sour cream.

Almond Cookies

Dessert

250 ml (1 cup) unsalted soft butter
125 ml (½ cup) sugar
1 egg yolk
175 ml (¾ cup) ground almonds
15 ml (1 tablespoon) vanilla extract
500 ml (2 cups) sifted flour
whole almonds for garnish

Preheat oven to 180°C (350°F).

In electric mixer, cream butter, sugar, and egg yolk 2 minutes. Add remaining ingredients and mix until well blended.

Shape dough into small balls. Place on greased cookie sheet. Lightly press 1 almond on each cookie.

Bake 10 to 12 minutes. Cool on wire rack.

Traditional Sugar Cookies

125 ml (½ cup) sugar
125 ml (½ cup) unsalted butter
2 eggs
125 ml (½ cup) sour cream
5 ml (1 teaspoon) baking soda
625 ml (2½ cups) sifted flour

Preheat oven to 190°C (375°F).
Lightly butter and flour cookie sheet.
Cream sugar and butter in electric mixer. Add eggs and mix well. Add sour cream; mix well.
Sift baking soda with flour; incorporate to mixture. Blend well.
Flour counter top well. Roll dough until thin. Using cookie cutter, form desired shapes.
Cook on cookie sheet 8 to 10 minutes. Cool on wire rack.

Sauté Chicken, European Style

Serves 4

30 ml (2 tablespoons) shortening
1.8 kg (4 pound) chicken cut into 8 pieces
125 ml (½ cup) flour
15 ml (1 tablespoon) paprika
1 Spanish onion, finely chopped
1 green pepper, diced into small pieces
1 red pepper, diced into small pieces
3 tomatoes, peeled, seeds removed, chopped
250 ml (1 cup) hot chicken stock
45 ml (3 tablespoons) 35% cream
salt and pepper

Preheat oven to 180°C (350°F).
Melt shortening into large ovenproof casserole.
Dredge chicken pieces with flour, season with salt and pepper and sauté for 3 to 4 minutes on each side.
Add paprika, onions, green and red pepper; mix well.
Add tomatoes and chicken stock; stir and bring to boil. Season well. Cover and cook in oven for 40 minutes.
Remove casserole from oven and stir in 35% cream.
Serve with peas.

Meat Broth Ukrainian Style

Serves 4

900 g (2 pounds) stewing beef
900 g (2 pounds) shredded cabbage
2 carrots, thinly sliced
1 turnip, thinly sliced
2 onions, thinly sliced
2 potatoes, thinly sliced
salt and pepper

Place beef in large saucepan. Cover with cold water and bring to boil. Skim and drain water. Cover beef with fresh water; season well.
Partly cover saucepan, bring to boil, and cook 2½ to 3 hours. 40 minutes before cooking end, add vegetables. Season well.
Serve in large soup tureen and season well.

Ukrainian church near Sheho, Saskatchewan.

Walnut Apple Cake
Serves 6 to 8

125 ml (½ cup) butter
375 ml (1½ cups) sugar
15 ml (1 tablespoon) vanilla
175 ml (¾ cup) flour
227 g (8 ounces) cream cheese, softened
2 eggs
5 apples, cored, peeled, and sliced
30 ml (2 tablespoons) rum
125 ml (½ cup) chopped walnuts

Preheat oven to 220°C (425°F).

Cream butter and 125 ml (½ cup) sugar in bowl. Add vanilla and flour. Blend dough well and roll.

Butter 1 – 23 cm (9 inch) springform mold. Line bottom with dough.

Cream cheese and 125 ml (½ cup) sugar in bowl. Add eggs and mix with electric beater. Spread mixture over dough.

Mix apples with remaining sugar. Pour in rum and toss. Arrange apples evenly over cream cheese filling.

Sprinkle apples with walnuts. Cook in oven 40 to 45 minutes.

Cool and serve with heavy cream.

Gingerbread
Serves 6 to 8

175 ml (¾ cup) lard
175 ml (¾ cup) sugar
2 eggs
425 ml (1¾ cups) sifted flour
5 ml (1 teaspoon) chopped ginger
5 ml (1 teaspoon) cinnamon
2 ml (½ teaspoon) nutmeg
5 ml (1 teaspoon) baking soda
250 ml (1 cup) boiling water
125 ml (½ cup) molasses
pinch salt

Preheat oven to 180°C (350°F).

Using electric beater, cream lard with sugar in bowl. Add eggs, one at a time, beating between additions.

Sift all dry ingredients together. Incorporate half to creamed mixture; mix well.

Blend in half of boiling water; mix well. Add molasses, mix very well, and beat in remaining water. Add remaining sifted ingredients and beat until smooth.

Pour into buttered teflon, 20 cm (8 inch) square mold. Bake in oven 40 to 45 minutes.

Club Steaks with Gherkin Sauce

Serves 4

60 ml (4 tablespoons) melted butter
2 onions, peeled and thinly sliced
2 gherkins, sliced
30 ml (2 tablespoons) tomato paste
45 ml (3 tablespoons) dry white wine
50 ml (¼ cup) hot beef stock
3 club steaks, deboned and cut in 2.5 cm (1 inch) slices
45 ml (3 tablespoons) sour cream
salt and pepper

Heat 15 ml (1 tablespoon) butter in frying pan. Add onions, season well, and cook 6 to 7 minutes over medium heat.

Add gherkins, mix, and stir in tomato paste. Stir well and pour in wine and beef stock.

Mix sauce well and cook 3 to 4 minutes over low heat.

Heat 25 ml (1½ tablespoons) butter in separate frying pan. Sauté half of meat 1 minute each side. Remove and repeat procedure with remaining butter and meat. Season well.

Mix meat with sauce and serve with sour cream.

The Ukrainian Salad

Serves 4

375 g (¾ pound) cold pork, thinly sliced
375 g (¾ pound) cold chicken, thinly sliced (remove skin)
2 cooked beets, peeled and sliced
3 cooked potatoes, peeled and sliced
½ cucumber, seedless and sliced
15 ml (1 tablespoon) chopped parsley
2 hard boiled eggs, sliced
1 gherkin, sliced
30 ml (2 tablespoons) vinegar
60 ml (4 tablespoons) oil
salt and pepper

Place all salad ingredients in large bowl. Add vinegar and oil; toss well.
Serve on lettuce leaves.

Alberta Rib Roast

2.7 to 3.2 kg (6 to 7 pound) rib roast
45 ml (3 tablespoons) sea salt
2 onions, peeled and diced
1 ml (¼ teaspoon) thyme
500 ml (2 cups) beef stock
pepper from the mill

Preheat oven to 240°C (450°F).

Remove excess fat from roast. Season very generously with salt and pepper. Set in roasting pan, fatty side up. Place in oven and sear 20 minutes.

Reduce heat to 190°C (375°F) and continue cooking 1½ hours. Baste with cooking fat occasionally.

When cooked, remove roast and let stand 15 minutes. Meanwhile set pan on stove top. Add onions and thyme; cook 6 to 7 minutes.

Drain most of fat from pan and replace with beef stock. Boil 7 to 8 minutes.

Pass sauce through sieve and serve with roast.

Sunset in the Gulf Islands, British Columbia.

CATCH OF THE DAY

Canada's coastline extends over 240,000 kilometers and, between fresh and salt water, the country boasts over 150 species of fish and shellfish. With this variety, Canada has become a nation of excellent fishermen and, not surprisingly, many citizens consider themselves seafood connoisseurs.

During the summer months many people visit the coasts each year to sample, discover, and savour the oceans' riches. Seafood festivals provide perfect opportunities to get acquainted with these food treasures, which are not only nutritious but extremely tasty.

With the advantages of modern technology most species are available year round, fresh or frozen, and in filets, steaks, or whole. Dungeness crabs, which are trapped off Graham Island and off the west coast of Vancouver Island, are constantly in demand. You may have to search a little longer to find them but your efforts will be well rewarded.

Along the Atlantic coast hide irresistible lobsters, which are trapped and immediately delivered to shore. Those of common size, around 2 kilograms, are left whole and sold fresh or frozen. Smaller and larger ones go to factories that produce canned meat, which is excellent in sandwiches, on canapes, and for innovative garnishes. Of course for a true seafood lover there is no substitute for fresh lobster and along the coast are lobster huts that pride themselves in offering the best boiled live lobsters. When cooking at home you too can claim the same by placing lobsters directly in boiling water and then reducing heat to a simmer. This method will assure tender and delicious meat every time.

Our collection of seafood recipes includes both old and new Canadian specialties. We hope you will discover some of your favourites and also some exciting new seafood fare.

Shrimp and Mushroom Salad

50 ml (¹/₄ cup) hazelnut oil
50 ml (¹/₄ cup) lemon juice
500 g (1 pound) cooked shrimp,
deveined and sliced in two
125 g (¹/₄ pound) fresh mushrooms,
cleaned and sliced
¹/₂ Boston lettuce, washed and dried
15 ml (1 tablespoon) chopped parsley
5 ml (1 teaspoon) fresh tarragon
few drops Tabasco sauce
salt and pepper

In a small bowl, combine oil and lemon juice. Season well and set aside.

Place shrimp, mushrooms, and lettuce in large salad bowl. Mix well. Season with salt and pepper.

Pour oil mixture over salad. Sprinkle with Tabasco sauce. Add spices and incorporate well.

Serve with garlic bread.

Shrimp Stuffed Eggs

8 cooked shrimp
12 hard boiled eggs
60 ml (4 tablespoons) mayonnaise
15 ml (1 tablespoon) chopped parsley
few drops Worcestershire sauce
few drops Tabasco sauce
lemon juice
salt and white pepper

Purée shrimp in blender. Set aside.

Cut each egg in two and remove yolk. Pass yolks through sieve. Add shrimp purée, mayonnaise, Worcestershire sauce, and Tabasco sauce. Season well. Sprinkle with lemon juice.

With spoon, stuff egg halves and sprinkle with parsley. Serve.

Pike Mousse

750 g (1¹/₂ pounds) boneless pike
2 egg whites
1 ml (¹/₄ teaspoon) nutmeg
750 ml (3 cups) 35% cream
salt and pepper
crushed ice

Preheat oven to 190°C (375°F).

Purée pike in blender. Pour contents into stainless steel bowl. Fill larger bowl with crushed ice. Set bowl containing fish on ice. Mix in egg whites. Sprinkle with nutmeg; season with salt and pepper.

Incorporate cream, very slowly, whisking constantly until mixture adheres to a spoon.

Fill a small, well buttered, ring mold. Set mold in pan containing 2.5 cm (1 inch) boiling water. Cook in oven 18 to 20 minutes.

Serve with Nantua sauce.

Skate with Capers

900 g (2 pound) skate, skinned
1.5 L (6 cups) water
¹/₂ onion, thinly sliced
15 ml (1 tablespoon) chopped parsley
30 ml (2 tablespoons) vinegar
50 ml (¹/₄ cup) butter
50 ml (¹/₄ cup) capers
juice 1 lemon
salt and pepper

Cut fish into medium size pieces and place in saucepan. Add water, onions, parsley, lemon juice, and vinegar. Season with salt and pepper; bring to boil. Continue cooking over very low heat for 3 minutes. Do not boil again.

Remove fish from saucepan and transfer to service platter.

Place butter and capers in frying pan. Pepper well and cook several minutes over high heat to brown.

Sprinkle with lemon juice and pour over fish.

Cod Filet Platter

Serves 4

375 ml (1¹/₂ cups) sour cream
45 ml (3 tablespoons) horseradish
4 cod filets, poached and cold
30 ml (2 tablespoons) chopped fresh dill
4 stuffed eggs
1 cucumber, peeled, seeded, and sliced
2 large tomatoes, sliced
few drops Tabasco sauce
lemon juice
lettuce leaves, washed and dried
salt and pepper

In bowl, combine sour cream, horseradish, Tabasco sauce, and lemon juice. Season with salt and pepper.

Decorate service platter with lettuce leaves. Place fish on top and spread sauce over fish. Sprinkle with dill. Refrigerate for 10 minutes.

Garnish with stuffed eggs, cucumbers, and tomatoes. Sprinkle with lemon juice. Serve.

Hollandaise Sauce

170 g (6 ounces) unsalted butter
15 ml (1 tablespoon) white vinegar
2 egg yolks
juice ¹/₄ lemon
crushed white peppercorns
salt

Melt butter in double boiler and skim. Set aside.

In stainless steel bowl, combine vinegar and crushed peppercorns. Place on stove top and cook 2 minutes to reduce vinegar. Remove and cool.

Add egg yolks; mix well.

Set bowl over saucepan containing warm water. Add butter in thin stream, mixing constantly with whisk.

Sprinkle with lemon juice, season well, and serve.

Lighthouse on Campobello Island, New Brunswick. American President Franklin D. Roosevelt spent many summers on the island at his summer cottage.

Pacific Halibut with Garlic Sauce

Serves 4

4 halibut steaks
50 ml (¹/₄ cup) flour
30 ml (2 tablespoons) oil
3 garlic cloves, smashed and chopped
2 egg yolks
125 ml (¹/₂ cup) olive oil
cayenne pepper
lemon juice
salt and pepper

Season halibut steaks well and dredge with flour.

Heat oil in frying pan. Add fish; cook 8 to 10 minutes over medium heat, depending on thickness.

Meanwhile, place garlic in mortar. Add egg yolks and with pestle mix well.

Incorporate olive oil, drop by drop at first, mixing constantly. Finish incorporating oil in thin steady stream.

Mixture should become like mayonnaise. Sprinkle with lemon juice and cayenne pepper.

Place mixture on top of fish.

Serve with green beans and sautéed potatoes.

Eggs Surprise

Serves 4

4 English muffins, sliced in two and toasted
8 thin slices smoked salmon
8 poached eggs
250 ml (1 cup) Béarnaise sauce
lemon slices for garnish

Preheat oven to 190°C (375°F).

Place toasted muffins on ovenproof platter.

Set salmon slices on top of muffins. Top with poached eggs and cover with Béarnaise sauce.

Cook in oven for 2 minutes. Serve.

Mussels Marinière

Serves 4

1.4 kg (3 pounds) mussels
60 ml (4 tablespoons) butter
1 small onion, finely chopped
50 ml (¹/₄ cup) white dry wine
15 ml (1 tablespoon) chopped parsley
50 ml (¹/₄ cup) light cream
pepper from mill

Scrub mussels well and rinse several times in cold water to remove all sand. With kitchen shears, remove beards.

Melt 30 ml (2 tablespoons) butter in large saucepan. Add onions, cover and cook 4 minutes over low heat.

Add wine and cook, uncovered, for 2 minutes.

Add mussels, cover and cook 4 minutes stirring once during cooking.

Remove mussels from saucepan and place on service platter. Keep hot.

Strain liquid into small saucepan. Add parsley, butter and cream; bring to boil. Season with pepper.

Pour sauce over mussels. Serve with french bread.

The fishing village of Burgeo, Newfoundland.

Stuffed Dungeness Crab
Serves 4

4 – 900 g (2 pounds) live crabs
30 ml (2 tablespoons) butter
2 shallots, chopped
250 g (½ pound) fresh chopped
mushrooms
375 ml (1½ cups) hot white sauce
125 ml (½ cup) grated Gruyère cheese
Tabasco sauce
salt and pepper

Preheat oven to 220°C (425°F).
Wash crab and plunge in large saucepan containing 4 L (16 cups) boiling, salted water. Crabs must be fully covered with water.

Cover and cook 20 to 25 minutes over medium heat. Remove and cool.

To remove flesh: break upper shell and pull halves. Discard dead fingers. Remove white flesh.

Break small and large claws and remove flesh. Set aside.

Before stuffing shells, wash well.

Melt butter in saucepan. Add shallots and mushrooms. Season well and cook 5 to 6 minutes over high heat.

Add white sauce, Tabasco sauce, and stir. Add crab meat, season well, and mix.

Stuff shells and sprinkle with cheese. Broil 5 to 6 minutes and serve.

Frogs Legs à l'ail
Serves 4

16 to 18 frog legs
300 ml (1¼ cups) milk
1 beaten egg
375 ml (1½ cups) flour
15 ml (1 tablespoon) oil
45 ml (3 tablespoons) butter
3 garlic buds, smashed and chopped
30 ml (2 tablespoons) chopped parsley
juice 1 lemon
salt and pepper

Preheat oven to 200°C (400°F).
Mix milk with egg. Dip frog legs in mixture. Dredge with flour.

Heat oil and 25 ml (1½ tablespoons) butter in frying pan. Cook frog legs over medium heat, 4 minutes each side.

Set pan in oven and continue cooking 15 to 17 minutes. Time will vary depending on size of legs. Turn twice during cooking. When done, meat should separate from bones.

Transfer frog legs to service platter. Place frying pan on stove top. Add remaining butter and garlic; cook 2 minutes.

Add parsley and lemon juice; cook 1 minute. Pour over frog legs and serve.

Oysters Florentine
Serves 4

Mornay sauce:
45 ml (3 tablespoons) butter
60 ml (4 tablespoons) flour
750 ml (3 cups) hot milk
50 ml (¼ cup) grated Gruyère cheese
pinch nutmeg
salt, pepper, paprika

Melt butter in saucepan. Add flour; mix and cook 2 minutes.

Incorporate milk and stir with whisk. Season well and cook 10 minutes over low heat.

Add paprika, nutmeg, and cheese; mix well and set aside.

24 large oysters
500 g (1 pound) spinach, washed,
steamed and chopped
60 ml (4 tablespoons) grated cheese
(parmesan, gruyère, etc.)
Mornay sauce

Wash shells, open and remove oysters. Reserve shells.

Place oysters and juice in saucepan and bring to boil. Remove from stove. Allow oysters to poach 3 minutes.

Place one layer spinach in bottom of each shell. Set poached oyster on top and cover with Mornay sauce. Sprinkle with cheese.

Broil 3 minutes and serve.

Crabmeat Coquille

Serves 4

45 ml (3 tablespoons) butter
30 ml (2 tablespoons) chopped onions
750 g (1½ pounds) fresh crabmeat
250 g (½ pound) fresh mushrooms,
washed and sliced
500 ml (2 cups) light fish stock, hot
45 ml (3 tablespoons) flour
15 ml (1 tablespoon) chopped parsley
125 ml (½ cup) grated Gruyère cheese
paprika
lemon juice
salt and pepper

Melt 15 ml (1 tablespoon) butter in saucepan. Add onions; cover and cook 3 minutes over low heat.

Add crabmeat and mushrooms. Season to taste; cover and cook 2 to 3 minutes.

Add fish stock; cook 2 to 3 minutes. Then remove crabmeat and mushrooms and set aside. Reserve cooking liquid.

Melt remaining butter in small saucepan. Add flour; mix and cook 1 minute.

Add cooking liquid. Season to taste, stir with a whisk; cook 5 to 6 minutes over medium heat.

Remove saucepan from stove. Add crabmeat and mushrooms. Sprinkle with parsley; mix and fill shell-shaped dishes. Sprinkle with cheese.

Place under broiler and cook 3 to 4 minutes.

Sprinkle with lemon juice. Serve.

Baked Coho Salmon
Serves 4

1 boneless Coho salmon, sliced open
250 ml (1 cup) dry white wine
15 ml (1 tablespoon) olive oil
2 ml (½ teaspoon) thyme
30 ml (2 tablespoons) fresh chopped dill
juice ¼ lemon

Preheat oven to 180°C (350°F).

Place 1 sheet of aluminum foil in long baking dish. Set salmon on top.

Mix wine, lemon juice, olive oil, and spices together. Pour over fish. Seal with foil and marinate 1 hour.

Bake salmon 45 minutes and serve with white fish sauce.

White fish sauce:
5 ml (1 teaspoon) butter
30 ml (2 tablespoons) chopped shallots
50 ml (¼ cup) dry white wine
375 ml (1½ cups) white sauce
15 ml (1 tablespoon) chopped dill
15 ml (1 tablespoon) chopped parsley
white pepper
few drops lemon juice

Heat butter in saucepan. Add shallots and cook 1 minute.

Pour in white wine; cook 3 to 4 minutes over high heat. Add remaining ingredients, season, and mix. Simmer 5 to 6 minutes. Stir in few drops lemon juice.

Carp Braised in Beer
Serves 4

30 ml (2 tablespoons) melted butter
2 onions, thinly sliced
1 celery stalk, thinly sliced
1 garlic bud, smashed and chopped
1 – 1.8 kg (4 pounds) carp, cleaned and
cut into 12 to 14 pieces
500 ml (2 cups) light beer

1 ml (¼ teaspoon) caraway seeds
15 ml (1 tablespoon) cornstarch
30 ml (2 tablespoons) water
15 ml (1 tablespoon) chopped parsley
salt and pepper

Heat butter in sauté pan. Add onions, celery, and garlic. Cover and cook 3 minutes.

Add carp pieces and cook, uncovered, 2 minutes. Stir in beer and caraway seeds; cover and cook over low heat 5 minutes.

Remove carp; transfer to service platter. Simmer cooking liquid for 5 minutes. Mix cornstarch with water and stir into pan. Season well.

Replace carp in pan. Garnish with parsley and serve.

Nantua Sauce
Serves 4

30 ml (2 tablespoons) melted butter
30 ml (2 tablespoons) diced onions
1 carrot, diced
30 ml (2 tablespoons) diced celery
8 scampi shells
30 ml (2 tablespoons) cognac
125 ml (½ cup) dry white wine
2 tomatoes, peeled and diced
30 ml (2 tablespoons) tomato paste
375 ml (1½ cups) hot white fish sauce
pinch thyme
several drops Tabasco sauce
salt and pepper

Heat butter in saucepan. Add onions, celery, and carrots. Cover and cook over medium heat 2 to 3 minutes.

Add scampi shells; continue cooking 4 to 5 minutes, uncovered. Add cognac and flambé.

Pour in wine. Cover and cook 5 to 6 minutes.

Mix in tomatoes and tomato paste; cook 8 to 10 minutes over low heat.

Add white sauce, thyme, and season. Sprinkle with Tabasco. Cook 10 minutes over low heat.

Pass through sieve and serve.

Deep-Fried Silvergrey Rockfish Filets

Serves 4

8 silvergrey rockfish filets
50 ml (¼ cup) flour
250 ml (1 cup) milk
3 beaten eggs
375 ml (1½ cups) soda cracker crumbs
125 ml (½ cup) Tartar sauce
salt and pepper
lemon slices for garnish

Heat peanut oil in deep-fryer to 180°C (350°F).

Season filets well and dredge with flour.

Mix milk and beaten eggs. Dip filets in mixture, then roll in cracker crumbs. Deep-fry 3 minutes.

Garnish with lemon juice and serve with Tartar sauce.

Tartar sauce:
125 ml (½ cup) mayonnaise
30 ml (2 tablespoons) chopped gherkins
15 ml (1 tablespoon) chopped capers
5 ml (1 teaspoon) chopped parsley
few drops Tabasco sauce
few drops Worcestershire sauce
several drops anchovy essence

Combine all ingredients in small mixing bowl. Correct seasoning.

Poached Pacific Cod with Egg Sauce

Serves 4

1.5 L (6 cups) water
4 cod filets
juice 1 lemon
salt

Pour water in sauté pan. Add lemon juice and salt; bring to boil.

Set fish in liquid; reduce heat to low. Cook 8 to 10 minutes over very low heat.

Serve with egg sauce, parsley boiled potatoes, and glazed carrots.

Egg sauce:
45 ml (3 tablespoons) butter
2 shallots, chopped
250 ml (1 cup) fresh mushrooms, finely chopped
45 ml (3 tablespoons) flour
30 ml (2 tablespoons) hot milk
2 hard boiled eggs, chopped
few drops lemon juice
few drops Tabasco sauce
salt and pepper

Place butter, shallots, and mushrooms in saucepan. Season to taste; cook 3 to 4 minutes.

Add flour; mix well and cook 1 minute.

Incorporate milk with a whisk. Correct seasoning.

Add eggs, lemon juice, and Tabasco sauce. Simmer 2 minutes over low heat and serve.

Shad Filets Maître d'Hotel

Serves 4

8 shad filets
125 ml (½ cup) olive oil
1 ml (¼ teaspoon) thyme
2 bay leaves
15 ml (1 tablespoon) chopped parsley
juice 1 lemon
Maître d'Hotel butter
salt and pepper

Place filets in baking dish. Add ¾ of oil, lemon juice, thyme, bay leaves, and parsley. Pepper well.

Marinate in refrigerator 30 minutes.

Heat remaining oil in frying pan. Add filets; cook 3 minutes each side. Season well.

Set filets in ovenproof platter. Place slice of butter on each. Sprinkle with lemon juice. Broil 2 minutes.

Serve.

15 ml (1 tablespoon) chopped parsley
125 g (¼ pound) mushrooms, chopped
250 g (½ pound) shrimp, shelled and
deveined
750 g (1½ pounds) clams, washed and
brushed
500 ml (2 cups) water
salt and pepper from mill

Heat 25 ml (1½ tablespoons) butter in frying pan. Add shallots, parsley, and mushrooms. Season and cook 3 to 4 minutes.

Place filets flat in baking dish. Spread mushroom stuffing on top, roll, and secure with toothpicks. Set aside.

Place shrimp in small saucepan; cover with cold water. Bring to boil and remove from stove. Let stand 3 to 4 minutes; drain, and set aside.

Place clams in saucepan; add 500 ml (2 cups) cold water. Cover and bring to boil. Stir and cook 3 to 4 minutes. Remove clams from shells; set aside. Reserve liquid.

Place rolled filets in small buttered saucepan. Add 375 ml (1½ cups) reserved liquid. Bring to boil. Turn filets.

Remove from heat and let stand.

Heat remaining butter in frying pan. Add shrimp and clams; sauté 3 minutes. Add parsley and season well.

Place filets in service platter. Garnish with clams and shrimp. Serve.

Poached Salmon Steaks
Serves 4

1 L (4 cups) hot fish stock
4 salmon steaks, 125 g (4 ounces) each
30 ml (2 tablespoons) butter
8 small potatoes, boiled and peeled
1 small cucumber, peeled, seeded, and
sliced 2.5 cm (1 inch) thick
250 ml (1 cup) Hollandaise sauce

Pour fish stock into sauté pan and bring to boil. Reduce heat to very low and set fish in liquid. Poach for 10 minutes.

Melt butter in small saucepan. Simmer potatoes and cucumbers for 5 minutes.

Remove fish from pan and transfer to service platter. Remove skin around fish and center bone.

Arrange vegetables and serve with Hollandaise sauce.

Perch Filets Stuffed with Shrimp and Clams
Serves 4

4 large perch filets
45 ml (3 tablespoons) butter
2 shallots, chopped

B.C. Clam Chowder
Serves 8

750 g (1½ lbs) fresh shucked clams
250 ml (1 cup) cold water
4 slices chopped bacon
1 large onion, chopped
60 ml (4 tablespoons) butter
625 ml (2½ cups) peeled and diced
potatoes
750 ml (3 cups) clam nectar
1 L (4 cups) milk
30 ml (2 tablespoons) butter
30 ml (2 tablespoons) flour
salt and pepper to taste

Sauté bacon and onions in butter until bacon is done.

Finely chop clams, and put into a large soup pot with bacon and onions.

Add potatoes and clam nectar and cover pot. Simmer until potatoes are tender.

Add milk and mix.

Melt butter in pan, sprinkle with flour and blend.

Simmer for 15 minutes and season with salt and pepper as desired.

Red Mullet, Devil Sauce

Serves 4

Devil sauce:
15 ml (1 tablespoon) butter
2 dry shallots, finely chopped
15 ml (1 tablespoon) chopped parsley
45 ml (3 tablespoons) wine vinegar
500 ml (2 cups) very light brown sauce
juice ¹/₄ lemon

Melt butter in saucepan. Add shallots and parsley; cover and cook 2 minutes.

Add wine vinegar. Cook, uncovered, 3 minutes over high heat until most of vinegar is evaporated.

Add brown sauce and lemon juice. Stir and simmer 10 to 12 minutes over low heat. Set aside.

4 — 180 to 250 g (6 to 8 ounce) red mullet, cleaned
50 ml (¹/₄ cup) flour
45 ml (3 tablespoons) oil
lemon juice
salt and pepper

Preheat oven to 220°C (425°F).

Wash fish under cold water; pat dry. Make 4 incisions on each side of fish. Dredge mullets with flour.

Mix oil and lemon juice in small bowl. Brush fish with mixture. Set fish in small, hot oiled roasting pan.

Cook under broiler 6 to 7 minutes. Baste fish during cooking.

Serve with devil sauce.

Stuffed Sea Trout

Serves 2

45 ml (3 tablespoons) butter
2 dry shallots, chopped
10 fresh mushrooms, washed and chopped
1 ml (¹/₄ teaspoon) tarragon
30 ml (2 tablespoons) chopped parsley
50 ml (¹/₄ cup) 35% cream
1 – 1.4 kg (3 pound) sea trout
lemon juice
salt and pepper

Preheat oven to 200°C (400°F).

Melt 30 ml (2 tablespoons) butter in saucepan. Add shallots, mushrooms, tarragon and parsley. Season well and cook 5 to 6 minutes over medium heat.

Remove saucepan from stove and stir in cream.

Season sea trout with salt and pepper and stuff with mixture. Tie fish with string and place in roasting pan.

Melt remaining butter and pour over fish. Sprinkle with lemon juice. Cook 15 minutes at 200°C (400°F).

Reduce heat to 190°C (375°F) and continue to cook fish for 20 minutes.

Serve with melted butter and lemon juice.

Boiled Live Lobsters

Serves 4

4 – 750 g (1¹/₂ pounds) live lobsters
125 ml (¹/₂ cup) melted unsalted butter
white pepper
lemon juice

Place deep saucepan on top of stove, fill with water and bring to boil.

Holding each lobster by the body, with claws away from you, plunge it into boiling water. Cover and cook 16 to 18 minutes over low–medium heat (water must simmer only).

Serve with melted butter well peppered and lemon juice.

Pacific Cod Fish with Anchovies

Serves 4

4 cod filets
50 ml (¹/₄ cup) flour
30 ml (2 tablespoons) oil
30 ml (2 tablespoons) butter
4 anchovy filets, drained and chopped
15 ml (1 tablespoon) chopped parsley
juice 1 lemon
few drops Tabasco sauce
salt and pepper

Season filets with salt and pepper; dredge with flour.

Heat oil in frying pan. Add fish; cook 4 minutes on each side. Transfer fish to hot service platter. Set aside.

Melt butter in frying pan. Add anchovies; mix and cook 1 minute.

Add parsley and lemon juice; mix and sprinkle with Tabasco sauce. Pour mixture over fish.

Serve with purée of vegetables.

Dungeness Crab Salad
Serves 4

Homemade mayonnaise:
15 ml (1 tablespoon) mustard
2 eggs
175 ml (³/₄ cup) olive oil
juice ¹/₂ lemon
salt and pepper

Place mustard in small bowl. Add eggs and lemon juice; mix well.

Incorporate oil, drop by drop, mixing with whisk. As soon as mixture thickens, add remaining oil in thin stream. Season well and set aside.

4 – 900 g (2 pounds) live crabs
1 celery stalk, diced
1 green pepper, diced
125 ml (¹/₂ cup) water chestnuts, diced
4 bamboo shoots, sliced
250 ml (1 cup) homemade mayonnaise
salt and pepper
garnish: lettuce, tomatoes, stuffed eggs, and cucumbers

Wash crabs and plunge in large saucepan containing 4 L (16 cups) boiling, salted water. Cook 20 to 25 minutes. Remove and cool.

Remove flesh and place in salad bowl. Add celery, green peppers, water chestnuts, and bamboo shoots. Mix and add mayonnaise. Mix again.

Decorate service platter with lettuce leaves. Place crab salad in center. Arrange garnish and serve.

Stuffed Clams
Serves 4

32 clams, brushed and cleaned
500 ml (2 cups) water
30 ml (2 tablespoons) butter
1 onion, finely chopped
15 ml (1 tablespoon) chopped fresh basil
125 g (¹/₄ pound) chopped fresh mushrooms
50 ml (¹/₄ cup) soda cracker crumbs
¹/₂ beaten egg
15 ml (1 tablespoon) chopped chives
pinch thyme
juice 1 lemon
few drops Tabasco sauce
salt and pepper

Preheat oven to 220°C (425°F).

Place clams in large saucepan. Add water and lemon juice; cover and bring to boil. Cook 4 to 5 minutes to open clams. Stir once during cooking process.

Remove clams from shells and chop coarsely.

Melt butter in saucepan. Add onions, thyme, basil; cook 3 minutes.

Add mushrooms, Tabasco sauce, and season well. Add cracker crumbs and beaten egg to bind mixture. Mix well.

Add chives and chopped clams. Mix and stuff shells. Cook in oven for 3 minutes. Serve.

Pike Filets Bordelaise

Serves 4

1 small onion, chopped
1 carrot, diced
½ celery stalk, diced
1 ml (¼ teaspoon) thyme
1 bay leaf
1 small garlic bud
4 pike filets
500 ml (2 cups) dry red wine
45 ml (3 tablespoons) butter
25 ml (1½ tablespoons) flour
15 ml (1 tablespoon) chopped parsley
salt and pepper
lemon slices for garnish

Heat a well buttered sauté pan. Add onions, carrots, and celery. Cover and cook 3 minutes over low heat.

Stir in spices and garlic. Set filets on top and add wine. Bring to gentle boil, reduce heat to very low and cook 3 to 4 minutes.

Remove filets and transfer to service platter.

Set sauté pan over high heat. Cook liquid 4 minutes. Mix butter with flour; stir into pan. Cook 2 minutes then pour over filets.

Garnish with parsley and lemon slices. Serve.

Shrimp Newburg

Serves 4

900 g (2 pounds) medium size shrimp,
shelled and deveined
45 ml (3 tablespoons) butter
30 ml (2 tablespoons) chopped dry
shallots
250 ml (1 cup) Madeira wine
375 ml (1½ cups) light cream
1 egg yolk, mixed with 45 ml
(3 tablespoons) cream
salt, pepper, paprika

Wash and pat dry shrimp.

Melt butter in frying pan. Add shrimp; season with salt and pepper. Do not stir and cook 3 minutes each side.

Remove shrimp from pan; set aside.

Place shallots in pan; cook 2 minutes.

Add wine and cook 3 minutes over medium heat. Incorporate cream and sprinkle with paprika. Stir 5 to 6 minutes.

Incorporate egg mixture and stir with whisk. Do not boil.

Replace shrimp in sauce; mix well and simmer 4 minutes.

Serve with pilaf rice.

Spawning sockeye salmon in the Adams River, British Columbia. Every October the fish travel 500 kilometres from the Pacific Ocean to spawn and die.

Flambéed Lobster

Serves 4

60 ml (4 tablespoons) butter
2 shallots, chopped
25 ml (1½ tablespoons) curry powder
30 ml (2 tablespoons) flour
500 ml (2 cups) light cream
15 ml (1 tablespoon) chopped parsley
4 lobsters, 750 g (1½ pounds) each
45 ml (3 tablespoons) brandy
paprika
salt and pepper

Melt 30 ml (2 tablespoons) butter in saucepan. Add shallots and curry powder; cook 3 minutes over low heat.

Add flour; mix and cook 2 minutes.

Incorporate cream; mix well. Sprinkle with paprika and chopped parsley. Simmer 2 minutes over low heat.

Remove meat from shells. Set aside.

Melt remaining butter in saucepan. Add lobster meat, pepper, and cook 2 minutes over high heat.

Add brandy and flambé. Add hot sauce and cook over very low heat for 4 minutes.

Serve with French bread.

Coquille St-Jacques, Maritime Style

Serves 4

500 g (1 pound) scallops
30 ml (2 tablespoons) chopped onions
1 bay leaf
24 mushrooms, washed and thinly sliced
50 ml (¼ cup) dry white wine
500 ml (2 cups) water
3 parsley sprigs
salt and pepper from mill

In well buttered sauté pan, place scallops, onions, bay leaf, mushrooms, wine, water, and parsley. Pepper well and bring to boil.

Remove pan from stove. Allow scallops to poach 3 minutes.

Remove scallops and mushrooms from pan; set aside.

Return pan to stove top and cook liquid 8 to 10 minutes. Pass through sieve and reserve.

45 ml (3 tablespoons) butter
1 chopped shallot
15 ml (1 tablespoon) chopped parsley
45 ml (3 tablespoons) flour
250 ml (1 cup) hot milk
250 ml (1 cup) cooking liquid from scallops
50 ml (¼ cup) bread crumbs
50 ml (¼ cup) grated parmesan cheese

Melt butter in sauté pan. Add shallots; cook 2 minutes. Add parsley and flour; mix well.

Incorporate hot milk and mix with whisk. Cook 4 to 5 minutes.

Add cooking liquid; mix and cook 4 to 5 minutes at medium heat. Add drained scallops and mushrooms. Season well and place mixture in scallop shells. Sprinkle with bread crumbs and grated cheese.

Broil 3 minutes. Serve.

Filet of Mackerel Sautéed with Peppers

Serves 4

*4 mackerel filets
50 ml (¼ cup) flour
45 ml (3 tablespoons) olive oil
1 green pepper, thinly sliced
1 red pepper, thinly sliced
15 ml (1 tablespoon) tomato paste
juice ½ lemon
salt and pepper*

Preheat oven to 100°C (200°F).

Season filets with salt and pepper; dredge with flour.

Heat oil in frying pan. Cook filets 3 to 4 minutes both sides. Transfer filets to service platter. Keep warm in oven.

Add green and red peppers to frying pan; cook 3 minutes over medium heat.

Sprinkle with lemon juice. Add tomato paste; mix well.

Pour over filets and serve with vegetables.

Lemon Sole

Serves 4

*8 sole filets
50 ml (¼ cup) flour
15 ml (1 tablespoon) oil
30 ml (2 tablespoons) butter
1 shallot, chopped
1 cucumber, peeled, seeded, and cut in
2.5 cm (1 inch) slices
30 ml (2 tablespoons) chopped
pimientos
lemon juice
salt and pepper*

Preheat oven to 100°C (200°F).

Season filets well and dredge with flour.

Heat oil and 15 ml (1 tablespoon) butter in frying pan. Cook filets 2 minutes each side. Remove filets and transfer to service platter. Keep warm in oven.

Melt remaining butter in pan. Add shallots and cucumbers. Season and cook 3 minutes over high heat.

Add pimientos and lemon juice. Pour over fish and serve.

Cream of Shrimp

Serves 4

*500 g (1 pound) shrimp, shelled and
deveined
45 ml (3 tablespoons) butter
2 shallots, chopped
45 ml (3 tablespoons) flour
500 ml (2 cups) hot milk
250 ml (1 cup) light cream
15 ml (1 tablespoon) parsley
few drops lemon juice
few drops Tabasco sauce
salt and white pepper*

Purée shrimp in blender. Set aside.

Melt butter in saucepan. Add shallots; cook 2 minutes. Add flour; mix well and cook 1 minute.

Incorporate hot milk, stir and season to taste. Bring to boil and continue cooking over low heat 6 to 7 minutes.

Incorporate shrimp purée and cream. Stir and simmer 4 to 5 minutes over low heat.

Sprinkle with Tabasco and lemon juice. Garnish with chopped parsley and serve.

Lobster, Cheese Sauce

Serves 4

*4 cooked lobsters, 750 g (1½ pounds)
each
30 ml (2 tablespoons) Madeira wine
45 ml (3 tablespoons) butter
2 dry shallots, chopped
250 g (½ pound) fresh mushrooms,
washed and cut in two
45 ml (3 tablespoons) flour
500 ml (2 cups) hot milk
125 ml (½ cup) light cream
125 ml (½ cup) grated Gruyère cheese
paprika
salt and pepper*

Preheat oven to 220°C (425°F).

Remove claws and legs from lobsters. Crack shells and remove flesh. Split lobsters in half, lengthwise, and remove flesh. Dice all flesh and place in bowl.

Add Madeira wine and marinate 15 minutes.

Melt butter in sauté pan. Add shallots; cook 2 minutes. Add mushrooms; season well with salt, pepper and paprika. Continue cooking 5 to 6 minutes.

Add marinade from lobsters and stir. Mix in flour. Incorporate milk mixing with whisk. Incorporate cream and half of cheese; mix well. Add lobster flesh and simmer over very low heat for several minutes.

Place lobster shells on service platter and fill with mixture. Sprinkle with remaining cheese and broil 3 minutes. Serve.

Poached Salmon with Fine Herbs

Serves 4

*4 B.C. salmon steaks, cut 2.5 cm (1 inch)
thick
1 leek, washed and thinly sliced
1 carrot, peeled and thinly sliced
1 ml (¼ teaspoon) thyme
1 bay leaf*

*12 whole peppercorns
50 ml (¼ cup) dry white wine (optional)
water
juice ½ lemon
salt and pepper*

Place salmon steaks in fish poacher or roasting pan. Add remaining ingredients, cover with water and bring liquid to a slow simmer over medium heat. Do not boil.

Let liquid simmer for 15 minutes over low heat.

Transfer salmon steaks to hot service platter. Serve with butter sauce.

Butter sauce:
*50 ml (¼ cup) melted unsalted butter
15 ml (1 tablespoon) chopped parsley
15 ml (1 tablespoon) chopped chive
juice ¼ lemon
pepper from mill*

Place all ingredients in small saucepan and cook over low heat for 2 minutes. Serve.

Sautéed Filet of Mackerel, with Gooseberries

Serves 4

250 g (1/2 pound) gooseberries, washed
45 ml (3 tablespoons) sugar
125 ml (1/2 cup) water
4 large mackerel filets
125 ml (1/2 cup) flour
30 ml (2 tablespoons) clarified butter
2 green onions, cut into small pieces
4 water chestnuts, thinly sliced
zest of 1/2 lemon, chopped
salt and pepper

Place gooseberries in saucepan. Add sugar, lemon zest, and water. Bring to boil; cook over low heat until tender. Set aside.

Season filets with salt and pepper; then flour.

Heat clarified butter in frying pan. Add filets; cook 3 minutes each side. Remove fish from pan and transfer to a service platter.

Add green onions and water chestnuts to pan. Cook 1 minute. Incorporate half of gooseberry sauce; stir and cook 2 minutes.

Pour mixture over fish. Serve with remaining sauce.

Poached Carp

Serves 4

1 – 1.6–1.8 kg (3 1/2–4 pounds) carp
4 bacon slices
30 ml (2 tablespoons) chopped fresh ginger
125 ml (1/2 cup) Madeira wine
500 ml (2 cups) chicken stock
2 green onions, cut into 2.5 cm (1 inch) pieces
3 parsley sprigs
lemon juice
salt and pepper

Clean and wash fish. Place carp in fish poacher. Set aside.

Heat bacon in saucepan. Add ginger and cook 2 minutes. Add remaining ingredients and bring to boil. Pour over fish; season well.

Cover poacher and cook 20 minutes over low heat. Turn fish over and continue cooking 10 to 15 minutes.

Serve with lemon juice.

Haddock Filets Flamande

Serves 4

30 ml (2 tablespoons) butter
4 haddock filets
1 onion, thinly sliced
125 g (1/4 pound) mushrooms, sliced
250 ml (1 cup) dry white wine
375 ml (1 1/2 cups) hot white fish sauce
15 ml (1 tablespoon) chopped parsley
salt and pepper
lemon slices for garnish

Preheat oven to 190°C (375°F).

Butter ovenproof dish. Add filets; cover with onions and mushrooms. Season and pour in wine. Cover and cook in oven for 10 minutes. Turn filets once during cooking time.

Transfer filets to service platter. Pour remaining ingredients from dish into saucepan. Cook on stove top 5 to 6 minutes. Stir in white sauce, bring to boil, then pour over filets.

Garnish with parsley and lemon slices. Serve.

Saturna Island Shrimp Pâté

Serves 10

700 g (1 1/2 lbs) cooked fresh shrimp, peeled and cleaned
125 ml (1/2 cup) softened butter
7 ml (1/2 tablespoon) lemon juice
7 ml (1/2 tablespoon) cooking sherry
2 ml (1/2 teaspoon) onion juice

2 ml (¹/₂ teaspoon) dry mustard
Mace, salt and freshly ground pepper

Put all the ingredients together in a blender or processor and whip until well blended.

May be combined by hand if the shrimp are mashed to a paste and then beaten into butter. Pack in a crock and chill in refrigerator for several hours before serving with crackers.

The catch of the day.

Broiled Trout
Serves 4

4 – 500 g (1 pound) trout, including tail,
cleaned
50 ml (¹/₄ cup) flour
50 ml (¹/₄ cup) melted butter
30 ml (2 tablespoons) chopped parsley
50 ml (¹/₄ cup) dry white wine
juice ¹/₂ lemon
salt and pepper

Preheat oven to 220°C (425°F).
Wash trout under cold water; pat dry. Make 4 incisions on both sides, on thickest part of fish.
Dredge fish with flour. Season well.
Pour melted butter in small bowl. Add chopped parsley and lemon juice. Mix well and brush fish with mixture.
Set fish in hot oiled roasting pan. Cook under broiler, 6 to 7 minutes each side.
3 minutes before end of cooking, pour wine over fish.
Serve with melted butter and lemon juice.

Ste-Thérèse-de-Gaspé is one of the numerous fishing villages on the south shore of the Gaspé Peninsula in Quebec.

Mackerel Filets Rosalie
Serves 4

4 mackerel filets
250 ml (1 cup) flour
45 ml (3 tablespoons) walnut oil
1 onion, finely chopped
125 g (¹/₄ pound) mushrooms, finely
chopped
2 shallots, chopped
15 ml (1 tablespoon) chopped parsley
salt and pepper
lemon juice

Dredge filets with flour. Heat 25 ml (1¹/₂ tablespoons) oil in frying pan. Cook filets, 3 to 4 minutes each side.
Transfer filets to ovenproof dish. Add remaining ingredients, including oil. Season well; cook 2 minutes on stove top.
Broil 4 minutes. Serve with lemon juice.

Shad Filets Florentine

Serves 4

4 large shad filets
1 beaten egg
125 ml (¹/₂ cup) milk
250 ml (1 cup) flour
30 ml (2 tablespoons) oil
15 ml (1 tablespoon) butter
2 packages spinach, washed, cooked,
and chopped
125 ml (¹/₂ cup) hot white sauce
30 ml (2 tablespoons) cream
pinch nutmeg
salt and pepper
lemon slices for garnish

Mix egg and milk together in small bowl. Season filets, then dip into mixture. Dredge filets with flour.

Heat oil in frying pan. Add filets; cook 2 to 3 minutes each side.

Remove filets and transfer to ovenproof service platter. Keep hot in oven at 70°C (150°F).

Heat butter in saucepan. Add spinach; cook 2 to 3 minutes. Mix in white sauce, cream, and nutmeg. Cook 2 to 3 minutes.

Serve sauce with filets. Garnish with lemon slices.

Paupiettes of Salmon Stuffed with Pike Mousse

Serves 4

250 ml (1 cup) pike mousse
8 very thin slices B.C. salmon
30 ml (2 tablespoons) butter
2 dry shallots, chopped
30 ml (2 tablespoons) fresh chopped
tarragon
250 ml (1 cup) dry white wine
500 ml (2 cups) hot Nantua sauce
pepper

Preheat oven to 180°C (350°F).

Place 15 ml (1 tablespoon) pike mousse on each salmon slice. Roll slices.

Well butter a baking dish. Add shallots and tarragon. Arrange salmon rolls in dish. Pour in wine and pepper well. Cover and cook in oven 10 to 12 minutes.

Remove fish and transfer to service platter.

Place baking dish on stove top; reduce liquid by ³/₄. Mix in Nantua sauce and cook over low heat 2 minutes.

Pour sauce over fish and serve.

Commercial fishboat gillnetting in the Fraser River near Steveston, British Columbia.

Longhouses, 'Ksan Indian Village, British Columbia

THE
FIRST
PEOPLE

The first people of Canada were semi-nomadic groups, isolated by the vast distances of the rugged Canadian landscape, that learned to rely on every resource that nature could provide. Representative of Canada from the Atlantic to the Pacific, Canadian Indian cookery is a refreshing reminder of the first people's appreciation for the wealth of the land and the sea.

Plants, cultivated and wild, not only served as food but were used in religious rituals and as medicine. To survive in an often difficult land, food was simple and nourishing — designed to maintain enough energy for hunting and trapping.

In keeping with the lifestyle, cooking techniques seldom wasted any part of the plant or animal. When stems, bark, or leaves of a plant were inedible, they were used for clothing or weapons. This logical and necessary way of life developed creativity in Indian cookery, and even today the same ideas are expressed.

Several varieties of fermented beverages were created from the wide selection of wild berries, and these were often served during annual celebrations. Berries also were used to create most of the Indian desserts.

The recipes in this section are a selection of the finest authentic Canadian Indian cookery, although some have been carefully adapted for today's cooking. Some of the produce, though unfamiliar, can be obtained in specialty shops. The extra shopping trip will be well worth your while! Whether you try Moose Shoulder Roast or Berry soup, newcomers to Indian cookery will enjoy the difference, simplicity, and distinctive flavour of this cuisine.

Indian Seafood, Modern Style

Serves 4 to 6

2 lobsters, cooked 10 minutes in boiling
sea water (with seaweed if available)
14 scallops
14 shrimp, shelled and deveined
12 wild onions
50 ml (¼ cup) bacon fat, melted

Cut lobster flesh into cubes. Alternate scallops, shrimp, lobster, and onions on skewers. Brush well with melted bacon fat.

Cook over a wild fire or barbecue for 3 minutes. Turn and cook 2 more minutes. Serve.

Berry Sauce

500 g (1 pound) chokecherries
500 g (1 pound) blackberries
375 ml (1½ cups) maple syrup
250 ml (1 cup) cider
15 ml (1 tablespoon) white alcohol

Place all ingredients in saucepan and stir. Cook 40 minutes over medium heat, cool, and serve.

Wild Rice

Serves 4 to 6

500 ml (2 cups) wild rice, washed
750 ml (3 cups) water
30 ml (2 tablespoons) sunflower oil
250 g (½ pound) wild mushrooms,
washed and cut in two
250 ml (1 cup) corn
2 wild onions, chopped
several sorrel leaves, chopped
salt and pepper

Preheat oven to 160°C (325°F).

Place rice in saucepan and pour in water. Cover and bring to boil. Cook 10 to 12 minutes.

Remove saucepan from stove. Let stand, covered, for 30 minutes or until water is absorbed.

Heat oil in sauté pan. Add mushrooms, sorrel leaves, corn, and onions. Stir and cook 3 minutes; season well.

Transfer rice to casserole dish. Incorporate mushroom mixture and cook 25 minutes in oven.

Serve as vegetable or with meat.

Fried Trout

Serves 6 to 8

375 ml (1½ cups) corn flour
1 wild onion, very finely chopped
1 branch wild thyme
6 to 8 small trout, washed and cleaned
125 ml (½ cup) corn or nut oil
salt and pepper

Combine flour, onion, and thyme in bowl. Roll fish in mixture and season well.

Heat oil in frying pan; add fish. Cook 4 minutes each side. Serve.

Blueberry Pancakes

Serves 6 to 8

500 ml (2 cups) blueberries, washed
125 ml (¹/₂ cup) maple syrup
750 ml (3 cups) flour
3 eggs
1 egg white, beaten stiff
sunflower oil
maple syrup

Place blueberries in sieve. Using spoon, mash to remove some of the juice.

Transfer berries to mixing bowl. Stir in maple syrup, flour, and whole eggs. Mix well and fold in egg white; mix again.

Heat enough oil to coat bottom of frying pan. When hot, use ladle to form small pancakes. Cook pancakes until golden on both sides.

Serve with maple syrup.

Pumpkin with Maple Syrup

Serves 6 to 8

1 medium pumpkin, washed
375 ml (1¹/₂ cups) maple syrup
15 ml (1 tablespoon) corn syrup
375 ml (1¹/₂ cups) cranberries, washed
50 ml (¹/₄ cup) melted butter

Preheat oven to 180°C (350°F).

Wrap pumpkin in aluminum foil and cook in oven 1 hour.

Remove pumpkin and slice off top. Using large spoon, scoop out loose flesh and seeds. Set pumpkin and top aside.

Combine maple syrup, corn syrup, cranberries, and butter in saucepan. Bring to boil and cook 6 minutes.

Generously brush inside of pumpkin with syrup mixture. Replace top and wrap in aluminum foil. Cook in oven for 35 minutes. Baste several times during cooking.

To serve, remove foil and pumpkin top. Slice pumpkin into large quarters and sprinkle with warmed syrup mixture.

Crab with Wood Sorrel

Serves 4 to 6

375 ml (1¹/₂ cups) crab meat
750 ml (3 cups) wood sorrel, washed
and chopped
¹/₂ wild onion, chopped
30 ml (2 tablespoons) corn flour
1 egg
75 ml (5 tablespoons) bacon fat or
butter
salt and pepper

Squeeze excess juice from crab meat. Place meat in bowl; mix in wood sorrel and onion. Season well and stir in flour.

Incorporate egg and shape into small pancakes.

Heat fat in frying pan. Cook pancakes, 3 minutes each side. Serve.

Succotash

Serves 4 to 6

2 onions, chopped
1 red pepper, chopped
1 green pepper, chopped
750 ml (3 cups) fresh yellow corn
500 ml (2 cups) water
500 ml (2 cups) shelled lima beans
45 ml (3 tablespoons) butter
salt and pepper

In large saucepan, place onions, peppers and corn; mix well.

Add water; season with salt and pepper.

Add lima beans and butter; mix well. Correct seasoning. Cover and cook 20 to 25 minutes over low heat. Serve.

Wild Stuffed Duck

Serves 4

2 wild ducks, feathers, tails, and necks removed
15 ml (1 tablespoon) sunflower oil
4 apples, cored, peeled, and cut in 4
125 ml (¹/₂ cup) sweet berries, washed
50 ml (¹/₄ cup) maple syrup
2 mint leaves, chopped
sea salt and pepper from mill

Preheat oven to 200°C (400°F).

Remove livers from ducks and chop; set aside. Wash ducks inside and out; pat dry. Season cavities with salt and pepper.

Heat oil in sauté pan. Add apples, berries, maple syrup, and mint leaves. Mix, cover, and cook 10 to 12 minutes.

Transfer stuffing to bowl. Add chopped liver to sauté pan; cook several minutes. Season well then add to bowl.

Stuff ducks and secure with kitchen string. Set in roasting pan and prick skins with paring knife.

Cook 1 hour in oven. Reduce heat to 190°C (375°F) and continue cooking 30 minutes.

Serve with berry sauce.

Wild Rice with Tomatoes

Serves 4 to 6

500 ml (2 cups) wild rice, washed and drained
1.5 L (6 cups) water
2 onions, diced
250 ml (1 cup) shelled hazelnuts, chopped
2 large tomatoes, quartered
salt and pepper

In large saucepan, combine wild rice, water and onions. Bring to boil, cover and cook for 35 to 40 minutes over medium heat or until most water is absorbed.

Add chopped hazelnuts and tomatoes. Season to taste and mix well. Cover and continue to cook for 20 to 25 minutes, stirring occasionally. Serve.

Savoury Bannock

Serves 2

250 ml (1 cup) whole wheat flour
5 ml (1 teaspoon) baking powder
5 ml (1 teaspoon) salt
2 ml (¹/₂ teaspoon) each sage, garlic and thyme
50 ml (¹/₄ cup) chopped onions
15 ml (1 tablespoon) lard
water

Mix flour, baking powder, salt and spices together. Add onion.

Cut lard into mixture and blend thoroughly.

Add just enough water to form a stiff dough.

Form patty about ³/₄″ thick and place in greased frying pan. Cook over medium heat 10 minutes each side.

Squash Soup

Serves 6 to 8

2 squash, peeled and cubed
3 green onions, thinly sliced
30 ml (2 tablespoons) maple syrup
1.5 L (6 cups) water
15 ml (1 tablespoon) oil
15 ml (1 tablespoon) chopped dill
salt and white pepper

In large saucepan, place squash, green onions and maple syrup. Season with salt and pepper.

Add water and oil; stir. Cover and cook 25 to 30 minutes over low heat or until squash is done. Pour mixture into blender and purée.

Return purée to saucepan. Add dill and correct seasoning. Simmer 5 minutes. Serve with fresh bread.

Venison Roast
Serves 4 to 6

750 ml (3 cups) cider
2 wild onions
45 ml (3 tablespoons) maple syrup
50 ml (1/4 cup) juniper berries, washed
2 ml (1/2 teaspoon) wild thyme
4 to 6 small hazelnuts
2.3 kg (5 pound) venison roast
30 ml (2 tablespoons) nut oil

Preheat oven to 190°C (375°F).

Place cider, onions, maple syrup, berries, thyme, and hazelnuts in saucepan. Bring to boil and cook 6 minutes.

Pour marinade over roast and refrigerate overnight.

Remove roast from marinade and transfer to roasting pan; reserve remaining marinade. Brush roast with oil and place in oven. Cook 1½ hours, basting frequently with marinade.

Serve with baked potatoes and dandelion salad.

Mussels Huron Style
Serves 4

48 mussels
500 ml (2 cups) water
50 ml (1/4 cup) butter
2 ml (1/2 teaspoon) wild thyme
45 ml (3 tablespoons) wild watercress,
chopped
pepper from mill

Wash mussels under cold water. Remove beard with small paring knife and scrub well with brush.

Rinse mussels again and place in large saucepan. Add remaining ingredients. Cover and bring to boil.

Cook 3 minutes over low heat; stir during process to evenly cook. Over cooking will result in toughness.

Remove mussels with slotted spoon; transfer to service platter.

Continue cooking sauce 3 to 4 minutes. Pour over mussels and serve.

Rabbit Stew
Serves 8

2 rabbits, cleaned
30 sheep sorrel leaves
1.2 L (5 cups) water
45 ml (3 tablespoons) nut oil
12 sweet crab apples, cored, peeled, and
cut in two
3 wild onions, chopped
500 ml (2 cups) fiddleheads, washed and
steamed
pinch wild thyme
sea salt and pepper

Preheat oven to 180°C (350°F).

Cut rabbits in pieces. Remove and chop livers; set aside.

Place sheep sorrel leaves in saucepan. Cover with water and bring to boil. Simmer 20 minutes. Strain liquid and reserve 500 ml (2 cups).

Heat oil in large sauté pan. Add rabbit, season well with sea salt, and brown 10 to 12 minutes over high heat.

Add apples, onions and chopped livers. Mix well, then stir in thyme and reserved sheep sorrel liquid. Season well.

Cover and cook in oven 1½ hours. 8 minutes before end of cooking, add fiddleheads. Serve.

Potato Soup

Serves 6

6 potatoes, peeled and cubed
6 fresh tomatoes, washed and diced
3 cooking apples, peeled, cored and
cubed
125 ml (½ cup) chopped fresh mint
2 L (8 cups) water
15 ml (1 tablespoon) cornmeal
2 bayberry leaves
250 ml (1 cup) fresh dillweed, chopped
pinch basil
salt and pepper

In large saucepan, place potatoes, tomatoes, apples, mint and water; stir. Season with salt and pepper.

Add cornmeal; mix again. Cover and cook over low heat for 2 hours, stirring occasionally.

Add herbs, stir and continue to cook for 8 to 10 minutes. Serve.

Stew, Huron Style

Serves 6 to 8

900 g (2 pound) lamb shoulder
900 g (2 pound) veal leg
1 rabbit cut into pieces
375 ml (1½ cups) dry white beans,
soaked 12 hours in cold water
375 ml (1½ cups) cooked corn
2 wild garlic cloves
50 ml (¼ cup) maple syrup

Preheat oven to 140°C (275°F).
Cut meat into 2.5 cm (1 inch) pieces.
Place meat in large ovenproof casserole. Season well.

Add remaining ingredients. Correct seasoning. Cover and cook 8 hours in oven. Serve.

Indian children at the Calgary Stampede.

Berry Soup

Serves 6 to 8

10 scallions, washed and sliced
12 dried juniper berries
250 ml (1 cup) shelled sunflower seeds
2 fresh mint leaves
2.5 L (10 cups) water
fresh chopped dill to taste

Place all ingredients in large stock pot. Bring to boil, partly cover, and cook 1 hour over low heat. Serve.

Apple Sauce Dessert

Serves 4 to 6

1.4 kg (3 pounds) cooking apples, cored and cut in 4
500 g (1 pound) sweet berries, washed
250 ml (1 cup) maple syrup
250 ml (1 cup) water
fresh cream

Place all ingredients in large saucepan, except cream, and cover. Bring to boil.
Mix well and continue cooking 1 hour over very low heat.
Cool and serve with fresh cream.

Moose Shoulder Roast

Serves 4 to 6

50 ml (¹/₄ cup) vegetable oil
125 ml (¹/₂ cup) white alcohol
2 onions, sliced
3 wild garlic cloves
15 ml (1 tablespoon) fresh ginger, chopped
125 ml (¹/₂ cup) molasses
30 ml (2 tablespoons) soya sauce
1 – 2.3 kg (5 pound) moose boneless shoulder roast

Preheat oven to 180°C (350°F).
In bowl, combine oil, alcohol, onions, garlic, ginger, molasses and soya sauce. Pour mixture over roast and marinate for 2 hours.
Transfer roast to roasting pan and place in oven. Cook, uncovered, for 1¹/₂ hours basting often with marinade.
Serve.

Indian Beverage

Serves 8 to 10

2 L (8 cups) water
375 ml (1¹/₂ cups) honey
white alcohol or rum

Place water and honey in large saucepan. Bring to boil and cook 12 minutes. Cool.
To serve, mix with white alcohol or rum.

Roast Wild Goose

Serves 6 to 8

50 ml (¼ cup) white alcohol
2 wild onions, chopped
3 to 4 fresh dillweed leaves, chopped
1-4.5 to 5.4 kg (10 to 12 pounds) goose,
cleaned, giblets removed and chopped
45 ml (3 tablespoons) nut oil
250 g (½ pound) wild mushrooms,
chopped
6 crab apples, cored, peeled, and sliced
125 ml (½ cup) cornmeal
250 ml (1 cup) cooked wild rice
pinch wild thyme
several leaves wild watercress, chopped
salt and pepper

Preheat oven to 180°C (350°F).

Combine alcohol, onions, thyme, and dillweed in small bowl. Mix well and pour into goose. Set goose aside for 1 hour.

Heat 30 ml (2 tablespoons) oil in frying pan. Add giblets, mushrooms, and apples; season well. Cover and cook 8 minutes.

Add cornmeal, rice, and watercress; mix well. Cook 3 minutes.

Stuff goose and secure with kitchen string. Place in roasting pan and brush goose with remaining oil. Cook in oven 3½ to 4 hours, depending on size. Prick skin during cooking to allow fat to escape. Baste frequently.

Serve goose with berry sauce.

Moose and Fish Stew

Serves 8

900 g (2 pound) trout, deboned and cut
into large pieces
900 g (2 pound) salmon, deboned and
cut into large pieces
1.4 kg (3 pounds) moose meat, cut into
3.8 cm (1½ inch) cubes
900 g (2 pounds) red kidney beans,
soaked in cold water for 12 hours
500 g (2 cups) corn

3 wild onions, chopped
2 ml (½ teaspoon) wild thyme
50 ml (¼ cup) maple syrup
sea salt and pepper

Preheat oven to 120°C (250°F).

Place all ingredients in large cast iron pot. Cover with water, mix and season well.

Cover and cook 8 hours in oven. Serve.

Moose Steak

Serves 4

45 ml (3 tablespoons) nut oil
2 wild onions, chopped
30 ml (2 tablespoons) white alcohol
2 ml (½ teaspoon) wild thyme
1.6 kg (3½ pound) moose steak, 3.8 cm
(1½ inch) thick
sea salt and pepper

Combine oil, onions, alcohol, thyme, and pepper in small bowl. Mix well and season.

Using small paring knife, make several incisions in meat on both sides. Brush marinade over meat.

Broil in oven 35 to 40 minutes, basting meat occasionally. Slice and serve.

Salmon Steaks Broiled over Coals

Serves 4

4 wild onions, chopped
60 ml (4 tablespoons) nut oil
3 mint leaves, chopped
4 salmon steaks, 3 cm (1¼ inch) thick
pinch wild thyme

Combine onions, oil, chopped mint, and thyme in bowl; mix well.

Brush salmon steaks well with mixture. Cook salmon over hot coals, 4 to 5 minutes each side. Baste during cooking. Serve.

CANADA'S
INTERNATIONAL

CITIES

C anada's international cities from coast to coast house a wide selection of multicultural cuisine. Cookery native to all parts of the world can be found in Canadian cities, where it charms and continually delights guests.

Over the years, Canadian cities have become known for their special ethnic cuisines. Montreal, for instance, is recognized for delicious French food stemming from the great cuisine of France. Typically French style, cozy, bistro-like indoor and outdoor cafés line cobblestone single lane streets in fashionable Old Montreal. This is a delightful way to spend an afternoon or evening, just relaxing and eating.

Vancouver, with its enviable climate, has attracted those from the Far East for years. Together Chinese and Japanese cuisines have enlightened many and continue to please many more.

In Vancouver's "Chinatown," residents and visitors are able to experience authentic Far East cookery, along with yearly traditional festivals and celebrations. Vancouver market places are super spots to spend an hour rummaging for perfectly ripe fruits and flawless vegetables. Armed with fresh produce, Far East cookery can be tackled justly.

Toronto, perched dock-side on Lake Ontario, welcomes the greatest selection of multicultural cuisine. Visitors flock to this sophisticated city to enjoy regional Italian cooking. Toronto's Italian neighbourhoods match the charm and warmth of the homeland. Small grocery stores overflow with delicious breads, cold meat, and many specialty items.

To the west and east of these three cities are a handful more that eagerly await your visit. But satisfy your appetite, for now, by trying some of the following recipes.

Calgary, Alberta; site of the 1988 Winter Olympic Games.

Sole Filets with Garlic and Tequila Carrots

Serves 4

4 carrots, sliced
30 ml (2 tablespoons) butter
45 ml (3 tablespoons) tequila
50 ml (¼ cup) olive oil
3 garlic buds, smashed and chopped
4 large sole filets
juice 1 lime
fresh chopped dill
salt and pepper

Place carrots in saucepan filled with 500 ml (2 cups) boiling water. Cook 5 to 6 minutes, depending on thickness.

Drain carrots and replace in saucepan. Stir in butter and tequila. Sprinkle with chopped dill and keep warm.

Heat half of oil in frying pan. Add garlic and cook 2 minutes. Set aside.

Heat remaining oil in separate frying pan. Add sole and cook 3 minutes. Turn fish and season well. Continue cooking 2 minutes.

When cooked, transfer sole to service platter.

Replace frying pan containing garlic on stove top. When hot, add lime juice. Simmer several minutes.

Pour garlic sauce over sole and serve with carrots.

Broccoli alla Romana

Serves 4

1 large fresh bunch broccoli
50 ml (¼ cup) olive oil
2 garlic buds, smashed and chopped
15 ml (1 tablespoon) chopped chives
15 ml (1 tablespoon) chopped parsley
125 ml (½ cup) dry white wine
500 ml (2 cups) cheese sauce, well seasoned
dash paprika
salt and pepper

Cut flowerets from stalks and wash well. Slice stalks and set broccoli aside.

Heat oil in large sauté pan. Add garlic and cook 2 minutes over low heat.

Add flowerets and sliced stalks to garlic. Season with salt and pepper. Cook 3 to 4 minutes over high heat.

Add chives and parsley; mix well. Pour in wine and cover. Continue cooking 6 to 7 minutes.

Add cheese sauce and paprika; simmer several minutes.

Serve.

Chicken Pie Niçoise

Serves 4

4 small frozen pastry shells
1½ chicken breasts, deboned and skinned
750 ml (3 cups) water
½ celery stalk
1 carrot, thinly sliced
30 ml (2 tablespoons) olive oil
1 onion, peeled and chopped
1 garlic bud, smashed and chopped
3 large tomatoes, peeled and chopped
20 olives, pitted and chopped
15 ml (1 tablespoon) chopped parsley
5 ml (1 teaspoon) tarragon
45 ml (3 tablespoons) tomato paste
salt and pepper

Bake frozen pastry shells as directed on package.

Place chicken in large sauté pan. Cover with water and add celery and carrots. Season well. Bring to boil and cook 12 minutes over low heat.

When cooked, remove meat and vegetables; slice thinly. Reserve 125 ml (½ cup) of cooking liquid.

Heat oil in frying pan. Add onions and garlic; cook 3 minutes over low heat. Add tomatoes, olives, and reserved cooking liquid. Mix in all spices and cook 8 minutes.

Stir in tomato paste. Add chicken, season well, and simmer 3 to 4 minutes.

Fill pastry shells and serve.

Super Chef's Salad
Serves 4

1 head Romaine lettuce, washed and dried
1 head Boston lettuce, washed and dried
1 bunch fresh spinach, washed, dried, and stems trimmed
½ English cucumber, peeled and sliced
75 ml (⅓ cup) pine nuts
2 large ripe tomatoes, quartered
125 g (¼ pound) fresh mushrooms, washed and sliced
250 ml (1 cup) cooked ham, cut into strips
125 ml (½ cup) Gruyère cheese, cut into strips
sour cream dressing
salt and pepper

Break lettuce and spinach into bite–size pieces. Place in large salad bowl.

Add cucumbers, nuts, tomatoes, and mushrooms. Season well.

Pour in sour cream dressing and toss until evenly coated.

Add ham, toss again. Serve in individual bowls and top with cheese.

Sour cream dressing:
1 ml (¼ teaspoon) salt
5 ml (1 teaspoon) Dijon mustard
15 ml (1 tablespoon) finely chopped dry shallots
5 ml (1 teaspoon) finely chopped parsley
1 ml (¼ teaspoon) finely chopped fresh dill
50 ml (¼ cup) wine vinegar
150 ml (⅔ cup) olive oil
30 ml (2 tablespoons) sour cream
pepper
juice ¼ lemon

Whisk salt, pepper, mustard, shallots, parsley, dill, and wine vinegar together in bowl.

Add olive oil in thin steady stream, whisking constantly.

Sprinkle with lemon juice, correct seasoning, and blend well.

Stir in sour cream and mix again.

Shrimp in Black Bean Sauce
Serves 4

45 ml (3 tablespoons) vegetable oil
750 g (1½ pounds) shrimp, shelled and deveined
2 garlic buds, smashed and chopped
30 ml (2 tablespoons) salted black beans, chopped
30 ml (2 tablespoons) chopped ginger root
3 scallions, chopped
1 green pepper, thinly sliced
1 red pepper, thinly sliced
1 Chinese cabbage leaf, cut in 1.3 cm (½ inch) strips
15 ml (1 tablespoon) soya sauce
30 ml (2 tablespoons) sake
15 ml (1 tablespoon) maple syrup
375 ml (1½ cups) hot chicken stock
15 ml (1 tablespoon) cornstarch
45 ml (3 tablespoons) water
salt and pepper

Heat oil in sauté pan. Add shrimps and season. Cook 3 to 4 minutes over medium heat. Remove and set aside.

Add garlic, beans, and ginger. Stir and add scallions, green and red peppers and cabbage. Season and cook 3 to 4 minutes over medium heat. Stir twice during cooking.

Mix in soya sauce, sake, and maple syrup. Cook 2 minutes.

Add chicken stock, reduce heat to low, and simmer 3 minutes.

Mix cornstarch with water; incorporate to sauce. Mix and simmer several minutes.

Add shrimps, bring to boil and stir. Simmer 2 minutes.

Serve.

Shrimp Marinara
Serves 4

30 ml (2 tablespoons) olive oil
24 jumbo shrimp, shelled, deveined,
and washed
3 garlic buds, smashed and chopped
15 ml (1 tablespoon) chopped parsley
4 anchovy filets, finely chopped
15 ml (1 tablespoon) chopped parsley
500 ml (2 cups) light tomato sauce
few drops Tabasco sauce
salt and pepper

Heat oil in frying pan. Add shrimp, season and cook 3 to 4 minutes. Remove shrimp and set aside.

Add garlic, parsley, anchovies, and chives to pan. Mix well and cook 1 minute.

Stir in tomato sauce and bring to boil over medium heat.

Replace shrimp, sprinkle with Tabasco sauce, and simmer 3 to 4 minutes over very low heat.

Serve with rice.

Quiche Lorraine
Serves 4

30 ml (2 tablespoons) butter
1 onion, peeled and finely chopped
85 g (3 ounces) diced smoked ham
85 g (3 ounces) diced smoked pork
flaky dough for bottom crust
125 ml (½ cup) grated Gruyère cheese
3 egg yolks
375 ml (1½ cups) 35% cream
pinch nutmeg

Preheat oven to 220°C (425°F).

Heat butter in small saucepan. Add onions, cover and cook 4 minutes. Stir in ham and pork; cook 2 minutes. Set aside.

Roll dough and line 23 cm (9 inch) flan dish. Prick dough with fork.

Spoon onion mixture into pie shell. Sprinkle half of cheese over top.

Mix egg yolks with cream; season well. Pour into pie shell and top with remaining cheese.

Cook in oven 4 to 5 minutes. Reduce heat to 190°C (375°F); continue cooking 25 to 30 minutes.

Serve.

Apple and Celery Soup
Serves 4

45 ml (3 tablespoons) butter
1 onion, peeled and thinly sliced
60 ml (4 tablespoons) flour
2 celery stalks, sliced
3 apples, cored, peeled, and sliced
1.2 L (5 cups) hot light chicken stock
salt and pepper
sour cream to taste
thin slices of apple for garnish

Heat butter in large saucepan. Add onions, cover and cook 3 minutes.

Stir in flour, continue cooking 3 to 4 minutes over low heat.

Add celery and apples; mix well. Pour in chicken stock, mix, and season well.

Bring to boil and continue cooking 35 to 40 minutes over medium heat.

Pass through food mill. Serve with 15 ml (1 tablespoon) sour cream and garnish with several slices of apple.

Traditional costume at the Oktoberfest in Kitchener, Ontario.

Montreal Bouillabaisse

750 g (1¹/₂ pound) lobster
30 ml (2 tablespoons) butter
45 ml (3 tablespoons) cognac
125 ml (¹/₂ cup) dry white wine
2 salmon steaks, skinned and cut in 2
18 shrimp, shelled, deveined, and washed
12 scallops
15 ml (1 tablespoon) oil
1 carrot, thinly sliced
1 leek, white section only, washed and cut in 4
1 garlic bud, smashed and chopped
796 ml (28 ounce) can tomatoes, drained and chopped
1 L (4 cups) fish stock

1 bay leaf
pinch thyme
chopped fresh parsley
salt and pepper

Remove head from lobster and discard. Crack claws and remove. Section body into 4 or 5 pieces.

Heat butter in frying pan. Add lobster pieces and claws; cook 3 to 4 minutes. Add cognac and flambé.

Season well, pour in wine and remaining fish. Simmer 5 minutes.

Heat oil in separate frying pan. Sauté carrots, leeks, and garlic 3 to 4 minutes. Add tomatoes, season and mix.

Transfer fish to large ovenproof casserole. Add sautéed vegetables and cooking liquid from fish.

Pour in fish stock, season and bring to boil. Add all spices and cook 15 minutes over low heat.

Serve with garlic bread.

126

Mexican Fruit Salad

Serves 4

1 large papaya, peeled, seeded, and cut in 0.62 cm (¼ inch) slices
½ cantaloupe, seeded and sliced
4 slices water melon, seeded, peeled, and cut in 3
1 banana, peeled and sliced
50 ml (¼ cup) shredded fresh coconut
45 ml (3 tablespoons) brown sugar
30 ml (2 tablespoons) liquid honey
625 ml (2½ cups) yogurt
125 ml (½ cup) granola
125 ml (½ cup) chopped walnuts
50 ml (¼ cup) slivered almonds
lettuce leaves

Place all fruit in large bowl. Toss lightly.

Add sugar and honey; mix well. Pour in yogurt and toss until blended.

Sprinkle with granola and nuts.

Serve over several lettuce leaves. Ideal for breakfast after a morning run through Stanley Park.

Braised Chinese Cabbage

Serves 4

1 large Chinese cabbage, washed
50 ml (¼ cup) vegetable oil
125 g (¼ pound) mushrooms, washed and sliced
15 ml (1 tablespoon) chopped fresh ginger
1 bamboo shoot, sliced
500 g (1 pound) shrimp, shelled and cut in half
375 ml (1½ cups) hot chicken stock
15 ml (1 tablespoon) cornstarch
30 ml (2 tablespoons) water
salt and pepper

Discard top leaves from cabbage. Slice remaining cabbage.

Heat half of oil in wok. When very hot, add cabbage and cook 3 minutes. Stir constantly.

Remove cabbage and set aside. Heat remaining oil. Cook mushrooms, ginger, bamboo shoot, and shrimp 3 minutes over high heat. Season well.

Add chicken stock and bring to boil. Reduce heat.

Mix cornstarch with water; incorporate to sauce. Continue cooking 2 minutes.

Replace cabbage in sauce, mix, and simmer 2 minutes. Serve.

Meatball Soup

Serves 4 to 6

3 garlic buds
15 ml (1 tablespoon) vegetable oil
1 large onion, peeled and diced
1 leek, cut in 4, washed, and sliced
2 carrots, peeled and thickly sliced
1 head cabbage, washed and sliced
2 bay leaves
3 parsley sprigs
1 ml (¼ teaspoon) coriander
50 ml (¼ cup) pimiento, chopped
3 L (12 cups) water
1 beef bone
1 large egg
salt and pepper

Peel 1 garlic bud and slice in half. Smash and chop remaining garlic; set aside.

Heat oil in large sauté pan. Add all vegetables and garlic halves; season well. Cover and cook 7 to 8 minutes over low heat.

Stir in all spices. Add water and beef bone; bring to boil. Skim and cook 2 hours over low heat.

Strain and replace liquid in sauté pan. Simmer over low heat.

Place meat, vegetables, and egg in blender. Mix until well blended.

Using hands form into meatballs. Drop meatballs into simmering stock and cook 4 to 5 minutes over very low heat.

Serve with boiled potatoes, carrots, and sour cream.

Vietnamese Pork (Adapted for North America)

Serves 4

900 g (2 pounds) lean leg of pork, cut in 2.5 cm (1 inch) squares
4 scallions, diced
2 leaves Chinese cabbage, sliced
30 ml (2 tablespoons) sesame oil
45 ml (3 tablespoons) nuoc-mam (Vietnamese fish stock)
1 green pepper, sliced
125 g (¼ pound) mushrooms, washed and sliced
1 carrot, thinly sliced
1 bunch broccoli, flowerets only
salt and pepper

Place meat in sauté pan and cover with scallions and cabbage. Season and cover with water. Bring to boil over medium heat.

Cover and continue cooking 2 hours over low heat.

When meat is cooked and most of water is evaporated, add oil. Stir in nuoc-mam and vegetables. Continue cooking 15 to 16 minutes, uncovered, over medium-high heat.

Serve and garnish with chopped chives if available.

Garlic Bread with Feta Cheese

250 ml (1 cup) butter
4 garlic buds, smashed and chopped
30 ml (2 tablespoons) chopped parsley
125 ml (½ cup) feta cheese
few drops lemon juice
slices French bread
pepper from mill

Preheat oven to 180°C (350°F).

Place butter in bowl. Add garlic, parsley, and pepper. Mix until well combined.

Add lemon juice and mix. Spread mixture over bread slices and top with feta cheese.

Bake in oven 5 to 6 minutes.

Serve with ouzo!

Lobster Pekin

Serves 4

45 ml (3 tablespoons) melted butter
4 green onions, chopped
625 ml (2¹/₂ cups) cooked lobster, diced
15 ml (1 tablespoon) Saki wine
375 ml (1¹/₂ cups) bamboo shoots
250 ml (1 cup) pea pods, cooked 3
minutes in boiling water
15 ml (1 tablespoon) soya sauce
2 eggs, lightly beaten
15 ml (1 tablespoon) cornstarch
30 ml (2 tablespoons) water
salt and pepper

Heat butter in large sauté pan. Add onions and lobster; cook 2 minutes. Stir in wine; continue cooking 2 minutes.

Remove lobster from pan and set aside. Add bamboo shoots, pea pods, and soya sauce to sauté pan. Mix very well and season. Cook 3 minutes.

Add eggs and remove pan from heat. Mix cornstarch with water; incorporate to sauce.

Replace pan on stove top. Cook 1 minute over low heat. Mix in lobster meat and simmer 2 minutes.

Serve over rice.

Strawberries Romanoff

Serves 6 to 8

1 L (4 cups) strawberries
50 ml (¹/₄ cup) fine sugar
30 ml (2 tablespoons) Cointreau
30 ml (2 tablespoons) Grand Marnier
375 ml (1¹/₂ cups) vanilla ice cream
500 ml (2 cups) whipped cream

Wash and hull strawberries. Place in mixing bowl.

Sprinkle with sugar, Cointreau, and Grand Marnier. Mix well and marinate 15 minutes.

Beat ice cream until soft. Incorporate to strawberries and fold in whipped cream.

Serve in dessert cups with lady fingers.

Veal Italienne

Serves 4

4 large veal scallops
125 ml (¹/₂ cup) flour
45 ml (3 tablespoons) butter
2 shallots, finely chopped
50 ml (¹/₄ cup) Marsala wine
375 ml (1¹/₂ cups) hot light chicken stock
15 ml (1 tablespoon) tomato paste
15 ml (1 tablespoon) cornstarch
30 ml (2 tablespoons) water
4 large slices Gruyère cheese
8 tomato slices
salt and pepper

Preheat oven to 200°C (400°F).

Set veal on wooden chopping board. If necessary, pound meat. Season generously with salt and pepper. Dredge scallops with flour.

Heat butter in frying pan. Add veal and cook 3 minutes each side. When cooked, remove and set aside.

Add shallots to pan and cook 1 minute. Mix in wine and reduce 3 minutes.

Stir in chicken stock and tomato paste. Mix cornstarch with water; incorporate to sauce. Simmer 3 minutes over low heat.

Arrange veal in large baking dish. Top scallops with cheese and tomatoes. Pour sauce over top.

Broil 3 to 4 minutes in oven. Serve.

Japanese Yakitori Chicken

Serves 8

500 g (1 lb) boneless chicken breasts
green onions in 2.5 cm (1") lengths
bamboo skewers
Marinade:
50 ml (4 tablespoons) soya sauce
50 ml (4 tablespoons) sake
25 ml (2 tablespoons) sugar
hot peppers

Cube chicken breasts into bite–size pieces, and thread onto bamboo skewers together with green onion.

Place ingredients for marinade in a saucepan and bring to a slow boil. Reduce liquid to half.

Remove from heat and let cool.

Place skewers of chicken in cooled marinade in a flat dish before grilling to taste.

Sprinkle with hot peppers and pour remaining marinade onto chicken. Serve.

Sour Schmurrbraten

Serves 4

4 rump steaks, flattened
2 garlic buds, peeled and cut in half
1 onion, peeled and sliced
1 carrot, sliced
1 bay leaf
3 parsley sprigs
2 cloves
500 ml (2 cups) wine vinegar
45 ml (3 tablespoons) melted butter
45 ml (3 tablespoons) flour
750 ml (3 cups) hot beef stock
4 large tomatoes, peeled, seeded, and chopped
chopped parsley
salt and pepper
boiled potatoes for garnish

Preheat oven to 180°C (350°F).

Rub meat on both sides with garlic. Place in small roasting pan and season well. Add all vegetables, bay leaf, parsley, and cloves.

Heat vinegar in small saucepan and cook 3 minutes. Pour over meat and cover roasting pan. Refrigerate 12 hours.

Remove meat and drain. Reserve 125 ml (½ cup) marinade.

Heat butter in sauté pan and add meat. Brown 4 minutes each side. Transfer meat to ovenproof casserole.

Add flour to sauté pan and brown over low heat. Mix in reserved marinade, beef stock, and tomatoes. Mix well. Bring to boil and season.

Pour over meat, cover casserole and cook 2 hours in oven.

When cooked remove meat and place on service platter. Cook sauce 3 to 4 minutes over high heat. Add chopped parsley and serve with beef. Garnish with boiled potatoes.

Pepper Salad

Serves 4

3 red peppers
3 green peppers
2 garlic buds, smashed and chopped
15 ml (1 tablespoon) chopped parsley
15 ml (1 tablespoon) chopped chives
45 ml (3 tablespoons) wine vinegar
135 ml (9 tablespoons) olive oil
few drops lime juice
salt and pepper

Preheat oven to 200°C (400°F).

Place peppers in roasting pan. Broil 12 to 15 minutes. Turn peppers 3 to 4 times during cooking.

Remove peppers from oven and core. Cut in half and remove seeds. Reserve juice and place peppers on service platter.

Place garlic, parsley, and chives in mixing bowl. Add vinegar and mix well.

Add salt and pepper. Add oil, in thin steady stream, whisking constantly. Add few drops lime juice and part of pepper juice. Blend well.

Pour over peppers and marinate for 15 minutes.

Serve.

Bamboo Shoots in Soya Sauce

Serves 4

8 large dried mushrooms
500 ml (2 cups) boiling water
60 ml (4 tablespoons) oil
8 bamboo shoots, thinly sliced
8 shrimps, shelled, deveined, and sliced in 4
1 garlic bud, smashed and chopped
2 slices ginger root, cut into julienne style
45 ml (3 tablespoons) soya sauce
15 ml (1 tablespoon) honey
5 ml (1 teaspoon) cornstarch
30 ml (2 tablespoons) water
salt and pepper

Place mushrooms in large bowl. Cover with boiling water and let stand 15 minutes. Drain and reserve 250 ml (1 cup) liquid. Slice mushrooms.

Heat oil in wok. When very hot, add bamboo shoots and shrimps. Season well and cook 4 minutes over medium heat.

Stir in garlic, ginger, and mushrooms. Continue cooking 3 minutes. Add soya sauce, honey, and reserved liquid.

Mix cornstarch with water; incorporate to sauce. Mix and cook 2 minutes.

Serve over rice.

Sweet and Sour Shrimp

Serves 4

2 eggs
1 ml (¼ teaspoon) salt
300 ml (1¼ cups) very cold water
500 ml (2 cups) all-purpose flour
15 ml (1 tablespoon) baking powder
900 g (2 pounds) shrimp , deveined, peppered, and sprinkled with lemon juice

Preheat peanut oil in deep fryer to 180°C (350°F).

Mix eggs and salt in bowl. Add half of water; stir well.

Sift flour and baking powder together; add to liquid. Blend and add remaining water. Mix very well.

Pass batter through sieve. Cover with wax paper and refrigerate until use.

Prepare sweet and sour sauce.

Coat shrimps in batter and deep fry 2 to 3 minutes. Serve with sauce.

Sweet and sour sauce:
250 ml (1 cup) water
60 ml (4 tablespoons) vinegar
50 ml (¼ cup) ketchup
50 ml (¼ cup) brown sugar
25 ml (1½ tablespoons) cornstarch
30 ml (2 tablespoons) water
4 litchi fruit, diced

Pour water into small saucepan. Add vinegar and bring to boil. Add ketchup, mix well, and stir in sugar. Mix and cook 3 to 4 minutes over medium heat.

Mix cornstarch with water; incorporate to sauce. Cook 1 minute. Add fruit and simmer few minutes.

Serve sauce with deep fried shrimps.

Crêpes Normande

Serves 4

8 crepes
45 ml (3 tablespoons) melted butter
3 apples, cored, peeled, and thinly sliced
175 ml (¾ cup) 35% cream
125 ml (½ cup) sugar
60 ml (4 tablespoons) rum

Preheat oven to 200°C (400°F).

Set 4 crepes flat in baking dish. Brush with half of melted butter. Cover with remaining crepes and brush again with butter.

Evenly spread apple slices over crepes. Cover with cream and sprinkle with sugar.

Cook in bottom of oven for 7 to 10 minutes.

Flambé with rum and serve.

Cover and continue to cook in oven for 45 minutes.

Discard berries, bay leaf and onion.

Serve with hot mustard.

Japanese Mayonnaise (Tempura Sauce)

Serves 6 to 8

3 egg yolks
15 ml (1 tablespoon) onion juice
300 ml (1¼ cup) vegetable oil
15 ml (1 tablespoon) ginger syrup
5 ml (1 teaspoon) sherry wine
25 ml (1½ tablespoons) Shoyu sauce
30 ml (2 tablespoons) chopped
preserved ginger
juice 2 limes
salt and pepper

Place egg yolks in bowl. Add onion juice and lime juice; season well.

Add oil, in thin stream, whisking constantly. As soon as mayonnaise becomes thick, add remaining ingredients. Mix until well blended.

Serve with shrimp or other fish.

Tempura Fried Shrimp

Serves 4

24 large shrimps, shelled and deveined
5 ml (1 teaspoon) baking powder
125 ml (½ cup) flour
1 small egg
125 ml (½ cup) water
few drops lemon juice
salt and pepper

Rinse shrimps in cold water. Fill large bowl with water and add shrimps. Sprinkle with lemon juice and let stand 15 minutes.

Drain shrimps and transfer to service platter. Season well with salt and pepper.

Sift dry ingredients together in bowl. Add

Sauerkraut Garnie

Serves 4

30 ml (2 tablespoons) lard
750 g (1½ pounds) sauerkraut, drained
5 slices back bacon
2 whole carrots, peeled
1 large onion studded with 1 clove
1 bay leaf
6 to 8 peppercorns
8 juniper berries
125 ml (½ cup) dry white wine
4 thick slices smoked ham
4 large knockwurst sausages
4 potatoes cooked with skin

Preheat oven to 180°C (350°F).

With lard, grease ovenproof casserole. Cover bottom with one layer of sauerkraut. Add bacon, carrots, onion, spices, berries and peppercorns. Cover with remaining sauerkraut and wine. Cook, covered, in oven for 1 hour.

Add smoked ham, sausages and potatoes.

egg and water; mix well. Pass batter through sieve.

Coat shrimps in batter and fry in olive oil for 4 to 5 minutes.

Serve with raw vegetables and Tempura sauce.

Chicken au Gratin

Serves 4

1.8 kg (4 pound) chicken
30 ml (2 tablespoons) oil
30 ml (2 tablespoons) butter
4 large endives, washed
125 ml (¹/₂ cup) water
4 slices smoked ham
125 ml (¹/₂ cup) grated Gruyère cheese
few drops lemon juice
salt and pepper

Preheat oven to 200°C (400°F).

Clean chicken inside and out. Dry well and season cavity with salt and pepper. Brush skin with oil and set in roasting pan. Cook in oven 1¹/₂ hours, basting occasionally.

Heat butter in sauté pan. When melted, add endives, lemon juice, and water. Cover, bring to boil, and cook 18 to 20 minutes. Drain and set aside endives.

When chicken is cooked, remove breasts and legs. Place pieces in ovenproof dish.

Cover chicken pieces with ham and top with endives. Sprinkle with cheese. Broil in oven 3 minutes.

Serve.

Hawaiian Curried Chicken

Serves 4

1.8 kg (4 pounds) chicken, skinned and cut into 8 pieces
250 ml (1 cup) flour
50 ml (¹/₄ cup) vegetable oil
2 onions, peeled and finely chopped
45 ml (3 tablespoons) curry powder
2 garlic buds, smashed and chopped

1 small can tomatoes, chopped (reserve juice)
250 ml (1 cup) hot chicken stock
1 ml (¹/₄ teaspoon) sage
1 red pepper, thinly sliced
50 ml (¹/₄ cup) raisins
50 ml (¹/₄ cup) slivered almonds
salt and pepper

Preheat oven to 180°C (350°F).

Wash chicken pieces thoroughly and dry on paper towel. Season well with salt and pepper. Dredge in flour.

Heat oil in sauté pan. Add onions and cover; cook 3 minutes. Stir in curry powder and continue cooking 3 minutes over low heat.

Add chicken pieces and garlic. Mix well and cook 7 to 8 minutes over medium heat. Add tomatoes and season.

Pour in chicken stock. Add sage and red pepper. Bring to boil, then cover. Cook 40 minutes in oven.

When chicken is cooked, remove and transfer to service platter.

Set sauté pan on stove top. Cook sauce 3 to 4 minutes over high heat. Add chicken pieces, raisins, and almonds. Simmer several minutes and transfer to service platter.

Serve.

Baked Eggplant and Zucchini

Serves 4

2 large eggplants
30 ml (2 tablespoons) olive oil
2 garlic buds, smashed and chopped
1 onion, finely chopped
2 zucchini, unpeeled and diced
3 tomatoes, peeled, seeded, and
chopped
2 ml (½ teaspoon) oregano
2 ml (½ teaspoon) tarragon
125 ml (½ cup) grated mozzarella cheese
salt and pepper

Preheat oven to 220°C (425°F).

Place eggplants in small roasting pan. Cook in oven for exactly 30 minutes.

Remove eggplants from oven. Cut lengthwise and remove flesh, leaving enough to support skin. Chop flesh and set aside.

Heat oil in sauté pan. Add garlic and onions; cover and cook 2 minutes over low heat.

Stir in zucchini, season well and cover. Continue cooking 6 to 7 minutes.

Add eggplants and tomatoes; mix well. Season and add spices. Cook, uncovered, for 18 to 20 minutes over medium heat.

Arrange eggplant skins on ovenproof platter. Fill with mixture and sprinkle with cheese. Broil 6 to 7 minutes.

Serve.

Moussaka

Serves 4

2 large eggplants
45 ml (3 tablespoons) olive oil
45 ml (3 tablespoons) butter
1 large onion, peeled and chopped
2 garlic buds, smashed and chopped
2 ml (½ teaspoon) oregano
1 ml (¼ teaspoon) thyme
1 ml (¼ teaspoon) nutmeg
500 g (1 pound) ground lamb
250 g (½ pound) ground veal

3 tomatoes, peeled, seeded, and
chopped
250 ml (1 cup) hot tomato sauce
1 beaten egg
250 ml (1 cup) grated kefalotyri cheese
few crushed red peppers
salt and pepper

Preheat oven to 190°C (375°F).

Cut eggplants into 1.3 cm (½ inch) slices. Heat oil in frying pan then add slices. Cook 3 to 4 minutes each side. Drain and set aside.

Heat butter in sauté pan. Add onions, garlic, and spices. Cook 2 to 3 minutes over low heat. Add lamb and veal; cook 4 to 5 minutes. Season well.

Stir in tomatoes and tomato sauce; season well. Continue cooking 15 to 18 minutes over low heat. Remove pan from heat and stir in egg.

Well butter soufflé dish. Arrange layer of eggplant on bottom. Cover with ⅓ of meat mixture. Sprinkle with part of cheese. Repeat procedure, ending with layer of eggplant.

Cook 40 minutes in oven and serve with tomato sauce.

Pork alla Oneglia

Serves 4

2 garlic buds, smashed and chopped
1 ml (¼ teaspoon) salt
1 ml (¼ teaspoon) oregano
1 ml (¼ teaspoon) thyme
2 ml (½ teaspoon) tarragon
30 ml (2 tablespoons) olive oil
8 pork chops, deboned and fat trimmed
125 ml (½ cup) Chianti wine
796 ml (28 ounce) can tomatoes,
drained and chopped
30 ml (2 tablespoons) tomato paste
30 ml (2 tablespoons) butter
2 red peppers, thinly sliced
250 g (½ pound) mushrooms, washed
and thinly sliced
salt and pepper

Place garlic, salt, and remaining spices in mortar. Using pestle, blend well until smooth.

Heat 15 ml (1 tablespoon) oil in frying pan. Add 2 pork chops and cook 3 minutes each side over medium heat. Time may vary depending on thickness.

Repeat procedure for remaining chops. When cooked set chops aside and keep warm.

Heat 15 ml (1 tablespoon) oil in sauté pan. Add garlic mixture and cook 1 minute. Stir in wine and cook 2 to 3 minutes.

Add tomatoes, mix well, and stir in tomato paste. Season well and cook 7 to 8 minutes over low heat.

Heat butter in frying pan. Add red pepper and mushrooms; cook 4 minutes. Stir once during cooking.

Replace chops in sauce and garnish with pepper mixture. Simmer several minutes.

Serve.

Eggplant Salad

Serves 4 to 6

15 ml (1 tablespoon) butter
2 garlic buds, smashed and chopped
3 shallots, chopped
2 large eggplants

15 ml (1 tablespoon) chopped parsley
30 ml (2 tablespoons) wine vinegar
175 ml (³/₄ cup) olive oil
juice 2 limes
few drops Tabasco sauce
salt and pepper

Preheat oven to 220°C (425°F).

Heat butter in small saucepan. Add garlic and shallots; cook 3 minutes over low heat. Set aside.

Score eggplants in criss-cross pattern. Set in roasting pan and cook 45 to 50 minutes, depending on size. Turn several times during cooking.

When cooked, remove from oven. Cool and peel skin. Scoop out flesh and place in blender.

Add garlic, shallots, parsley, and lime juice. Blend for 5 minutes. Season well.

Add vinegar and Tabasco sauce. Pour oil in thin steady stream, mixing at low speed.

Arrange salad on lettuce leaves. Garnish with black olives and cherry tomatoes.

Serve with toasted bread.

Many Canadians of East Indian descent are involved in farming in British Columbia's fertile Fraser Valley.

Expo 86 and the Vancouver skyline.

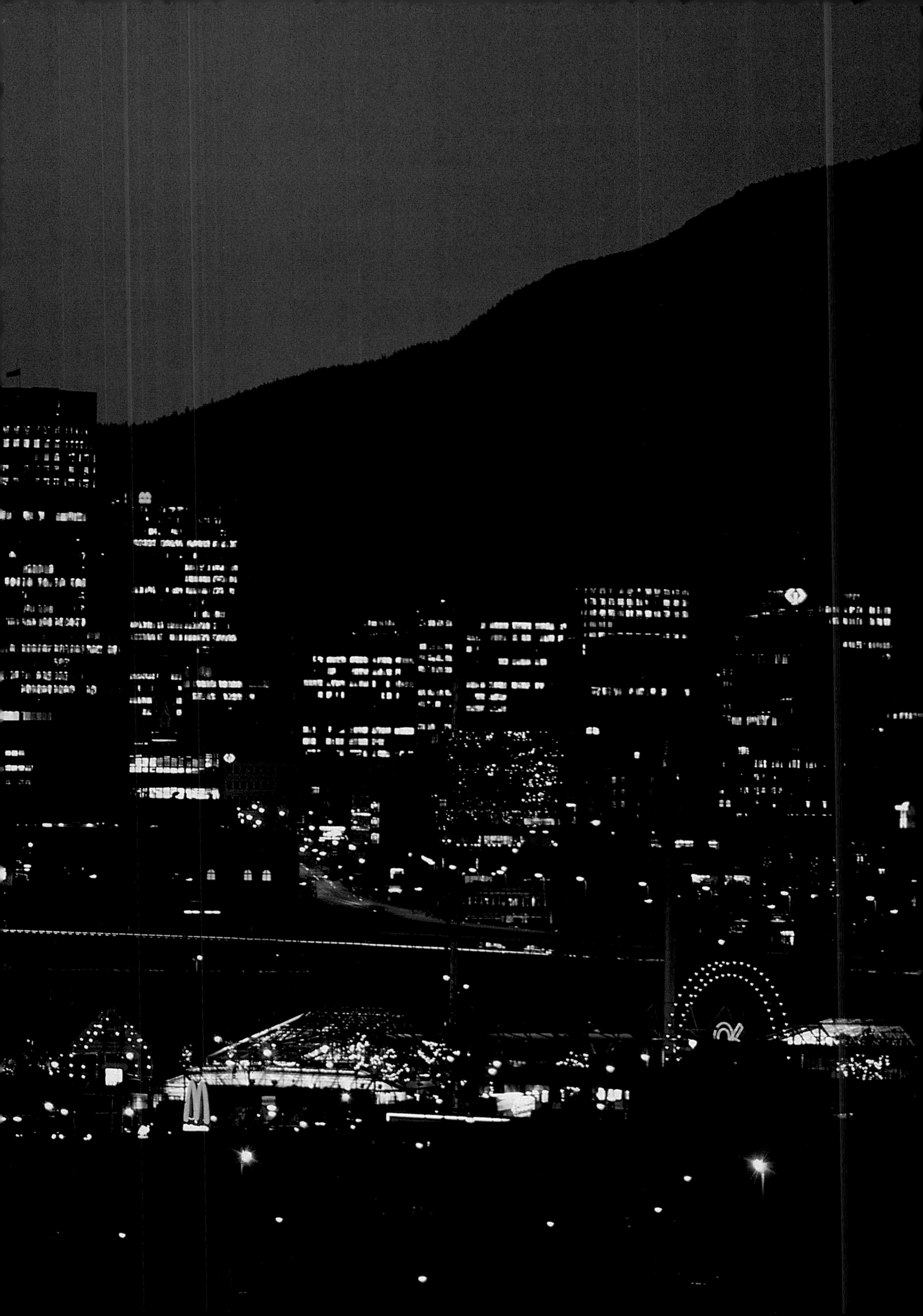

Linguine à la Carbonara
Serves 4

15 ml (1 tablespoon) olive oil
1 small onion, peeled and finely chopped
375 g (³/₄ pound) prosciutto, diced
3 eggs, lightly beaten
250 ml (1 cup) hot 15% cream
500 g (1 pound) linguine, cooked and drained
(reserve 125 ml (¹/₂ cup) cooking liquid)
125 ml (¹/₂ cup) grated Parmesan cheese
pepper from mill

Heat oil in large saucepan. Add onions and prosciutto; cook 5 minutes over medium–low heat. Stir once during cooking.

Mix eggs and cream together. Remove saucepan from heat and stir in mixture.

Add linguine and mix. Replace saucepan on stove top and continue cooking 2 to 3 minutes over very low heat. The mixture must thicken.

Add half of cheese and mix. Cook 1 minute and season with pepper. Add reserved linguine liquid and toss.

Serve and sprinkle with remaining cheese.

Potato Pancakes
Serves 4 to 6

6 large peeled potatoes
1 onion, peeled and grated
2 large eggs, beaten
30 ml (2 tablespoons) flour
5 ml (1 teaspoon) baking powder
1 ml (¹/₄ teaspoon) nutmeg
chicken or bacon fat
salt and pepper

Place potatoes in large saucepan and cover with cold water. Let stand 2 hours, changing water once during soaking process.

Remove potatoes and grate into bowl. Add onions and eggs; mix well.

Sift flour, baking powder, and nutmeg together. Incorporate to potatoes and mix well.

Season to taste. If mixture does not adhere, add a bit of flour.

Heat fat in large frying pan or griddle. Drop a large spoonful of batter into hot fat. Cook 3 minutes each side over medium heat. Repeat process for desired quantity.

Serve pancakes with sour cream.

Dango Meatballs
Serves 6 to 8

15 ml (1 tablespoon) oil
1 onion, peeled and finely chopped
2 green onions, chopped
1 small bell pepper, finely chopped
15 ml (1 tablespoon) chopped ginger
500 g (1 pound) lean ground beef
250 g (¹/₂ pound) lean ground pork
50 ml (¹/₄ cup) cracker crumbs
1 egg
few drops Worcestershire sauce
peanut oil
salt and pepper

Heat oil in small sauté pan. Add all onions, bell pepper, and ginger. Mix and cook 2 minutes over low heat.

Place beef, pork, and sauté pan contents in mixing bowl. Mix for 1 minute.

Add crackers, egg, and Worcestershire sauce. Season and mix 1¹/₂ minutes.

Shape into small balls and cook in peanut oil. When cooked, drain on paper towel.

Serve with sweet and sour sauce.

Chili Dip
Serves 8 to 10

2 garlic buds, smashed and chopped
5 ml (1 teaspoon) olive oil
4 bacon slices, thinly sliced
2 onions, peeled and finely chopped
2 green onions, finely chopped
796 ml (28 ounce) can tomatoes,
drained and chopped
50 ml (1/4 cup) green chilies, chopped
125 ml (1/2 cup) grated strong cheddar
cheese
few drops Tabasco sauce
dash cayenne pepper
salt and pepper

Place garlic in mortar. Add Tabasco sauce, 2 ml (1/2 teaspoon) salt, and pepper. Mix until well blended.

Heat oil in frying pan. Add bacon and cook 4 minutes. Stir in onions and mix well. Continue cooking 3 minutes over low heat.

Add remaining ingredients and spices, except cheese. Cook 18 to 20 minutes over low heat. Stir occasionally. Season well.

When cooked, transfer to mixing bowl. Incorporate cheese.

Serve dip with corn chips.

Filet Mignon with Liver Pâté
Serves 4

60 ml (4 tablespoons) melted butter
2 shallots, finely chopped
250 g (1/2 pound) mushrooms, washed
and cut in 2
45 ml (3 tablespoons) cognac
25 ml (1 1/2 tablespoons) green
peppercorns
300 ml (1 1/4 cups) 35% cream
5 ml (1 teaspoon) fresh chopped
tarragon
5 ml (1 teaspoon) fresh chopped parsley
4 filet mignons
4 slices liver pâté
salt and pepper

Preheat oven to 200°C (400°F).

Heat 30 ml (2 tablespoons) butter in sauté pan. Add shallots and mushrooms; season well. Cook 5 minutes over high heat.

Add cognac and flambé.

Mix peppercorns with 30 ml (2 tablespoons) cream in mortar; crush using pestle or spoon.

Pour into sauté pan, add remaining cream and herbs. Season well and cook 7 to 8 minutes over low heat.

Heat remaining butter in separate sauté pan. Add beef and cook 8 minutes, turn 2 to 3 times.

When cooked, transfer to ovenproof service platter. Place liver pâté on top and cover with sauce.

Broil 3 to 4 minutes.

Serve.

Ratatouille
Serves 4 to 6

45 ml (3 tablespoons) olive oil
1 large onion, peeled and chopped
1 large eggplant, sliced 2.5 cm (1 inch)
thick
2 large zucchini, thickly sliced
1 red pepper, thinly sliced
3 large tomatoes, peeled and chopped
3 garlic buds, smashed and chopped
15 ml (1 tablespoon) chopped parsley
2 ml (1/2 teaspoon) rosemary
pinch thyme
salt and pepper

Heat oil in sauté pan. When hot, add onions and cover. Cook 6 to 7 minutes over low heat.

Add eggplant, season well and cover. Continue cooking 15 minutes over low heat. Mix twice during cooking.

Add all remaining ingredients. Mix well and season. Cook, uncovered, 15 to 18 minutes over medium heat. Stir frequently.

Serve.

Steak Tartare

Serves 4

*900 g (2 pounds) beef tenderloin, finely
ground
30 ml (2 tablespoons) olive oil
5 ml (1 teaspoon) wine vinegar
5 ml (1 teaspoon) Dijon mustard
4 egg yolks
4 shallots, chopped
4 small gherkins, chopped
30 ml (2 tablespoons) capers
chopped parsley
salt and pepper*

Place meat in mixing bowl and season with salt and pepper. Mix well.

Mix oil, vinegar, and mustard together. Add to meat and mix well.

Shape meat into 4 small steaks. Arrange on service platter.

Set egg yolks over steaks and garnish with shallots, gherkins, and capers.

Sprinkle with parsley and serve.

German Mashed Potatoes

Serves 6

*1.4 kg (3 pounds) potatoes, unpeeled
and washed
60 ml (4 tablespoons) butter
300 ml (1¼ cups) hot milk
1 onion, peeled and sliced into rings
3 cooked bacon slices, diced
250 ml (1 cup) garlic croutons
salt and pepper*

Preheat oven to 190°C (375°F).

Cook unpeeled potatoes in boiling water. When cooked, peel and place in food mill. Purée.

Add half of butter and all of milk; mix well. Season very well and place in baking dish.

Heat remaining butter in frying pan. Add onion rings and cover. Cook 4 to 5 minutes.

Stir in bacon and croutons; cook, uncovered, 3 minutes.

Place mixture over potatoes. Bake 10 minutes in oven. Serve.

Scallopini Marsala

Serves 4

4 veal scallops, 170 g (6 ounces)
125 ml (¹/₂ cup) flour
45 ml (3 tablespoons) butter
1 green pepper, chopped
250 g (¹/₂ pound) mushrooms, washed
and sliced
125 ml (¹/₂ cup) Marsala wine
125 ml (¹/₂ cup) hot light brown sauce
salt and pepper

Trim scallops. Using flat portion of knife or heel of hand, pound meat. Dredge with flour and season well.

Heat butter in frying pan. Add veal and sauté 2 minutes each side. Remove veal and keep warm.

Add green peppers and mushrooms to pan; mix well. Continue cooking 3 to 4 minutes.

Stir in wine, continue cooking 2 to 3 minutes and add brown sauce. Mix and season well. Simmer 3 to 4 minutes.

Pour sauce over veal and serve.

Curried Apple and Potato Soup

Serves 4

45 ml (3 tablespoons) butter
1 onion, peeled and finely chopped
45 ml (3 tablespoons) curry powder
3 cooking apples, cored, peeled, and
sliced
2 large potatoes, peeled and sliced
1 ml (¹/₄ teaspoon) ground ginger
1.2 L (5 cups) hot chicken stock
175 ml (³/₄ cup) 35% cream
few drops lemon juice
salt and pepper

Heat butter in large saucepan. Add onions, cover and cook 2 to 3 minutes over low heat. Add curry powder, mix well and continue cooking 2 minutes.

Add apples and potatoes; sprinkle with lemon juice. Stir in ginger, cover and cook 2 minutes.

Add chicken stock and bring to boil. Continue cooking 20 minutes. Pass soup through food mill and stir in cream.

Correct seasoning and garnish with mint leaves. Serve.

Note: This soup could be served cold by adding more cream.

Snails à la Chablisienne

Serves 4

32 canned snails
45 ml (3 tablespoons) butter
250 g (¹/₂ pound) mushroom caps
2 shallots, finely chopped
50 ml (¹/₄ cup) dry white wine
250 ml (1 cup) 35% cream
few drops lemon juice
salt and pepper from mill

Wash snails under cold water.

Heat butter in frying pan. Add mushrooms and shallots; cook 3 minutes.

Stir in wine and cook 3 minutes over high heat. Add cream and bring to boil.

Cook 3 minutes, then add snails. Reduce heat and simmer 2 minutes. Season well and sprinkle with lemon juice.

Serve on toast.

Pickelsteiner Stew
Serves 4

45 ml (3 tablespoons) butter
250 g (¹/₂ pound) leg of veal, cut in
2.5 cm (1 inch) squares
250 g (¹/₂ pound) shoulder of lamb, cut
in 2.5 cm (1 inch) squares
500 g (1 pound) leg of pork, cut in
2.5 cm (1 inch) squares
1 large onion, peeled and finely chopped
45 ml (3 tablespoons) flour
500 ml (2 cups) tomato purée
500 ml (2 cups) hot chicken stock
1 bay leaf
1 ml (¹/₄ teaspoon) thyme
2 ml (¹/₂ teaspoon) chili powder
dash paprika
salt and pepper

Preheat oven to 180°C (350°F).

Heat butter in large ovenproof casserole. Add veal, lamb, and pork; cook 4 minutes each side over high heat.

Add onions, cook 3 minutes, and season well. Mix in flour and cook 2 minutes over low heat.

Add tomato purée, chicken stock, and spices. Bring to boil, cover and cook 2 hours in oven.

Serve with noodles.

Hambourg Steak
Serves 4

750 g (1¹/₂ pounds) lean ground beef
90 g (3 ounces) lean ground pork
15 ml (1 tablespoon) chopped parsley
1 large onion, peeled, chopped, and
cooked
2 slices white bread, crust trimmed and
soaked in milk
5 eggs
15 ml (1 tablespoon) oil
30 ml (2 tablespoons) butter
dash paprika
few drops Worcestershire sauce
salt and pepper

Place meat, parsley, and onions in mixing bowl. Season well and add Worcestershire sauce. Add bread and blend 30 seconds.

Add 1 egg and mix for 1 minute. Season with paprika and shape into patties.

Heat oil in frying pan. Add patties and cook 3 to 4 minutes each side. When cooked, transfer to service platter. Keep hot.

Heat butter in frying pan. Carefully break in remaining eggs. Cook over low heat 2 to 3 minutes.

Set eggs over patties and serve.

Toronto's Italian community, the largest outside of Italy, celebrate a victory by their mother nation's soccer team.

Chinese Canadians at Vancouver's Chinese New Year's Day Parade.

Curried Lobster

Serves 4

2.5 L (10 cups) water
2 live lobsters, 750 g (1½ pounds) each
30 ml (2 tablespoons) butter
1 large onion, peeled and chopped
1 garlic bud, smashed and chopped
2 green onions, diced
15 ml (1 tablespoon) chopped ginger
30 ml (2 tablespoons) curry powder
5 ml (1 teaspoon) ground cloves
250 ml (1 cup) coconut milk
1 cucumber, peeled, seeded, and diced
3 Chinese cabbage leaves, diced
salt and pepper

Pour water into large saucepan. Salt well and bring to boil. Plunge live lobsters in water and cover. Cook 12 to 15 minutes over low heat.

When cooked, remove lobsters and set aside. Continue cooking liquid 15 minutes over high heat. Reserve 250 ml (1 cup) of liquid.

Heat butter in large sauté pan. Add chopped onions and garlic; mix well. Stir in green onions and cook 2 to 3 minutes over low heat.

Add ginger, curry powder, and cloves. Mix, cover and cook 3 minutes over low heat. Season well.

Split lobsters lengthwise. Remove and dis-card dark vein and small sac below head. Remove meat, dice and set aside.

Chop shells into large pieces. Mix into sauté pan. Pour in milk and reserved cooking liquid. Add cucumbers, cabbage, and mix. Cook 12 minutes over low heat. Remove shells.

Stir in lobster meat, season, and simmer 3 to 4 minutes. Serve over rice.

Should you desire a thicker sauce, mix 15 ml (1 tablespoon) cornstarch with 30 ml (2 table-spoons) water and add to sauce. Stir and sim-mer 1 to 2 minutes before serving.

Greek Lemon Soup

Serves 4 to 6

2 fresh lemons
30 ml (2 tablespoons) butter
4 shallots, chopped
2 green onions, chopped
45 ml (3 tablespoons) flour
1.2 L (5 cups) hot chicken stock
3 egg whites
30 ml (2 tablespoons) light cream
125 ml (½ cup) 35% cream
2 egg yolks
well buttered custard dishes
salt and pepper

Preheat oven to 160°C (325°F).

Peel lemon zest and thinly slice. Reserve juice of 1½ lemons.

Heat butter in saucepan. Add lemon zest, shallots, and green onions. Cover and cook 3 minutes over low heat.

Add flour to saucepan and mix well. Pour in chicken stock, mix, and cook 20 minutes over medium heat. Season well.

6 minutes before end of cooking, add reserved lemon juice. When cooked, pass through sieve and replace in saucepan. Sim-mer.

Beat egg whites with fork and incorporate light cream. Pour mixture into prepared molds. Bake 6 to 7 minutes in oven.

When cooked, remove and unmold. Slice into large pieces.

Mix 35% cream with egg yolks and add to simmering soup. Mix and continue simmering for several minutes.

Serve lemon soup with baked egg whites.

Crab and Rice Salad
Serves 4

375 g (³/4 pound) cooked crab meat
375 ml (1¹/2 cups) cooked rice
1 garlic bud, smashed and finely chopped
1 red pepper, thinly sliced and blanched 3 minutes in boiling water
1 green pepper, thinly sliced and blanched 3 minutes in boiling water
375 ml (1¹/2 cups) sliced white mushrooms
24 stuffed olives, chopped
30 ml (2 tablespoons) chopped red pimientos
125 ml (¹/2 cup) chopped walnuts
125 ml (¹/2 cup) mustard vinaigrette

Place all ingredients in large bowl. Season well and add vinaigrette. Toss and marinate at room temperature for 30 minutes.

Serve on lettuce leaves.

Mustard vinaigrette:
25 ml (1¹/2 tablespoons) Dijon mustard
50 ml (¹/4 cup) wine vinegar
175 ml (³/4 cup) olive oil
50 ml (¹/4 cup) yogurt
lemon juice to taste
salt and pepper

Place mustard in small bowl. Add vinegar and mix with whisk. Season with salt and pepper; mix again.

Add oil, in thin steady stream, whisking constantly. Mix in yogurt and few drops lemon juice. Whisk until blended.

Sweet and Sour Pork
Serves 4

2 pork tenderloins, fat trimmed and thinly sliced
60 ml (4 tablespoons) soya sauce
125 ml (¹/2 cup) dry white wine
15 ml (1 tablespoon) chopped ginger
30 ml (2 tablespoons) cornstarch
30 ml (2 tablespoons) corn oil
2 garlic buds, smashed and chopped
4 green onions, thinly sliced
2 small carrots, thinly sliced
250 ml (1 cup) dried mushrooms, soaked and sliced
2 bamboo shoots, thinly sliced
1 red pepper, thinly sliced
30 ml (2 tablespoons) ketchup
30 ml (2 tablespoons) chili sauce
50 ml (¹/4 cup) sugar
250 ml (1 cup) hot chicken stock
45 ml (3 tablespoons) vinegar
2 pineapple slices, diced
30 ml (2 tablespoons) water
salt and pepper

Preheat deep fryer to 190°C (375°F).

Place pork in bowl and add 30 ml (2 tablespoons) soya sauce. Pour in wine and sprinkle with ginger. Add pepper and cover. Marinate 30 minutes in refrigerator.

Add 15 ml (1 tablespoon) cornstarch to marinade. Mix thoroughly, then remove meat and drain.

Deep fry pork 2 minutes. Set aside.

Heat oil in wok. Add garlic, onions, carrots and remaining vegetables. Cook 3 minutes over high heat.

Stir in ketchup, chili sauce, sugar, and chicken stock. Bring to boil. Add vinegar and pineapple; mix and correct seasoning.

Mix remaining cornstarch with water; incorporate to mixture. Add remaining soya sauce and boil 2 minutes.

Add meat, mix and simmer 1 minute. Serve.

Goulash, Hungarian Style
Serves 4

30 ml (2 tablespoons) vegetable oil
1 Spanish onion, thinly sliced
25 ml (1¹/2 tablespoons) paprika

1.4 kg (3 pound) blade steak cut
into 2.5 cm
(1 inch) cubes
30 ml (2 tablespoons) flour
1 L (4 cups) hot beef stock
30 ml (2 tablespoons) tomato paste
15 ml (1 tablespoon) chopped parsley
salt and pepper

Preheat oven to 180°C (350°F).

Heat oil in ovenproof casserole. Add onions and cook 2 to 3 minutes.

Sprinkle with paprika and continue to cook 3 to 4 minutes.

Add meat and sear 5 to 6 minutes over high heat.

Add flour, mix and continue cooking for 3 minutes stirring once during cooking process.

Add beef stock. Season to taste. Add tomato paste; mix well. Cover and cook in oven for 2 hours.

Sprinkle with chopped parsley and serve on buttered noodles.

Canada Day fireworks display in Vancouver.

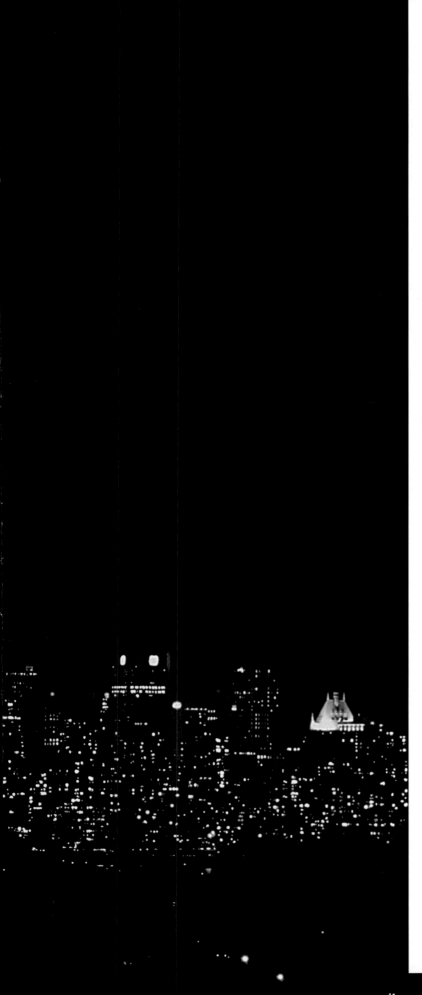

CANADIAN PARTY TIME

Canada has hosted a great many lavish affairs in her day, among them spectacular events for British Royalty, political officials, and foreign diplomats. And since the earliest times, parties have been an occasion to rejoice with family and friends.

Aside from traditional events, such as Christmas and Easter, Canadians have long enjoyed entertaining in their own homes, for there is something special in joining in a private party. Perhaps it is the open gesture of friendship and the sharing of fine fare among people that nourishes a sense of belonging, which cannot be duplicated even in the very best restaurant.

With Canada's diverse ethnic groups and seasons, there are frequent occasions for a party. Winter brings out the opportunity for cozy gatherings around a flaming fireplace with guests enjoying Baked Alaska and sipping a mug of Canadian Coffee. With summer's heat, thousands of people head to cottage country leaving the busy city behind. Casual affairs are preferred, serving delicious, refreshing salads and, for a super treat, cool and creamy Avocado Dip.

Not to be outdone, city entertaining is well worth the long, hot drive home. Tasteful cocktail parties are common events, often pool-side or on a rooftop terrace, featuring such delicacies as Liver Paté Puffs and Champagne Punch.

The party food that we have selected will meet any occasion. One tip though, treat party food the way Canadians do — make it the guest of honour.

Macaroni Salad

Serves 6

2 ml (¹/₂ teaspoon) salt
2 ml (¹/₂ teaspoon) white pepper
5 ml (1 teaspoon) dry mustard
30 ml (2 tablespoons) vinegar
60 ml (4 tablespoons) oil
175 ml (³/₄ cup) mayonnaise
1 L (4 cups) cooked macaroni elbows,
hot
4 hard boiled eggs, chopped
125 ml (¹/₂ cup) pitted black olives
¹/₂ cucumber, peeled, seeded and finely
diced
1 celery heart, finely diced
3 green onions, sliced
50 ml (¹/₄ cup) pimiento, diced

In mixing bowl, combine salt, pepper, dry mustard, vinegar and oil. Incorporate mayonnaise.

Add hot macaroni; mix well.

Incorporate remaining ingredients. Correct seasoning. Cool and refrigerate 1 hour. Serve.

Chicken Curry Crêpe

Serves 12

4 chicken breasts, deboned and skinned
1 celery stalk, diced
1 onion, sliced
2 L (8 cups) water
30 ml (2 tablespoons) curry powder
salt and pepper

Place all ingredients in large saucepan and bring to boil. Correct seasoning and cook 18 minutes over low heat.

Remove chicken and cool.

Pass liquid through sieve and reserve 750 ml (3 cups).

50 ml (¹/₄ cup) butter
1 onion, finely chopped
250 g (¹/₂ pound) fresh mushrooms,
washed and diced
750 ml (3 cups) cooking liquid (chicken
stock)
45 ml (3 tablespoons) flour
45 ml (3 tablespoons) curry powder
125 ml (¹/₂ cup) light cream
cooked chicken, diced
few drops Tabasco sauce
salt and pepper
12 crêpes

Melt butter in saucepan. Add onions and mushrooms. Season to taste; cover and cook 3 minutes.

Add curry powder and cook 4 to 5 minutes over low heat. Incorporate flour and cook 2 minutes.

Add cooking liquid, stir and cook 8 to 10 minutes over low heat. Add chicken, cream and Tabasco sauce. Correct seasoning; simmer 2 minutes.

Place small amount of mixture on each crêpe, roll and place on service platter. Pour remaining sauce over crêpes. Serve.

Cherry Tomato and Egg Canapés

Serves 6 to 8

12 slices white bread, toasted
50 ml (¹/₄ cup) mayonnaise
12 cherry tomatoes, cut in two
15 ml (1 tablespoon) olive oil
4 hard boiled eggs, sliced
few drops Worcestershire sauce
juice ¹/₂ lemon
salt and pepper

Cut 24 rounds of 4 cm (1¹/₂ inches) diameter from toasted bread slices. Spread mayonnaise on each.

Place tomatoes in bowl. Season with salt and pepper. Add lemon juice and Worcestershire sauce. Add oil and marinate 15 minutes.

Place one egg slice on each round and top with half cherry tomato. Serve cold.

Stuffed Mushroom Caps

Serves 10 to 12

36 large mushroom caps, cleaned
30 ml (2 tablespoons) butter
1 onion, finely chopped
2 garlic cloves, smashed and chopped
5 tomatoes, peeled, seeded and chopped
5 ml (1 teaspoon) sugar
45 ml (3 tablespoons) tomato paste
45 ml (3 tablespoons) parmesan cheese
salt and pepper

Preheat oven to 220°C (425°F).

Place mushrooms, hollow side up, on platter. Cook in oven at 220°C (425°F) for 8 minutes. Drain and set aside.

Melt butter in saucepan. Add onions; cook 2 minutes. Add garlic, tomatoes and sugar; season well and cook 6 to 7 minutes.

Add tomatoe paste; mix well and cook 3 minutes.

Stuff mushroom caps. Sprinkle with cheese and broil 3 minutes. Serve.

Ham and Mushroom Crêpes

Serves 12

50 ml (¹/₄ cup) butter
250 g (¹/₂ pound) fresh mushrooms,
washed and thinly sliced
2 dry shallots
50 ml (¹/₄ cup) flour
1 L (4 cups) milk
1 ml (¹/₄ teaspoon) nutmeg
175 ml (³/₄ cup) parmesan cheese
12 thin slices cooked Virginia ham
12 crêpes
30 ml (2 tablespoons) chopped parsley
salt and pepper

Preheat oven to 200°C (400°F).

Melt butter in saucepan. Add mushrooms and shallots; cook 5 minutes. Season to taste. Add flour; mix well. Incorporate milk and nutmeg; mix with whisk. Cook 10 to 12 minutes over low heat.

Place one crêpe on kitchen counter. Place one ham slice over crêpe and add 15 ml (1 tablespoon) of sauce. Sprinkle with cheese and fold in 4. Repeat for remaining crêpes.

Place stuffed crêpes in well buttered ovenproof dish; cover with sauce and sprinkle with cheese and parsley. Cook in oven for 12 minutes. Serve.

Crêpe Batter
20 Crêpes

250 ml (1 cup) flour
1 ml (¼ teaspoon) salt
3 large eggs
300 ml (1¼ cups) milk
30 ml (2 tablespoons) melted butter

Sift flour and salt into bowl. Add eggs and half of milk; beat well with whisk. Add remaining milk and melted butter; mix again.

Pass batter through sieve. Cover with wax paper and refrigerate 1 hour.

Lightly butter crêpe pan and heat. Add enough batter to cover pan bottom, tilt pan and remove excess batter. Cook 1½ minutes on one side. Turn crêpe over and continue to cook 1 minute. Remove and set aside.

Repeat to use remaining batter.

Chicken Salad
Serves 8 to 10

6 whole chicken breasts, deboned and skinned and cut in two
2 celery stalks, diced
1.5 L (6 cups) light chicken stock
salt and pepper

Place chicken in saucepan. Add celery and chicken stock. Season with salt and pepper; bring to boil. Cook 20 minutes over low heat.

Remove chicken from saucepan, cool and dice. Set aside.

5 ml (1 teaspoon) candied ginger
30 ml (2 tablespoons) port wine
45 ml (3 tablespoons) Dijon mustard
3 egg yolks
15 ml (1 tablespoon) soya sauce
15 ml (1 tablespoon) vinegar
375 ml (1½ cups) olive oil
125 ml (½ cup) chopped green onions
250 ml (1 cup) water chestnuts, thinly sliced
125 ml (½ cup) toasted slivered almonds

500 ml (2 cups) pea pods, cooked 4 minutes in boiling water
juice of 2 lemons

In mixing bowl, combine ginger, port wine, mustard and egg yolks. Season well with salt and pepper.

Add soya sauce, vinegar and lemon juice; mix well.

Add oil in thin stream mixing constantly with whisk.

Add green onions, water chestnuts, almonds, pea pods and diced chicken. Incorporate well.

Serve on bed of lettuce.

Liver Pâté Puffs

Gelatine coating:
½ envelope gelatine
1 can beef consommé
15 ml (1 tablespoon) brandy

Sprinkle gelatine over 50 ml (¼ cup) beef consommé in small saucepan. Let stand 3 minutes. Stir mixture over low heat until gelatine is dissolved.

Pour remaining consommé and brandy into the saucepan and bring to boil. Remove from stove and cool.

125 ml (½ cup) liver pâté
30 ml (2 tablespoons) butter
50 ml (¼ cup) 35% cream, lightly beaten
15 ml (1 tablespoon) cognac
250 ml (1 cup) gelatine coating
salt and pepper
18 to 20 small puffs

Place pâté and butter in blender. Season with salt and pepper. Mix well for 30 seconds.

Add cognac; mix again. Incorporate half of cream, mix and add remaining cream. Blend well.

Place pâté mixture in pastry bag fitted with star nozzle. Fill little puffs.

Glaze puffs with gelatine coating. Refrigerate 30 minutes. Serve.

Chicken Wings

Serves 8 to 10

36 chicken wings, washed and pat dried
125 ml (¹/₂ cup) maple syrup
2 garlic cloves, smashed and chopped
1 ml (¹/₄ teaspoon) chili powder
125 ml (¹/₂ cup) beer
30 ml (2 tablespoons) olive oil
juice of 1¹/₂ lemons
salt and pepper

Preheat oven to 200°C (400°F).

Place chicken wings in large saucepan. Season well with salt and pepper.

Combine all remaining ingredients in large mixing bowl. Pour mixture over chicken wings and marinate 30 minutes.

Remove and transfer chicken wings to baking pan. Broil in oven for 20 minutes, turning and basting wings often. Serve.

Cheese Tarts

4 beaten eggs
500 ml (2 cups) 35% cream
15 ml (1 tablespoon) cornstarch
30 ml (2 tablespoons) water
375 ml (1¹/₂ cups) grated Gruyère cheese
15 ml (1 tablespoon) chopped parsley
18 to 24 tarts, depending on size
paprika
salt and peper

Preheat oven to 190°C (375°F).

Mix eggs and cream in bowl.

Mix cornstarch with water. Incorporate to egg mixture. Add half of cheese. Season with salt, pepper and paprika.

Prick tart bottoms with fork. Pour cheese mixture into tart shells. Sprinkle with remaining cheese and parsley.

Bake in oven for 16 to 18 minutes. Serve.

Shrimp, Teriyaki Style
Serves 6

900 g (2 pounds) shrimp, peeled and deveined
125 ml (¹/₂ cup) teriyaki sauce
175 ml (³/₄ cup) olive oil
2 garlic cloves, smashed and chopped
50 ml (¹/₄ cup) port wine
5 ml (1 teaspoon) fresh ginger, chopped
1 ml (¹/₄ teaspoon) thyme
15 ml (1 tablespoon) chopped parsley
30 ml (2 tablespoons) peanut oil
juice of 1 lemon
few drops Tabasco sauce

Place shrimp in roasting pan. Set aside.

In large bowl, combine teriyaki sauce, olive oil, lemon juice, garlic, port wine, ginger, thyme and parsley. Sprinkle with Tabasco sauce.

Pour mixture over shrimp and marinate for 1 hour.

Heat half of peanut oil in frying pan. When oil is very hot, add half of shrimp and cook at very high heat 2 minutes on each side. Repeat with remaining shrimp.

Serve.

Chocolate Fondue

45 ml (3 tablespoons) honey
175 ml (³/₄ cup) light cream
255 g (9 ounces) milk chocolate cut into pieces
50 ml (¹/₄ cup) slivered almonds
30 ml (2 tablespoons) Cointreau
strawberries

Heat honey and cream in fondue pot. Add chocolate and continue to cook to melt chocolate, stirring constantly.

Incorporate almonds and Cointreau; cook for a few minutes.

Dip strawberries in chocolate fondue.

Green Pepper Rings
Serves 8 to 10

4 small green peppers
30 ml (2 tablespoons) butter
250 g (¹/₂ pound) fresh mushrooms, washed and chopped
1 package 250 g (8 ounces) cream cheese
125 g (¹/₄ pound) Roquefort cheese
45 ml (3 tablespoons) chopped pimiento
45 ml (3 tablespoons) pistachio nuts, chopped
Tabasco sauce
salt and pepper

Remove top edge of peppers. Remove seeds and stem along seeds. Place in saucepan containing 1 L (4 cups) salted boiling water; cook 3 minutes.

Drain well. Wipe inside. Set aside.

Melt butter in saucepan. Add mushrooms; cover and cook 3 to 4 minutes. Remove and transfer mushrooms to blender; purée and drain well to remove juice.

Return drained mushrooms to blender. Add remaining ingredients. Mix well. Refrigerate 15 minutes.

Stuff peppers with mushroom mixture and wrap in foil paper. Refrigerate 3 hours.

Cut pepper into 1.5 cm (¹/₂ inch) slices. Serve on bed of lettuce. Sprinkle with paprika.

Open Shrimp Sandwich

Serves 6

10 slices white bread, toasted and crust removed
500 g (1 pound) small baby shrimp, cooked and finely chopped
60 ml (4 tablespoons) mayonnaise
15 ml (1 tablespoon) chopped parsley
2 ml (1/2 teaspoon) curry powder
1 small bottle red caviar
lemon slices for garnish
soft butter
salt and pepper

Butter bread.

Mix shrimp, mayonnaise, parsley and curry powder. Season well.

Spread mixture over bread. Place 2 ml (1/2 teaspoon) caviar in center of each bread. Decorate with sliced lemon and chopped parsley. Serve.

Puff Dough

250 ml (1 cup) water
60 ml (4 tablespoons) butter
1 ml (1/4 teaspoon) salt
250 ml (1 cup) flour
5 eggs

Pour water into saucepan. Add butter and salt; bring to boil and cook 2 minutes to melt butter completely.

Remove saucepan from stove. Add flour and beat vigorously for 5 seconds. Return saucepan to stove top and continue beating, over low heat, until mixture becomes smooth and pulls away from sides.

Cool mixture for 3 minutes and transfer into electric mixer bowl. Add eggs, one at a time, beating at medium speed until dough forms a ball.

Preheat oven to 200°C (400°F).

Place dough in pastry bag fitted with plain nozzle. Drop batter on damp cookie sheet swirling top of each.

Flatten each puff with a fork dipped in beaten egg. Let puffs rest for 20 minutes at room temperature.

Cook in oven for 10 minutes at 200°C (400°F). Increase heat to 220°C (425°F) and continue cooking for 10 to 15 minutes depending on size.

When done, open oven door about 8 cm (3 inches) and let puffs stand for 25 minutes.

Remove, cut and fill with chosen filling.

Cocktail Meat Balls

Serves 6 to 8

60 ml (4 tablespoons) melted butter
1/2 small onion, finely chopped
1 garlic clove, smashed and chopped
50 ml (1/4 cup) soda cracker crumbs
375 g (3/4 pound) lean minced beef
375 g (3/4 pound) lean minced pork
1 egg
15 ml (1 tablespoon) tomato paste
1 ml (1/4 teaspoon) Worcestershire sauce
salt and pepper

Heat 15 ml (1 tablespoon) butter in saucepan. Add onions and garlic; cook 3 minutes.

Transfer onions to mixing bowl. Add cracker crumbs, meat, egg, tomato paste and Worcestershire sauce; blend well. Season with salt and pepper.

Form mixture into small balls. Season well.

Melt remaining butter in frying pan. Add half of meat balls and cook 2 minutes on each side.

Cook remaining meat balls.

Serve with spicy tomato sauce.

Turkey Vol-au-vent

Serves 12

60 ml (4 tablespoons) butter
4 green onions, finely chopped
900 g (2 pounds) fresh mushrooms, washed and cut in 2
2 green peppers, diced
2 red peppers, diced

1.5 L (6 cups) cooked turkey, diced
1.2 L (5 cups) hot white sauce
12 vol–au–vent shells, heated
30 ml (2 tablespoons) chopped parsley
juice 1 lemon
salt, pepper, paprika

Melt butter in large saucepan. Add green onions and cook for 2 minutes.

Add mushrooms and lemon juice. Season well and cook for 2 minutes.

Add red and green peppers; cover and cook for 4 minutes.

Add diced turkey and white sauce. Season well and cook 3 minutes over very low heat.

Fill heated vol–au–vent shells. Sprinkle with parsley. Serve.

Cheese Fondue

---

1 garlic clove, peeled and cut in two
500 ml (2 cups) white wine, Neuchatel, Chablis etc.
250 g (1/2 pound) Gruyère cheese, cut into small pieces
250 g (1/2 pound) Emmenthal cheese, cut into small pieces
45 ml (3 tablespoons) kirsch
30 ml (2 tablespoons) cornstarch
pepper from mill
few drops Tabasco sauce
French bread cut in 2.5 cm (1 inch) pieces

Rub inside ceramic fondue pot with garlic. Discard garlic.

Pour wine into fondue pot and bring to boil. Add half of cheese; mix and cook 2 minutes.

Add remaining cheese and season well with pepper and Tabasco sauce. Stir and continue to cook.

Mix cornstarch with kirsch and incorporate into cheese. Continue to cook until cheese melts totally.

Serve with French bread.

Cherries Jubilee

Serves 4

---

30 ml (2 tablespoons) sugar
2 oranges, juice only
1/2 lemon, juice only
2 cans pitted Bing cherries
5 ml (1 teaspoon) cornstarch
30 ml (2 tablespoons) cold water
45 ml (3 tablespoons) kirsch or other liqueur
vanilla ice cream

Place sugar, orange and lemon juice in saucepan. Bring to a boil and cook 3 minutes over medium heat.

Add 375 ml (1½ cups) juice from can of cherries; stir and cook 2 minutes.

Mix cornstarch with cold water and incorporate into sauce. Add cherries; mix and cook 1 minute.

Add kirsch and flambé. Pour over ice cream. Serve quickly.

Baked Alaska

Serves 4 to 6

24 lady fingers
500 g (1 pound) vanilla ice cream
6 egg whites
375 ml (1½ cups) granulated sugar
50 ml (¼ cup) rum
cherries for garnish

Place 6 lady fingers on ovenproof service platter. Place ice cream over lady fingers. Then cover ice cream with remaining lady fingers. Place in freezer.

Place eggs and sugar in double–boiler over medium heat. Beat ingredients until very stiff with an electric mixer.

Remove ice cream from freezer and cover with meringue. Place remaining meringue into pastry bag fitted with star nozzle and decorate Baked Alaska.

Place under broiler for 2 minutes to brown meringue. Remove from oven.

Heat rum and pour over Baked Alaska. Flambé. Garnish with cherries. Serve.

Champagne Punch

1 bottle champagne
50 ml (¼ cup) Cointreau
125 ml (½ cup) brandy
50 ml (¼ cup) granulated sugar
750 ml (3 cups) chilled soda
few slices lemon or orange
few mint leaves
ice cubes

Place ice cubes in large punch bowl. Add remaining ingredients. Stir and serve.

Rum Punch

550 ml (2¼ cups) dark rum
175 ml (¾ cup) brandy
50 ml (¼ cup) Triple–sec

125 ml (¹/₂ cup) lemon juice
500 ml (2 cups) orange juice
500 ml (2 cups) cold tea
50 ml (¹/₄ cup) granulated sugar
1 sliced orange for garnish
ice cubes

Place ice cubes in large punch bowl. Add remaining ingredients. Stir and garnish with orange slices.

Serve.

Clam and Spinach Canapés

Serves 6 to 8

30 ml (2 tablespoons) butter
250 ml (1 cup) cooked spinach, chopped
1 small can clams, drained and chopped
125 ml (¹/₂ cup) thick white sauce
45 ml (3 tablespoons) grated parmesan cheese
12 slices white bread, toasted
Tabasco sauce
salt and pepper

Preheat oven to 200°C (400°F).

Cut 24 rounds of 4 cm (1¹/₂ inches) diameter from bread slices. Set aside.

Melt butter in saucepan. Add spinach and clams. Season with salt and pepper; cook 2 minutes.

Incorporate white sauce and 15 ml (1 tablespoon) grated cheese. Stir and cook 1 minute. Sprinkle with few drops Tabasco sauce.

Spread mixture over bread. Sprinkle with cheese.

Broil 2 to 3 minutes. Serve.

Avocado Dip

2 medium ripe avocados, peeled and puréed
2 ripe tomatoes, peeled, seeded and

finely chopped
1 onion, chopped and cooked 3 minutes in boiling water
1 garlic clove, smashed and chopped
¹/₂ green chili, finely chopped
juice of 1 lemon
salt and pepper

Mix all ingredients in bowl. Correct seasoning.

Serve with crackers or toasted French bread.

Canadian Coffee

Serves 4

160 ml (6 ounces) Fine Canadian Whiskey
4 large glasses
hot strong coffee
lemon
sugar
whipped cream

Rub glass rim with slice of lemon and frost rim with sugar. Heat glass and pour in 40 ml (1¹/₂ ounces) whiskey.

Fill glass to 2.5 cm (1 inch) from brim with hot coffee. Top off with whipped cream. Do not stir. Serve.

The Great Outdoors.

THE
GREAT
OUTDOORS

Ah yes, the great outdoors certainly brings back many memories for almost everyone, with outstanding food usually at the top of the list. Summers rarely change and neither do the activities or the desire for down-to-earth cuisine. Canadians have a fantastic selection of recipes for outdoor cooking and if you want to cheat a little, some of them can be prepared inside with some conversions to your oven.

There's nothing quite like a weekend trip in Canada's great outdoors to relax the mind and rejuvenate the spirit. With sturdy backpacks overflowing with survival gear, Canadians from all provinces head off on foot through woods and fields. There they can experience the fun and enjoyment of food cooked over an open fire, and the opportunity to relax among family and friends, simply enjoying each other's company.

Aside from traditional barbecued meat and chicken dishes that most Canadians love, fish has become a super change for those Saturday afternoon gatherings. Taking a bite of Grilled Trout might remind you of the time you went fishing up north with a pal.

Sitting quietly, side by side, you'd fish for hours until the sunset signalled dinnertime and then the great feast would begin. Or perhaps you can remember those romantic picnics with just the two of you, savouring simple fare and special wine. Surrounded by luscious green trees in your favourite park, you both vowed that it had been the best meal ever.

It is true that the great outdoors have provided beautiful memories to share with others and will create many more. Begin some new remembrances by enjoying the best cuisine from Canada's backyard.

Whitewater rafting on the Thompson River.

B.B.Q. Pork Chops with Orange Sauce

Serves 4

50 ml (¹/₄ cup) brown sugar
125 ml (¹/₂ cup) water
2 mint leaves
4 pork chops, fat slashed diagonally to
prevent curling
juice 1¹/₂ oranges
pepper from mill

Place orange juice, brown sugar, water, mint leaves, and pepper in saucepan. Bring to boil and cook 3 to 4 minutes over high heat.

Remove and cool liquid. Brush pork chops generously with sauce. Cook on barbecue 8 to 10 minutes depending on size. Turn 3 times during cooking and baste with sauce 4 times.

Serve with green salad and potatoes in foil.

Venison Steaks

Serves 4

60 ml (4 tablespoons) butter
30 ml (2 tablespoons) port wine
30 ml (2 tablespoons) currant jelly
4 venison steaks, cut from leg
salt and pepper

Mix butter, wine, and jelly together in bowl. Season and mix again.

Brush steaks with mixture. Cook venison on barbecue grill, 7 to 8 minutes depending on thickness. Baste frequently during cooking.

Serve with steamed broccoli and sautéed potatoes.

Green Salad with Mustard Vinaigrette

Serves 4

Mustard vinaigrette:
15 ml (1 tablespoon) Dijon mustard
60 ml (4 tablespoons) wine vinegar
175 ml (³/₄ cup) oil
few drops lemon juice
salt and pepper

In small bowl, combine mustard, vinegar, salt and pepper. Add oil in thin stream mixing constantly with whisk. Sprinkle with lemon juice. Season to taste. Set aside.

Salad:
1 chicory lettuce, washed and dried
1 romaine lettuce, washed and dried
¹/₂ red pepper, thinly sliced
175 ml (³/₄ cup) mustard vinaigrette
few slices red onions
few drops lemon juice
salt and pepper

Place lettuce and red peppers into large salad bowl. Season to taste.

Add vinaigrette; mix well.

Sprinkle with lemon juice.

Decorate with sliced onions. Serve.

Pork Tenderloin Barbecued Style

Serves 4

45 ml (3 tablespoons) oil
2 garlic buds, smashed and chopped
15 ml (1 tablespoon) soya sauce
45 ml (3 tablespoons) chili sauce
5 ml (1 teaspoon) prepared mustard
2 pork tenderloins, skin and fat
removed, split in 2
juice ¼ lemon
salt and pepper

Mix oil, garlic, soya sauce, chili sauce, mustard, and lemon juice in bowl. Season with pepper; mix well.

Brush mixture over pork. Cook on barbecue grill 18 minutes. Turn pork 2 to 3 times and baste occasionally.

Serve with baked potatoes.

Chili Burgers

Serves 4

900 g (2 pounds) lean ground beef
250 ml (1 cup) chili sauce
2 ml (½ teaspoon) puréed garlic
1 ml (½ teaspoon) sugar
15 ml (1 tablespoon) chopped parsley
5 ml (1 teaspoon) horseradish
few drops Tabasco sauce
dash chili powder
salt and pepper
buns or kaisers

Place meat in bowl and add 50 ml (½ cup) chili sauce. Sprinkle with Tabasco and mix well until meat is supple.

Shape beef into patties and place on plate. Cover with wax paper and refrigerate for 15 minutes.

Place remaining chili sauce in saucepan. Add garlic, sugar, parsley, horseradish, and chili powder.

Mix well and bring to boil. Reduce heat to low and cook 4 minutes.

Place beef patties on barbecue and brush generously with sauce. Cook 3 minutes each side, depending on size. Baste frequently during cooking.

Serve on buns with tomato slices and garnish with remaining sauce.

Sweet and Sour Barbecue Sauce

15 ml (1 tablespoon) melted butter
1 onion, peeled and chopped
2 garlic buds, puréed
30 ml (2 tablespoons) wine vinegar
125 ml (½ cup) dry white wine
250 (1 cup) crushed pineapple
30 ml (2 tablespoons) brown sugar
30 ml (2 tablespoons) pimientos
few drops Tabasco sauce
few drops lemon juice
salt and pepper

Heat butter in saucepan; add onions and garlic. Cover and cook 2 minutes.

Add vinegar and wine; cook uncovered 3 to 4 minutes, reducing wine by half.

Add remaining ingredients, cover and cook 8 minutes over low heat.

Zesty B.B.Q. Chicken Wings

Serves 4

24 chicken wings
45 ml (3 tablespoons) wine vinegar
75 ml (5 tablespoons) maple syrup
45 ml (3 tablespoons) oil
15 ml (1 tablespoon) prepared mustard
5 ml (1 teaspoon) soya sauce
3 garlic buds, smashed and chopped
juice 1/2 lemon
salt and pepper

Place all ingredients, except chicken, in bowl. Combine well and season.

Add chicken and marinate 35 minutes.

Place wings on barbecue grill, 18 cm (7 inches) away from coals. Cook 16 to 18 minutes, basting frequently. Turn wings 3 to 4 times during cooking. Serve with rice or vegetables.

Pepper Steak with Brandy

Serves 4

45 ml (3 tablespoons) melted butter
5 ml (1 teaspoon) brandy
1 ml (1/4 teaspoon) basil
1/2 garlic bud, smashed and chopped
30 ml (2 tablespoons) black peppercorns
4 New York cut steaks, 3 cm (1 1/4 inches)
thick
4 tomatoes, cut in 2

Mix butter, brandy, basil, and garlic in bowl. Blend well.

Using rolling pin, coarsely crush peppercorns. Coat steaks, both sides, in peppercorns.

Generously brush sauce over meat; set aside 15 minutes.

Cook on barbecue grill, 4 minutes each side, basting 2 to 3 times. Barbecue tomato halves 2 minutes each side. Serve.

Deluxe Italian Cheeseburgers

Serves 4

900 g (2 pounds) lean ground beef
50 ml (1/4 cup) chili sauce
1 onion, peeled, chopped, and cooked
1 garlic bud, smashed and chopped
50 ml (1/4 cup) grated parmesan cheese
30 ml (2 tablespoons) oil
tomato slices
mozzarella slices
hamburger buns

Place meat in mixing bowl and add chili sauce, onions, and garlic. Mix well, then add parmesan cheese. Mix and shape into patties.

Brush patties with oil. Cook on barbecue, 3 to 4 minutes each side depending on size.

2 minutes before end of cooking add slices of tomato and top with mozzarella.

Serve on hamburger buns.

Charcoal Porterhouse Steaks

Serves 2

45 ml (3 tablespoons) melted butter
2 garlic buds, smashed and chopped
15 ml (1 tablespoon) Worcestershire
sauce
2 porterhouse steaks, 3.8 cm (1 1/2 inches)
thick
juice 1 lemon
pepper from mill

Mix butter, garlic, Worcestershire sauce, and lemon juice in bowl.

Score meat edges to prevent curling. Brush sauce over steaks. Cook on barbecue grill, 12 to 14 minutes for rare.

Turn meat 2 to 3 times and baste occasionally. Season well.

Serve with roquefort salad and potatoes.

London Broil with Horseradish Sauce

Serves 4

Sauce:
45 ml (3 tablespoons) prepared
horseradish
250 ml (1 cup) sour cream
5 ml (1 teaspoon) chopped parsley
5 ml (1 teaspoon) chopped chives
few drops Tabasco sauce
few drops Worcestershire sauce
pepper from mill

In small bowl or glass jar, mix all ingredients together. Refrigerate 1 hour.

8 London broil, prepared by butcher
50 ml (¹/₄ cup) vegetable oil
30 ml (2 tablespoons) brown sugar
5 ml (1 teaspoon) soya sauce
30 ml (2 tablespoons) grated onions
lemon juice to taste
salt and pepper

Place meat on service platter. Mix all remaining ingredients together and brush over meat.

Cook on barbecue grill 8 to 10 minutes, depending on thickness. Turn meat 3 times during cooking and baste occasionally.

Serve with horseradish sauce.

The Elfin Lakes in Garibaldi Provincial Park, British Columbia. Garibaldi Park is a popular camping and hiking area within easy reach of Vancouver and Fraser Valley.

Chicken on Skewers
Serves 4

15 ml (1 tablespoon) soya sauce
30 ml (2 tablespoons) vegetable oil
1 garlic bud, smashed and chopped
1 chicken breast, cubed
1 green pepper, cubed
1 red pepper, cubed
8 cooked bacon slices, cut in 2
1/2 zucchini, cubed
20 large mushrooms, washed
lemon juice to taste
salt and pepper

In small bowl, mix soya sauce, oil, and garlic. Set aside.

Alternate remaining ingredients on skewers. Brush well with marinade and season.

Cook on barbecue grill 10 to 12 minutes, turning skewers twice. Season and serve.

Marinated Lamb Shish Kebabs
Serves 4

750 g (1 1/2 pound) boneless leg of lamb,
cut into 2.5 cm (1 inch) cubes
2 garlic buds, smashed and chopped
2 ml (1/2 teaspoon) rosemary
500 ml (2 cups) dry white wine
45 ml (3 tablespoons) walnut oil
3 mint leaves
5 bacon slices, cooked and cut in half
1 large red onion, wedged
1 large green pepper, cut into 2.5 cm
(1 inch) cubes
12 mushroom caps
4 bay leaves
salt and pepper from mill

Place lamb in large bowl. Add garlic, rosemary, wine, oil, and mint leaves. Pepper well and marinate 2 to 3 hours.

Remove meat from marinade. Skewer lamb

and rolled bacon, alternately with vegetables on metal skewers.

Brush with oil and cook on barbecue grill 8 minutes. Serve with caesar salad.

Venison Steaks with Marinated Onions
Serves 4

30 ml (2 tablespoons) oil
3 onions, peeled and very finely
chopped
250 ml (1 cup) walnut oil
4 venison steaks
salt and pepper

Heat 30 ml (2 tablespoons) oil in sauté pan. Add onions; cook 7 to 8 minutes.

Cool and add walnut oil. Season and mix well.

Brush over steaks. Cook on barbecue grill, 3 to 4 minutes each side, basting occasionally.

Serve.

Alpine meadows, Mount Revelstoke, British Columbia.

Barbecued Steaks

Serves 4

4–250 g (8 ounce) New York–cut steaks
15 ml (1 tablespoon) soya sauce
15 ml (1 tablespoon) vegetable oil
1 garlic clove, smashed and chopped
few drops Tabasco sauce
salt and pepper

Trim excess fat.

In a small bowl, combine soya sauce, oil, Tabasco sauce, garlic and pepper. Brush steaks with mixture.

Place steaks on barbecue grill and cook 3 to 4 minutes on each side. Brush meat during cooking. Season with salt and pepper.

Allow 2 more minutes on each side for well done steaks.

Serve with buttered potatoes and steamed asparagus.

Potatoes in Foil

Serves 4

12 to 14 small potatoes
30 ml (2 tablespoons) butter
15 ml (1 tablespoon) chopped chives
salt

Scrub potatoes well and place in aluminum foil. Salt and add butter. Seal tightly.

Cook on barbecue 40 to 50 minutes.

3 to 4 minutes before end of cooking, add chives.

Serve with butter.

Grilled Trout with Fennel

Serves 4

4 fennel sprigs
4 fresh trout, cleaned and seasoned
90 ml (6 tablespoons) butter
4 lemon slices

few drops of lemon juice
chopped parsley
salt and pepper

Place fennel sprigs in trout. Spread butter inside and outside; season well. Add lemon slices and juice.

Set fish on oiled aluminum foil and wrap tightly. Barbecue 25 to 30 minutes. Turn once during cooking.

5 to 6 minutes before cooking end, sprinkle fish with lemon juice and chopped parsley. Serve.

Garlic Honey Chicken

Serves 4

50 ml (¹/₄ cup) melted butter
90 ml (6 tablespoons) clear honey
15 ml (1 tablespoon) Dijon mustard
15 ml (1 tablespoon) lemon juice
1 garlic bud, smashed and chopped
1.8 kg (4 pound) chicken, cleaned and cut into 10 to 12 pieces
few drops Tabasco sauce
salt and pepper

In small saucepan, combine butter and honey. Add mustard, lemon juice, and garlic.

Mix well; season with Tabasco sauce, salt, and pepper. Cook 2 minutes.

Brush mixture over chicken pieces. Cook chicken on barbecue grill 20 to 25 minutes, depending on size. Baste frequently.

Serve with spinach and mushroom salad.

Barbecued Red Snapper

Serves 4

4 – 250 g (¹/₂ pound) red snapper, dressed, with head, fins and tail removed
45 ml (3 tablespoons) oil
juice 1¹/₂ lemons
salt and pepper

Rinse fish well; pat dry with paper towels.

Season fish with salt and pepper. Cut 4 shallow incisions on both sides of fish.

Mix oil and lemon juice in small bowl. Brush fish with mixture. Cook on barbecue grill 8 to 10 minutes on each side.

Brush fish during cooking.

Serve with melted butter and chopped parsley.

B.B.Q. Short Loin Ribs

Serves 4

50 ml (¹/₄ cup) soya sauce
45 ml (3 tablespoons) maple syrup
30 ml (2 tablespoons) vegetable oil
30 ml (2 tablespoons) wine vinegar
15 ml (1 tablespoon) lemon juice
15 ml (1 tablespoon) grated ginger
2 garlic buds, puréed
4 short loin ribs, 2.5 cm (1 inch) thick
few drops Tabasco sauce

Mix all ingredients together, except ribs, in bowl. Add ribs and refrigerate 3 hours. Turn ribs twice while marinating.

Remove ribs, drain, and cook on barbecue grill 35 to 40 minutes. Baste frequently during cooking. Serve.

Lamb Kebabs

Serves 4

1 – 800 g (1³/₄ pound) lamb tenderloin
30 ml (2 tablespoons) oil
15 ml (1 tablespoon) soya sauce
1 onion cut into 5 cm (2 inch) cubes
1 green pepper cut into 5 cm (2 inch) cubes
¹/₂ red pepper cut into 5 cm (2 inch) cubes
8 cherry tomatoes
8 fresh mushroom caps
juice 1 lemon
salt and pepper

Trim fat from tenderloin. Cut meat into 2.5 cm (1 inch) cubes.

Mix lemon juice, oil and soya sauce in a small bowl. Add meat and marinate 1 hour.

Skewer lamb cubes alternately with vegetables on all–metal skewers. Reserve marinade.

Brush lamb kabobs with marinade and cook on barbecue grill for 5 to 6 minutes on each side. Brush meat during cooking.

Serve with rice.

Calf Liver and Bananas

Serves 4

30 ml (2 tablespoons) vegetable oil
30 ml (2 tablespoons) maple syrup
5 ml (1 teaspoon) soya sauce
4 slices calf liver
2 unpeeled bananas
few drops lemon juice
salt and pepper

Mix oil, maple syrup, and soya sauce together in bowl. Season with pepper and lemon juice.

Brush liver with sauce. Place liver and whole bananas on barbecue grill. Cook 3 minutes each side, basting liver occasionally. Season well.

When cooked, peel bananas, slice in half and serve with liver. Garnish with green salad.

Spicy Grilled Salmon Steaks

Serves 4

30 ml (2 tablespoons) melted butter
5 ml (1 teaspoon) Worcestershire sauce
5 ml (1 teaspoon) fresh chopped tarragon
5 ml (1 teaspoon) fresh chopped fennel

5 ml (1 teaspoon) walnut oil
4 salmon steaks
juice 1/2 lemon
salt and pepper

Mix butter with Worcestershire sauce in small bowl. Stir in spices, oil, and lemon juice.

Brush salmon steaks with mixture; cook on barbecue grill 6 to 7 minutes each side. Time may vary depending on thickness. Flesh should be firm when cooked.

Serve with vegetables.

Barbecued Apple Surprise

Serves 4

4 apples, cored
30 ml (2 tablespoons) butter
15 ml (1 tablespoon) cinnamon
30 ml (2 tablespoons) maple syrup
few drops lemon juice

Using sharp knife, score around middle of apples. Place apples on double sheet of aluminum foil.

Dab butter amongst apples and add remaining ingredients. Wrap tightly.

Set on barbecue grill, 18 cm (7 inches) away from coals. Cook 35 to 40 minutes. Turn if needed to avoid burning.

Serve with whipped cream.

Deluxe Hamburger
Serves 4

5 ml (1 teaspoon) butter
1 onion, finely chopped
625 g (1¼ pound)
extra lean ground beef
1 egg
15 ml (1 tablespoon)
chopped parsley
15 ml (1 teaspoon) oil
few drops Worcestershire sauce

pinch nutmeg
salt and pepper

Melt butter in small saucepan. Add onions and cook 2 minutes over low heat.

Place meat in mixing bowl. Add cooked onions, egg, Worcestershire sauce, parsley, nutmeg, salt and pepper. Mix well for 2 minutes.

Shape beef mixture in 4 patties and brush with oil. Cook over barbecue grill 5 to 6 minutes on each side depending on thickness of patties.

Serve on toasted buns with sliced tomato and onion.

Heli-skiing in the Bugaboos, British Columbia.

HEARTY WINTER FARE

Canadian winters for the most part are for those who appreciate peaceful, white-covered rolling hills, glistening ice-trimmed pine trees, and crystal clear evening skies. Often referred to as a winter wonderland, Canada boasts many wintertime activities and among them satisfying hearty winter appetites is by far the national favourite.

With the first true snowfall, Canadians head north to secluded cozy chalets and ski lodges, where they begin a seasonal tradition of savouring wholesome, piping hot cuisine. In country and city homes, classic soups and stews, laden with meats and vegetables, are prepared in steamy kitchens. Immense batches of spaghetti and heaping bowls of chili become everyday fare. For winter in its white disguise masks the reality for calorie-counting individuals and provides temporary shelter for tempted tasters.

In the 1900s the presence of snow meant idle days — a time to enjoy the good food reaped from the summer's labour. Today's Canada continues the tradition but attemps to balance indulgence by plunging into an endless array of activities. Whether it be skating on a tree-sheltered pond or joining in dog-sledding, people burst into activity.

During the Christmas season, Roast Turkey is an absolute favourite, bursting at the seams with Apple Stuffing. And if that is not enough, Christmas Cake and English Pudding and even a selection of mouth-watering cookies are just within a hand's reach. To end a perfect evening, a steaming brew of Spirited Coffee is ideal, with just enough zest to warm the blood of those gathered around the flickering fireplace.

For those of you who have yet to experience these winter festivities, begin by sampling the recipes in this chapter, and without a doubt you will soon be knocking on Canada's door for more, much more.

The Ice-Castle at the Québec Winter Carnival, Quebec City.

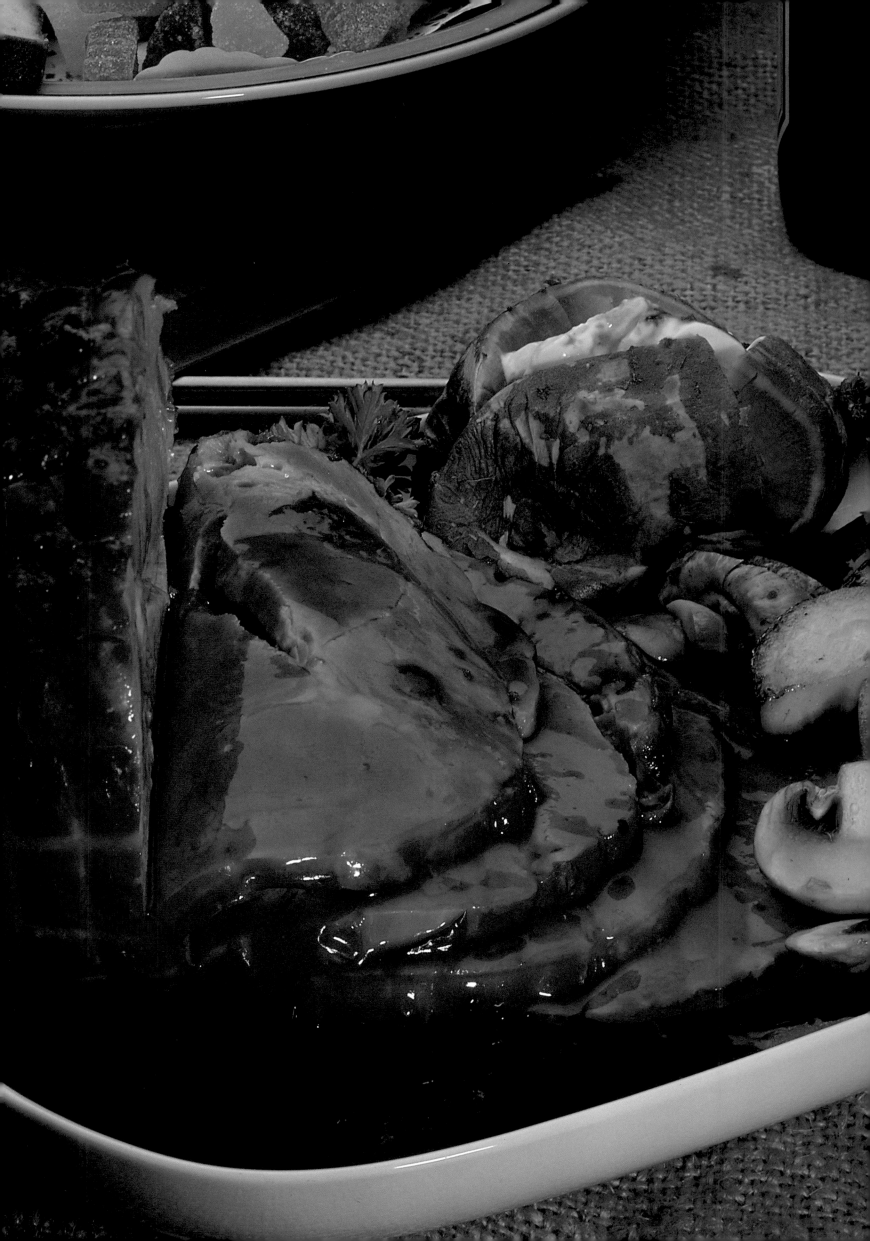

Braised Ham with Madeira Wine
Serves 10 to 12

3.6 to 4.5 kg (8 to 10 pound) ham
500 ml (2 cups) Madeira wine
50 ml (¼ cup) brown sugar
750 ml (3 cups) hot brown sauce

Preheat oven to 180°C (350°F).
Soak ham in cold water for 12 hours.
Cook ham in large saucepan covered with water. Bring to boil and continue cooking 3 to 3½ hours over low heat.
Remove ham from saucepan. Separate pelvic bone and discard. Remove skin and trim fat.
Place ham in roasting pan and pour in wine. Cover with aluminum foil and cook 1 hour in oven.
Remove roasting pan from oven. Transfer ham to ovenproof platter. Sprinkle with brown sugar and broil in oven until melted. Remove and keep warm.
Set roasting pan on stove top. Reduce wine by half. Add brown sauce, stir, and cook 15 minutes over low heat.
Serve sauce with ham and sweet potatoes.

Boiled Beef Brisket
Serves 4 to 6

1.8 kg (4 pounds) beef brisket
1 thyme sprig
2 cloves
3 parsley sprigs
3 bay leaves
1 turnip, peeled and cut in 4
2 large carrots, peeled
4 onions, peeled
4 leeks, white section only, washed and tied
1 small cabbage, cut in 4
sea salt and pepper from mill

Place meat in large saucepan. Cover with water and bring to boil. Skim and continue boiling 8 minutes. Skim again.
Add thyme, cloves, parsley, and bay leaves. Season well with salt and pepper. Partly cover and cook 2½ hours over low heat.
40 minutes before end of cooking, add turnip. 10 minutes later add carrots, onions, leeks, and cabbage.
When meat is cooked, carve and place on service platter. Moisten with cooking liquid and garnish with vegetables.
Serve beef with gherkins and mustard.
Note: The cooking liquid can be reserved for soup stock.

English Pudding
Serves 12 to 16

375 ml (1½ cups) golden seedless raisins
227 g (8 ounces) currants
175 ml (6 ounces) rum
142 g (5 ounces) suet
500 ml (2 cups) sifted pastry flour
625 ml (2½ cups) white breadcrumbs
250 ml (1 cup) sugar
2 ml (½ teaspoon) salt
5 eggs
140 ml (5 ounces) milk
175 ml (¾ cup) mixed candied fruits
5 ml (1 teaspoon) cinnamon
5 ml (1 teaspoon) nutmeg
30 ml (2 tablespoons) cognac

Place raisins and currants in mixing bowl. Add rum and marinate 2 hours.
Add suet to raisins and mix well. Incorporate flour, breadcrumbs, sugar, and salt. Blend well.
Add eggs, stirring after each addition. Mix in milk, candied fruits, and spices. Blend until well incorporated.
Pour batter into buttered mold. Press pudding with spatula and sprinkle with cognac.
Cover pudding with aluminum foil and set plate over top. Wrap mold with clean towel. Attach securely by tying ends over plate.
Set mold in saucepan containing 1.2 to 1.5 L (5 to 6 cups) water. Cover and bring to boil.
Continue cooking 6 hours over low heat.
Serve with a custard cream.

and continue to cook at 200°C (400°F) for 25 to 30 minutes. Baste hens during cooking.

Remove skillet from oven. Add parsley and chicken stock. Stir and serve.

Christmas Cake

Serves 10–12

625 ml (2¹/₂ cups) California golden raisins
500 ml (2 cups) raisins
625 ml (2¹/₂ cups) currants
250 ml (1 cup) mixed candied fruits, chopped
125 ml (¹/₂ cup) candied cherries, sliced in half
125 ml (¹/₂ cup) slivered almonds
625 ml (2¹/₂ cups) flour
5 ml (1 teaspoon) baking soda
1 ml (¹/₄ teaspoon) salt
125 ml (¹/₂ cup) grated chocolate
300 ml (1¹/₄ cup) butter
300 ml (1¹/₄ cup) brown sugar
5 eggs
45 ml (3 tablespoons) rum
2 egg whites, beat stiff

Preheat oven to 150°C (300°F).

Line 23 cm (9 inch) springform mold with double wax paper.

Place raisins, currants, candied fruits, and almonds in large mixing bowl. Set aside.

In separate bowl, sift flour, baking soda, and salt together. Remove ¹/₃ of mixture and add to fruits. Toss to coat well.

Melt chocolate and cool.

Using spatula cream butter in large bowl. Blend in chocolate and gradually add sugar; mix well.

Add eggs, one at a time, mixing well between additions. Incorporate sifted flour and fruit mixture; blend well.

Add rum, stir, and fold in egg whites.

Spoon batter into mold and brush top with water. Cook 1¹/₂ hours in oven.

To test if cooked, insert toothpick and remove. Toothpick should be clean.

Cool cake on rack, then wrap in cheese-cloth. Keep in airtight container until use.

Rock Cornish Hens, Garden Style

Serves 4

4 Rock Cornish hens
30 ml (2 tablespoons) melted butter
24 Parisienne potatoes
3 carrots, peeled and cut in sticks
3 onions quartered
15 ml (1 tablespoon) chopped parsley
125 ml (¹/₂ cup) hot chicken stock
salt and pepper

Preheat oven to 220°C (425°F).

Rinse hens well; pat dry with paper towels. Season inside and outside with salt and pepper.

Place hens in large skillet and brush with melted butter. Cook in oven for 15 minutes.

Pour 500 ml (2 cups) salted water into saucepan and bring to boil. Add potatoes and carrots; cook for 5 minutes. Cool vegetables under cold water and drain.

Add potatoes, carrots and onions to skillet

Quail with Grapes

Serves 2

4 ready-to-cook quail
30 ml (2 tablespoons) melted butter
125 ml (¹/₂ cup) dry white wine
350 g (³/₄ pound) white and red seedless
grapes
500 ml (2 cups) hot beef stock
25 ml (1¹/₂ tablespoons) cornstarch
30 ml (2 tablespoons) cold water
15 ml (1 tablespoon) chopped parsley
salt and pepper

Preheat oven to 220°C (425°F).

Rinse quail well; pat dry with paper towels. Season with salt and pepper.

Brush quail with melted butter and place in ovenproof casserole. Cook at 220°C (425°F) for 20 minutes, basting during cooking.

Add white wine and grapes; continue cooking for 6 to 7 minutes.

Arrange quail on hot service platter. Set aside.

Place casserole on stove top and pour in beef stock.

Mix cornstarch with cold water. Incorporate mixture into sauce. Bring to boil and add parsley.

Pour sauce over quail. Serve.

Stuffed Cannelloni for Four

Serves 4

45 ml (3 tablespoons) melted butter
375 g (³/₄ pound) ground veal
1 onion, peeled and finely chopped
1 celery stalk, finely chopped
1 carrot, finely chopped
1 garlic bud, smashed and chopped
750 g (1¹/₂ pounds) spinach, cooked and
chopped
125 ml (¹/₂ cup) hot thick white sauce
1 ml (¹/₄ teaspoon) nutmeg
15 ml (1 tablespoon) chopped parsley

125 ml (¹/₂ cup) grated Gruyère cheese
4 portions cooked cannelloni
375 ml (1¹/₂ cups) hot tomato sauce
dash paprika
salt and white pepper

Preheat oven to 190°C (375°F).

Heat 30 ml (2 tablespoons) butter in frying pan. Add veal and season well. Cook 4 minutes then remove.

Add remaining butter and heat. Add onions, celery, carrots, and garlic. Season, cover, and cook 6 to 7 minutes over medium heat. Stir frequently.

Add spinach, mix well, and cook 3 minutes.

Transfer vegetables to blender and purée. Place in large bowl and mix in white sauce and nutmeg. Add parsley and 50 ml (¹/₄ cup) cheese; mix well.

Incorporate veal to mixture and season with paprika, salt, and pepper.

Stuff cannelloni and set in buttered baking dish. Pour tomato sauce on top and sprinkle with remaining cheese. Cook 18 minutes in oven.

Serve.

Chicken Casserole

Serves 4

30 ml (2 tablespoons) butter
1 carrot, sliced 1.3 cm (½ inch) thick
½ celery stalk, sliced 1.3 cm (½ inch) thick
1 onion, peeled and cut in 6
1 bay leaf
1 thyme sprig
2 parsley sprigs
1.8 kg (4 pound) chicken, cleaned and tied
50 ml (¼ cup) melted butter
50 ml (¼ cup) dry white wine
375 ml (1½ cups) hot thin brown sauce
30 ml (2 tablespoons) chopped parsley
salt and pepper

Preheat oven to 200°C (400°F).

Heat 30 ml (2 tablespoons) butter in ovenproof casserole. Add vegetables and all spices.

Set chicken, back bone against vegetables, and pour melted butter over top. Season, cover and cook 1½ to 1¾ hours in oven. Baste occasionally.

Test if chicken is cooked, by piercing leg. The juice should be clear.

When cooked, remove from oven and keep warm. Set casserole on stove top and discard most of fat. Add wine and cook 4 minutes.

Stir in brown sauce and continue cooking 3 to 4 minutes. Season, strain and add parsley.

Serve sauce with chicken and roast potatoes.

Chicken Poached in White Wine

Serves 4

1.8 kg (4 pound) chicken, cleaned
2 carrots, sliced
1 celery stalk, sliced
1 large onion, peeled and cut in 4
1 leek, cut in 4 and washed
375 ml (1½ cups) dry white wine
1.5 L (6 cups) water
1 bay leaf
3 parsley sprigs
60 ml (4 tablespoons) butter
75 ml (5 tablespoons) flour
1 egg yolk
125 ml (½ cup) heavy cream
15 ml (1 tablespoon) chopped parsley
juice 1 lemon
salt and pepper

Place chicken in large saucepan. Add carrots, celery, onions, and leek. Pour in white wine and water; season well.

Add bay leaf, parsley sprigs, and lemon juice. Cover and bring to boil. Continue cooking 40 to 50 minutes over low heat.

When chicken is cooked, remove and set aside. Continue cooking liquid 10 minutes over high heat. Reserve 750 ml (3 cups).

Heat butter in saucepan. Add flour and mix well. Cook 2 to 3 minutes. Stir in reserved liquid and continue cooking 8 to 10 minutes.

Mix egg yolk with cream; incorporate to sauce. Simmer 2 minutes.

Pour sauce over chicken and sprinkle with parsley. Serve.

Turkey Apple Stuffing

45 ml (3 tablespoons) melted butter
2 onions, peeled and chopped
1 celery stalk, chopped
500 ml (2 cups) cooking apples, cored, peeled, and sliced
5 ml (1 teaspoon) sage
500 ml (2 cups) crumbled day old white bread
salt and pepper

Heat butter in large sauté pan. Add onions and celery; cook, covered, 6 to 7 minutes.

Add apples and sage; mix and continue cooking 18 to 20 minutes over medium heat.

Mix in bread and season. Stuff turkey.

Après-ski Chili
Serves 4

30 ml (2 tablespoons) beef drippings
1 large onion, peeled and chopped
30 ml (2 tablespoons) chili powder
5 ml (1 teaspoon) cumin
750 g (1½ pounds) lean ground beef
375 ml (1½ cups) cooked kidney beans
796 ml (28 ounce) can tomatoes,
drained and chopped
50 ml (¼ cup) hot beef stock
(if necessary)
few drops Tabasco sauce
dash paprika
salt and pepper from mill

Heat drippings in sauté pan. Add onions, chili powder, and cumin. Cook 2 to 3 minutes over low heat.

Add beef, season well, and continue cooking 3 to 4 minutes or until brown.

Stir in beans, tomatoes, Tabasco sauce, and paprika. Mix well. If mixture is too thick, add beef stock.

Cover and cook 60 minutes over low heat. Serve with toast.

Meatballs à la Bourguignonne
Serves 4

15 ml (1 tablespoon) melted butter
1 onion, peeled and finely chopped
2 garlic buds, smashed and chopped
750 g (1½ pounds) lean ground beef
15 ml (1 tablespoon) tomato paste
1 egg
30 ml (2 tablespoons) oil
4 bacon slices, diced
125 g (¼ pound) mushrooms, washed
and cut in half
250 ml (1 cup) dry red wine
1 bay leaf
2 parsley sprigs

1 ml (¼ teaspoon) thyme
500 ml (2 cups) hot brown sauce
dash paprika
crushed peppers to taste
salt and pepper

Preheat oven to 180°C (350°F).

Heat butter in small saucepan. Add onions and garlic; cover and cook 3 minutes over low heat.

Remove onions and place in blender. Add meat, tomato paste, paprika, and crushed peppers. Break in egg and mix 1 minute.

Shape mixture into small meatballs. Heat oil in sauté pan and add meatballs. Brown on all sides over medium heat. Remove and set aside.

Add bacon and mushrooms to sauté pan; season well. Cook 6 to 7 minutes. Pour in wine and continue cooking 3 minutes over high heat.

Add all spices and brown sauce. Simmer several minutes then replace meatballs in pan. Cover and cook 15 to 16 minutes in oven. Serve.

The Tombstone Range, Yukon.

Roast Turkey

Serves 10 to 12

4.5 to 5.4 kg (10 to 12 pound) turkey
50 ml (¹/₄ cup) melted butter
turkey apple stuffing
salt and pepper

Preheat oven to 180°C (350°F). Allow 20 minutes per 500 g (1 pound).

Remove giblets and neck; wash and set aside. Singe any pin feathers to remove. Wash turkey thoroughly inside and out; dry with paper towel.

Season cavities with salt and pepper. Stuff neck cavity and secure with string. Stuff main cavity, secure, and truss.

Set turkey in roasting pan and season well. Brush with melted butter. Cook in oven and baste frequently.

Gravy:
1 onion, peeled and cut in 4
2 carrots, diced
1 celery stalk, diced
2 cloves
3 parsley sprigs
1 bay leaf
1 L (4 cups) water
45 to 60 ml (3 to 4 tablespoons) turkey drippings
60 ml (4 tablespoons) flour
giblets
neck
salt and pepper

Place giblets, neck, onions, carrots, celery, cloves, parsley, and bay leaf in large saucepan. Add water and season.

Bring to boil and cook 1½ hours over low heat. Partly cover.

After 15 minutes of cooking, remove liver and set aside.

Place turkey drippings in saucepan and add flour. Mix and cook over low heat until browned.

Strain stock and add to browned flour in thin steady stream. Mix constantly.

Season gravy and continue cooking 15 minutes. Chop liver and add to sauce. (optional)

Pour into gravy boat and serve with roast turkey.

New York Cut Tyrolienne

Serves 4

30 ml (2 tablespoons) oil
2 dry shallots, chopped
1 garlic bud, smashed and chopped
796 ml (28 ounce) can tomatoes, drained and chopped
15 ml (1 tablespoon) tomato paste
1 large Spanish onion, peeled and sliced in 0.6 cm (¹/₄ inch) rings
250 ml (1 cup) flour
2 beaten eggs
375 ml (1¹/₂ cups) breadcrumbs
4 New York cut steaks, 2.5 cm (1 inch) thick
salt and pepper
peanut oil for deep fryer

Heat half of oil in sauté pan. Add shallots and garlic; mix, cover and cook 2 minutes.

Add tomatoes, season well and continue cooking 3 to 4 minutes over high heat. Stir in tomato paste, mix and simmer 6 to 7 minutes over low heat.

Dredge onion rings with flour. Dip in eggs and coat with breadcrumbs. Deep fry several minutes before serving steaks.

Heat remaining oil in sauté pan. Add steaks and cook 3 minutes each side. Season well.

When steaks are cooked, remove and serve with sauce and onion rings.

Leek Soup au Gratin

Serves 4

30 ml (2 tablespoons) butter
1 small onion, peeled and chopped
3 large leeks, white section only, washed and sliced
1 ml (¹/₄ teaspoon) thyme
1 ml (¹/₄ teaspoon) fennel
1 bay leaf
15 ml (1 tablespoon) chopped parsley
3 potatoes, peeled and thinly sliced
1.5 L (6 cups) hot chicken stock
250 ml (1 cup) grated Gruyère cheese
dash paprika
salt and pepper

Preheat oven to 200°C (400°F).

Heat butter in sauté pan. Add onions and leeks; season well. Sprinkle in spices; stir slightly. Cover and cook 8 to 10 minutes.

Add potatoes and chicken stock; season well. Bring to boil and continue cooking 30 minutes over low heat. Partly cover.

Place soup in small serving bowl and sprinkle with cheese. Broil in oven 8 to 10 minutes. Serve.

Duckling Breast with Green Peppercorn Sauce

Serves 4

30 ml (2 tablespoons) butter
4 duckling breasts, skinned
1 small carrot, diced into small pieces
30 ml (2 tablespoons) diced onions
30 ml (2 tablespoons) diced celery
125 ml (¹/₂ cup) dry white wine
375 ml (1¹/₂ cups) hot chicken stock
30 ml (2 tablespoons) 35% cream
25 ml (1¹/₂ tablespoons) green peppercorns
15 ml (1 tablespoon) cornstarch
30 ml (2 tablespoons) cold water
30 ml (2 tablespoons) oil
250 g (¹/₂ pound) mushrooms, washed and diced
salt and pepper

Preheat oven to 190°C (375°F).

Season breasts with salt and pepper.

Melt butter in large skillet. Add breasts, carrots, onions and celery; cook 3 minutes on each side. Cover and transfer skillet to oven; continue to cook 7 to 8 minutes.

5 minutes before end of cooking, remove cover and add wine. Finish cooking process without cover.

Once breasts are done, remove from skillet and transfer to hot service platter.

Return skillet to stove top and stir in chicken stock. Cook for 2 minutes.

In small bowl, crush peppercorns in cream using back of spoon. Incorporate mixture into sauce.

Mix cornstarch with cold water and incorporate mixture into sauce. Return breasts to sauce and cook 2 minutes over low heat.

Heat oil in frying pan. Add mushrooms and cook for 3 minutes. Incorporate mushrooms to sauce. Serve.

Spaghetti with Shrimp Sauce

Serves 4

30 ml (2 tablespoons) oil
2 onions, peeled and finely chopped
2 garlic buds, smashed and chopped
1 small chili pepper, chopped
2 – 796 ml (28 ounces) can tomatoes,
drained and chopped
1 small can tomato paste
45 ml (3 tablespoons) butter
500 g (1 pound) shrimps, shelled and
deveined
125 g (1/4 pound) Parmesan cheese,
grated
uncooked spaghetti for 4
salt and pepper

Heat oil in large saucepan. Add onions, garlic, and chili pepper; mix well and cook 3 minutes over low heat.

Stir in tomatoes and tomato paste; mix and season well. Cook 30 minutes over low heat.

Prepare spaghetti following directions on package.

Meanwhile, heat butter in frying pan. Add shrimps, season, and cook 3 minutes. Mix once during cooking.

Transfer shrimps to sauce and simmer several minutes.

When spaghetti is cooked, drain and serve with sauce. Top with grated cheese.

Avocado Salad

Serves 4

1 avocado, peeled, cut in half, pitted,
and sliced
6 litchi nuts, drained
1 apple, peeled, cored, and thinly sliced
500 g (1 pound) cooked shrimps, shelled
and deveined
250 ml (1 cup) frozen peas, cooked
1 small stalk celery heart, sliced
250 ml (1 cup) tomato dressing
few drops lemon juice
salt and pepper
lettuce leaves for garnish

In large salad bowl place avocado, litchi nuts, apples, shrimps, peas, and celery. Toss lightly.

Season well and sprinkle with lemon juice; toss.

Pour in dressing and toss lightly. Arrange lettuce leaves on service platter and spoon salad over top.

Decorate with lemon wedges and serve.

Tomato dressing:
1 garlic bud, smashed and chopped
30 ml (2 tablespoons) lemon juice
45 ml (3 tablespoons) wine vinegar
15 ml (1 tablespoon) Dijon mustard
135 ml (9 tablespoons) olive oil
5 ml (1 teaspoon) maple syrup
30 ml (2 tablespoons) tomato sauce
pinch sugar
few drops Worcestershire sauce
salt and pepper

Place garlic, lemon juice, vinegar, and mustard in small bowl. Mix well with whisk.

Add oil, in thin steady stream, whisking constantly.

Mix in maple syrup, tomato sauce, and sugar. Season well and add Worcestershire sauce. Whisk and serve.

Quails with Vegetables and Wine

Serves 4

6 bacon slices, diced
45 ml (3 tablespoons) butter
8 quails, cleaned, seasoned, and trussed
250 ml (1 cup) pearl onions
250 ml (1 cup) small mushroom caps
50 ml (1/4 cup) dry white wine
300 ml (1 1/4 cup) hot brown sauce

Fresh snowfall at Lake O'Hara, Yoho National Park.

15 ml (1 tablespoon) tomato paste
15 ml (1 tablespoon) chopped parsley
salt and pepper

Preheat oven to 180°C (350°F).

Place bacon in large sauté pan and cook 3 minutes. Discard part of fat and add butter. Place quails in pan and brown 2 to 3 minutes over high heat.

Cover sauté pan and cook 10 to 15 minutes in oven.

Add onions, cover and continue cooking 8 minutes.

Add mushroom caps, cover and cook 7 minutes.

When quails are cooked, remove from sauté pan and transfer to service platter. Place sauté pan on stove top over high heat.

Add wine and cook 3 minutes. Stir in brown sauce, tomato paste, and parsley; season well. Cook 3 minutes.

Pour vegetable sauce over quails and serve with steamed broccoli.

Carbonnade of Beef

Serves 4 to 6

1 thick beef flank, cut into 8 small steaks
250 ml (1 cup) flour

60 ml (4 tablespoons) beef drippings
30 ml (2 tablespoons) butter
1 large Spanish onion, peeled and chopped
15 ml (1 tablespoon) brown sugar
250 ml (1 cup) beer
625 ml (2¹/₂ cups) hot brown sauce
15 ml (1 tablespoon) chopped parsley
15 ml (1 tablespoon) chopped chives
salt and pepper

Preheat oven to 180°C (350°F).

Season steaks well and dredge with flour.

Heat drippings in roasting pan on stove top. Add meat and brown on both sides. Remove steaks and set aside.

Drain excess fat from roasting pan, then add butter. Heat and add onions; cook 15 minutes over low heat. Stir frequently.

When onions are brown, add sugar and mix well. Add meat and beer; continue cooking 4 minutes.

Stir in brown sauce, parsley, and chives. Correct seasoning and mix.

Cover with aluminum foil and cook 2 hours in oven.

Serve with egg noodles.

Remove tenderloins from skillet and transfer to hot service platter. Return skillet to stove top.

Mix cornstarch with cold water. Incorporate mixture into sauce. Stir and correct seasoning. Cook 3 to 4 minutes over high heat.

Add orange zest and continue to cook for 1 minute.

Add orange sections to sauce; mix well.

Place pork tenderloins in sauce and cook for 2 minutes over low heat. Serve.

Mulled Burgundy Wine
Serves 8

250 ml (1 cup) water
90 ml (3 ounces) sugar
3 cloves
3 cinnamon sticks
2 bottles Burgundy wine
125 ml (4 ounces) hot brandy
zest 2 lemons, sliced

Pour water into saucepan. Add sugar, lemon zest, cloves, and cinnamon sticks. Boil 2 minutes and strain.

Heat wine in saucepan and bring to boiling point. Do not boil! Add spiced water and brandy. Stir slightly and simmer several minutes.

Serve.

Pork Tenderloin à l'orange
Serves 4

2 pork tenderloins
30 ml (2 tablespoons) melted butter
30 ml (2 tablespoons) chopped onions
375 ml (1¹/₂ cups) hot chicken stock
15 ml (1 tablespoon) cornstarch
30 ml (2 tablespoons) cold water
1 orange sectioned
juice 1¹/₂ oranges
zest of 1 orange
salt, pepper, paprika

Preheat oven to 180°C (350°F).

Remove fat and skin from pork tenderloins.

Heat butter in skillet over medium heat. Add onions and tenderloins; cook 3 to 4 minutes on each side. Season with salt, pepper and paprika.

Add orange juice and continue to cook for 2 minutes over high heat.

Add chicken stock; transfer skillet to oven and cook for 15 to 18 minutes depending on tenderloins thickness.

Turkey Breast with Mushroom Stuffing
Serves 4

1 turkey breast, deboned
50 ml (¹/₄ cup) melted butter
30 ml (2 tablespoons) unsalted butter
1 onion, peeled and chopped
15 ml (1 tablespoon) chopped parsley
125 g (¹/₄ pound) mushrooms, washed and chopped
1 apple, cored, peeled and chopped
125 ml (¹/₂ cup) seasoned croutons
45 ml (3 tablespoons) 35% cream

250 ml (1 cup) hot cranberry sauce
dash paprika
salt and pepper

Preheat oven to 180°C (350°F).

Place turkey in roasting pan and season well. Brush with melted butter and cook 20 minutes per 500 g (1 pound) in oven. Baste often.

Melt butter in saucepan. Add onions, parsley, and mushrooms; season well. Cover and cook 3 minutes over low heat.

Add apples and croutons. Correct seasoning.

Add paprika, cover and continue cooking 4 to 5 minutes.

Stir in cream and simmer several minutes.

Serve turkey with mushroom stuffing and cranberry sauce.

Roast Pheasant
Serves 4 to 6

125 ml (¹/₂ cup) Parisienne potatoes
125 ml (¹/₂ cup) carrot balls
125 ml (¹/₂ cup) turnip balls
50 ml (¹/₄ cup) melted butter
2 pheasants, washed, rubbed with
lemon juice and seasoned
45 ml (3 tablespoons) cognac
45 ml (3 tablespoons) Madeira wine
1 onion, peeled and finely chopped
1 ml (¹/₄ teaspoon) thyme
1 ml (¹/₄ teaspoon) chopped parsley
300 ml (1¹/₄ cup) hot brown sauce
salt and pepper

Place potatoes, carrots, and turnips in small saucepan containing 500 ml (2 cups) boiling salted water. Cook 6 to 7 minutes. Remove vegetables and cool under cold water.

Heat butter in large casserole dish. Add birds and brown on all sides over medium heat.

When brown, cover and cook 40 minutes over low heat, depending on size. Season and baste during cooking.

When pheasants are cooked, remove cover and add cognac. Flambé and simmer 2 minutes.

Remove birds and keep warm. Add wine, onions, and cooked vegetables to casserole. Cook 3 minutes.

Sprinkle in thyme and parsley; stir. Add brown sauce and simmer 5 to 6 minutes. Correct seasoning.

Serve vegetable sauce with pheasants.

Spirited Coffee
Serves 4 to 6

60 ml (4 tablespoons) sugar
15 ml (1 tablespoon) brown sugar
90 ml (3 ounces) cognac
30 ml (1 ounce) anisette
375 ml (1¹/₂ cups) whipped cream
hot strong black coffee
dash nutmeg

Place sugars in flambé pan. Cook until caramel coloured. Remove from heat.

Dip each glass rim in caramel, allowing sugar to drip down outside of glasses.

Mix cognac and anisette together; divide between glasses. Fill with coffee almost to rim.

Top with whipped cream and sprinkle with nutmeg. Serve.

Vineyard in the Okanagan Valley, British Columbia.

SWEET TREATS

Most people's tastebuds glow at the thought of a heavenly dessert, for there is no better crowning touch to a meal. Even when appetites are largely satisfied, the mere sight of an awaiting dessert revives the senses and challenges the will power. Time and time again, desserts succeed in tantalizing and manipulating the palate into submission.

Sweet treats appeal to almost everyone, for they can be as simple and light or as rich and luxurious as the creator wishes. Elegant glass coupes brimming with fresh, colourful fruit laced with sugar are a perfect ending to a heavy meal. Or if the occasion suggests a truly scrumptious dessert, thick and creamy cheesecake smothered in ripe, plump strawberries is a deserved reward. For a superb dessert designed to be the focal point of an entire meal, Paris-Brest is a classic finale. This extravaganza, oozing with mouth-watering whipped and pastry creams tucked between two cushions of light pastry, is a memorable experience.

Canadians take great pride in their splendid collection of fulfilling desserts. From old and new recipes, fabulous concoctions have emerged and become popular treats. Cakes and puddings served hot from the oven are still soothing endings on cold winter nights.

Regardless of the dessert or the occasion, presentation must justify the creation. Often several specks of grated chocolate sprinkled over a custard cream will give it the finishing touch. Or with an old-fashioned apple pie, a scoop of vanilla ice cream or a wedge of cheddar cheese is all that is needed to complete the fantasy.

These desserts are Canadian favourites. Remember to be imaginative when preparing these recipes, and with your individuality it is likely a new Canadian dessert will be born.

Crêpes Suzette
Serves 4

Batter:
> 250 ml (1 cup) all purpose flour
> 30 ml (2 tablespoons) sugar
> 3 large eggs
> 375 ml (1½ cups) half milk, half
> lukewarm water
> 30 ml (2 tablespoons) brandy
> 45 ml (3 tablespoons) melted butter
> pinch salt

Sift flour, salt and sugar in bowl. Add eggs and half of liquid; mix with whisk.

Add remaining liquid, brandy and butter; mix well.

Pass batter through sieve, cover and refrigerate for 1 hour.

Heat crêpe pan, butter and when very hot, add sufficient amount of batter to coat bottom of pan. Tip out surplus. Cook each crêpe 1 minute on one side and 30 seconds on other.

Sauce Suzette:
> 30 ml (2 tablespoons) butter
> 30 ml (2 tablespoons) sugar
> 30 ml (2 tablespoons) lemon zest
> 30 ml (2 tablespoons) brandy
> juice 2 oranges
> juice ½ lemon

Place butter and sugar in frying pan, mix and caramelize for 2 minutes.

Add orange and lemon juice; stir.

Arrange 8 crêpes folded in 4 in sauce and cook 1 minute on each side.

Add lemon zest and brandy. Light with a long match and let mixture flame. Serve.

Crêpes with Bananas
Serves 4

> 4 bananas, peeled and cut in half,
> lengthwise
> 50 ml (¼ cup) icing sugar
> 45 ml (3 tablespoons) rum
> 50 ml (¼ cup) slivered almonds
> 8 crêpes

Preheat oven to 200°C (400°F).

Set bananas in roasting pan and sprinkle with half of sugar. Add 15 ml (1 tablespoon) rum and broil 2 minutes, until brown.

Remove and sprinkle with almonds. Stuff crêpes with bananas and place in roasting pan.

Sprinkle with remaining sugar and broil 2 minutes. Flambé with remaining rum and serve.

Strawberry Cheesecake
Serves 6 to 8

> 300 ml (1¼ cups) cream cheese
> 30 ml (2 tablespoons) sour cream
> 175 ml (¾ cup) sugar
> 30 ml (2 tablespoons) lemon juice
> 20 ml (1¼ tablespoons) flour
> 15 ml (1 tablepoon) vanilla
> 4 egg yolks
> 1 cooked graham-cracker pie shell

Preheat oven to 220°C (425°F).

Place cheese in mixer. Add sour cream and sugar; mix 2 to 3 minutes.

Add lemon juice and flour; mix until blended. Fold in vanilla.

Add eggs, mixing after each addition. Thoroughly blend.

Set pie shell into mold and add filling. Cook 7 minutes in oven.

Reduce heat to 100°C (200°F) and continue cooking 20 minutes.

Topping:
> 1 quart strawberries, washed and hulled
> 50 ml (¼ cup) sugar
> 30 ml (2 tablespoons) lemon juice
> 15 ml (1 tablespoon) cornstarch

Purée strawberries in blender.

Transfer to saucepan and add remaining ingredients. Bring to boil, whisking constantly.

When almost boiling, remove from heat and cool. Pour over cake and decorate with strawberries.

Paris–Brest

250 ml (1 cup) water
2 ml (¹/₂ teaspoon) salt
60 ml (4 tablespoons) unsalted butter
250 ml (1 cup) sifted all–purpose flour
4 eggs
1 beaten egg
30 ml (2 tablespoons) slivered almonds
pastry cream
whipped cream

Preheat oven to 200°C (400°F).

Lightly butter and flour cookie sheet; set aside.

Place water in saucepan. Add salt and butter; bring to boil. Continue boiling 3 minutes.

Remove saucepan from heat and stir in flour. Mix rapidly with wooden spoon.

Replace saucepan over low heat. Continue stirring until dough forms ball and does not adhere to your fingers. This should take about 3 to 4 minutes.

Remove saucepan from heat and transfer dough to mixing bowl. Cool 8 minutes.

Add eggs, one at a time, stirring after each addition until smooth.

Spoon dough into pastry bag. Form 1 large ring on cookie sheet. Form another ring inside. Form last ring on top of the others.

Brush with beaten egg and sprinkle with slivered almonds. Set aside 20 minutes.

Bake 40 minutes in oven. Turn off oven and set door ajar; let stand 20 minutes.

Using long knife, slice pastry into 2 layers. Spread pastry cream over bottom layer and top with whipped cream. Replace top layer, decorate with whipped cream and serve.

Chocolate Squares

Serves 6 to 8

60 g (2 ounces) semi-sweet chocolate
125 ml (¹/₂ cup) unsalted butter
125 ml (¹/₂ cup) sugar
1 large egg
30 ml (2 tablespoons) rum
125 ml (¹/₂ cup) sifted flour
50 ml (¹/₄ cup) chopped walnuts
50 ml (¹/₄ cup) toasted slivered almonds
pinch salt

Preheat oven to 185°C (360°F).

Well butter 30 cm (12 inch) square baking pan.

Melt chocolate and butter in bowl set over saucepan filled with water, over low heat.

Add sugar and mix until blended. Mix egg with rum; incorporate to mixture.

Sift flour and salt into mixture and stir until blended.

Pour batter into baking pan and spread evenly with spatula. Sprinkle with walnuts and almonds.

Bake 15 to 18 minutes in oven.

When cooked, remove and immediately cut into 5 cm (2 inch) squares. Remove squares and cool before serving.

Pastry Cream

5 egg yolks
125 ml (¹/₂ cup) sugar
15 ml (1 tablespoon) vanilla
425 ml (1³/₄ cups) milk
125 ml (¹/₂ cup) flour
30 ml (2 tablespoons) Cointreau or Triple-Sec
15 ml (1 tablespoon) unsalted butter

Place egg yolks in mixer. Add sugar and vanilla; mix 2 to 3 minutes at medium speed.

Pour milk into saucepan and set over medium heat.

Meanwhile, add flour to mixer and blend well. Add Cointreau and continue mixing 30 seconds.

Pour half of hot milk into mixer. Mix until blended.

When remaining milk begins to boil, add flour mixture. Incorporate with whisk.

Continue cooking over low heat, mixing constantly with whisk. Cream should thicken.

When cream turns yellow and forms ribbons, remove from heat. Add butter and mix well.

Transfer to bowl and cover with buttered wax paper. The paper must touch surface. Cool on counter top and refrigerate.

This cream can be used to fill éclairs, cream puffs, Paris-Brest, etc.

Date Squares

Serves 6 to 8

125 ml (¹/₂ cup) maple syrup
125 ml (¹/₂ cup) corn syrup
125 ml (¹/₂ cup) golden raisins
375 ml (1¹/₂ cups) pitted dates
5 ml (1 teaspoon) vanilla
30 ml (2 tablespoons) lemon juice
15 ml (1 tablespoon) orange juice
375 ml (1¹/₂ cups) flour
375 ml (1¹/₂ cups) brown sugar
5 ml (1 teaspoon) baking powder
375 ml (1¹/₂ cups) rolled oats
250 ml (1 cup) soft butter

Preheat oven to 180°C (350°F).

Butter 23 cm (9 inch) square cake pan; set aside.

In medium size saucepan, place maple syrup, corn syrup, raisins, dates, vanilla, lemon and orange juice. Cook 3 to 4 minutes.

Reduce heat to low and simmer 4 to 5 minutes. Mixture must thicken. Remove, set aside and cool.

Combine flour, sugar, baking powder, and rolled oats in large bowl. Add butter and incorporate well until crumbly.

Place half of flour mixture in bottom of cake pan. Cover with date mixture and add remaining flour mixture.

Cook 35 to 40 minutes in oven.

Cool before cutting into squares. Serve.

Omelet Soufflé

Serves 4 to 6

4 egg yolks
250 ml (1 cup) icing sugar
5 ml (1 teaspoon) vanilla
6 egg whites
500 ml (2 cups) fresh strawberries,
washed, stemmed and cut in two
30 ml (2 tablespoons) sugar
30 ml (2 tablespoons) liqueur of your
choice

Preheat oven to 190°C (375°F).

Place egg yolks in large mixing bowl. Add icing sugar; mix with an electric beater until mixture becomes very thick and pale yellow. Add vanilla and mix.

In stainless steel bowl, beat egg whites until very stiff. Then, fold into egg yolk mixture.

Place mixture into large ovenproof service platter and cook in oven for 16 minutes.

Combine sugar, strawberries and liqueur into saucepan. Cover and cook 4 to 5 minutes. Cool and pour over omelet. Serve.

English Trifle

Serves 6

750 ml (3 cups) fresh strawberries,
washed and stemmed
125 ml (1/2 cup) sugar
1 sponge cake layer
500 ml (2 cups) whipped cream
1 recipe of English cream
12 lady fingers
50 ml (1/4 cup) water
juice 1/2 lemon
zest of 1 lemon, cut julienne style

Combine strawberries, lemon juice and sugar in bowl. Marinate 15 minutes.

Place one layer of sponge cake into the bottom of large glass bowl. Garnish with one layer strawberries and one layer whipped cream. Pour ⅓ of English cream over whipped cream. Repeat to fill glass bowl.

Place lemon zest in small saucepan. Add water and cook 3 minutes. Cool.

Decorate trifle with lemon zest, lady fingers, whipped cream and strawberries. Serve.

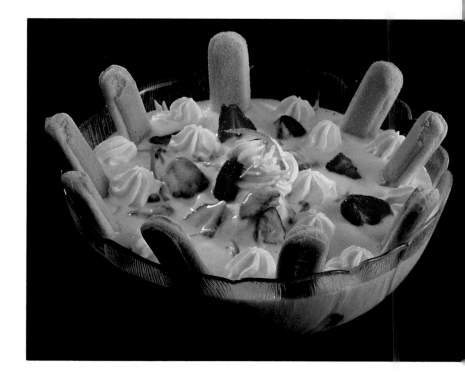

Cheese Crêpes

Serves 6 to 8

125 g (¼ pound) cream cheese
50 ml (¼ cup) sugar
30 ml (2 tablespoons) rum
1 egg yolk
45 ml (3 tablespoons) sour cream
50 ml (¼ cup) icing sugar
125 ml (½ cup) toasted slivered almonds
zest 1 lemon, cooked
zest 1 orange, cooked
crêpes

Preheat oven to 200°C (400°F).

Place cheese, sugar, rum and egg yolk in blender. Add sour cream, icing sugar, and zests. Blend 1 minute.

Spread mixture over crêpes and sprinkle with almonds. Roll and place on ovenproof service platter.

Broil 5 minutes, then serve.

Frozen Eggnog

Serves 4 to 6

4 egg yolks
125 ml (½ cup) fine sugar
75 ml (⅓ cup) brandy
4 egg whites
175 ml (¾ cup) whipped cream
few drops lemon juice

Place egg yolks in mixing bowl and beat with electric mixer. Add sugar and continue beating 2 to 3 minutes.

Add brandy and lemon juice; mix well.

Beat egg whites until stiff; incorporate to mixture. Fold in whipped cream and mix until blended.

Spoon eggnog into plastic container, cover and freeze.

Unmold and serve.

Pineapple Tart

Serves 6

4 pineapple rings, diced
15 ml (1 tablespoon) Cointreau
2 eggs
125 ml (½ cup) sugar
250 ml (1 cup) hot milk
lined 23 cm (9 inch) pie plate*

Preheat oven to 190°C (375°F).

Place pineapples in bowl and sprinkle with Cointreau. Marinate 5 minutes.

Using fork, prick bottom of pie shell. Add pineapples and set aside.

Place eggs in bowl and add sugar; mix well. Pour in milk and continue mixing until well blended.

Pour mixture over pineapples. Bake 30 to 35 minutes in oven. Serve.

*Use dough recipe from Alsatian Tart — p. 202.

Cherry blossoms near Queenston, Ontario

Cointreau Marble Cake

Serves 6 to 8

3 squares semi-sweet chocolate
550 ml (2¼ cups) sifted flour
2 ml (½ teaspoon) salt
15 ml (1 tablespoon) baking powder
175 ml (¾ cup) soft sweet butter
300 ml (1¼ cup) sugar
3 eggs
30 ml (2 tablespoons) Cointreau
125 ml (½ cup) milk

Preheat oven to 180°C (350°F).
Butter and flour 23 cm × 13 cm (9 in × 5 in) loaf pan.
Fill saucepan with water and place over low heat. Melt chocolate in bowl set over saucepan. Set aside.
Sift flour, salt, and baking powder together in mixing bowl.
Cream butter with sugar in separate bowl. Add eggs and incorporate with electric beater.
Add Cointreau and half of milk; mix with spatula. Sift flour mixture into bowl and blend dough well. Add remaining milk if necessary.
When incorporated, remove ⅓ of dough and place in bowl. Set aside.
Mix remaining dough with chocolate, using spatula. Add set aside dough and slightly incorporate with spatula.
Pour into mold and bake 60 to 70 minutes in oven.
Unmold, cool, and serve.

Cherry Flan

Serves 6 to 8

150 ml (⅔ cup) sifted all-purpose flour
325 ml (1⅓ cups) milk
3 eggs
30 ml (2 tablespoons) brown sugar
50 ml (¼ cup) sugar
30 ml (2 tablespoons) Cointreau
675 ml (2¾ cups) pitted cherries
pinch salt
icing sugar

Preheat oven to 180°C (350°F).
Well butter 23 cm (9 inch) flan dish.
Place flour in bowl and add salt; mix well.
Add milk, eggs, and sugars. Mix well and pass through sieve.
Stir in Cointreau and pour half of batter into flan dish. Cover with cherries and remaining batter.
Cook 50 to 55 minutes in oven.
Sprinkle with icing sugar and serve.

Alsatian Tart

Serves 6

The dough:

500 ml (2 cups) all-purpose flour
1 ml (¼ teaspoon) salt
175 ml (¾ cup) soft sweet butter
60 to 75 ml (4 to 5 tablespoons) cold water

Sift flour and salt together into mixing bowl. Make well in middle of flour and add butter. Incorporate with pastry cutter until dough resembles rolled oats.
Add water and form ball. Knead dough twice.
Wrap dough in pastry cloth and set aside 1 hour.

Filling:

60 ml (4 tablespoons) apricot jam
2 apples, peeled, cored, and sliced
175 ml (¾ cup) sugar
2 eggs
15 ml (1 tablespoon) cinnamon
45 ml (3 tablespoons) soft sweet butter
15 ml (1 tablespoon) Pernod

Preheat oven to 180°C (350°F).
Roll dough flat and line 23 cm (9 inch) pie plate. Using fork, prick bottom of dough and brush with jam.
Add apples to pie shell and set aside.
Place sugar in bowl. Add eggs and cinnamon; mix with whisk.
Add butter and mix well. Pour in Pernod and blend.
Pour mixture in pie shell. Cook 35 minutes. Serve.

Tia Maria Chocolate Treats

170 g (6 ounces) semi–sweet chocolate
2 egg yolks
30 ml (2 tablespoons) Tia Maria
15 ml (1 tablespoon) rum
30 ml (2 tablespoons) tepid milk
30 ml (2 tablespoons) unsalted butter
250 ml (1 cup) cocoa

Bring 750 ml (3 cups) water in saucepan to boil over medium heat. Place chocolate in stainless steel bowl and set over top. Reduce heat and melt.

Remove bowl and cool 2 minutes. Add egg yolks and mix well.

Stir in Tia Maria, rum, and milk. If mixture is too thick, replace over saucepan for 2 minutes.

Add butter, mix and cover. Refrigerate 12 hours.

Roll 15 ml (1 tablespoon) of mixture in cocoa. Repeat procedure.

Serve.

Doris Biscuits

Serves 12 to 16

500 g (1 pound) unsalted butter
250 ml (1 cup) icing sugar
250 ml (1 cup) cornstarch
750 ml (3 cups) flour
1 ml (¹/₄ teaspoon) salt
cherries for garnish

Preheat oven to 160°C (325°F).

Butter and flour cookie sheet.

Place butter in mixer. Add sugar and mix 1½ minutes. If using hand beater, mix 8 to 10 minutes.

Sift cornstarch into creamed mixture and mix 30 seconds.

Sift flour and salt together; add to mixture. Mix until all ingredients are well blended.

Using hands, roll dough into small balls and set on cookie sheet. Flatten with fork and place cherry on top.

Bake 10 to 15 minutes.

Cool on cookie rack and serve.

The British Columbia Parliament Buildings in Victoria. Located by the Inner Harbour the buildings were completed in 1898.

Cantaloup and Spanish Melon Flambé

Serves 4

15 ml (1 tablespoon) butter
30 ml (2 tablespoons) sugar
1/2 large cantaloup, seeded and diced
1/2 large Spanish melon, seeded and diced
5 ml (1 teaspoon) cornstarch
30 ml (2 tablespoons) cold water
50 ml (2 ounces) cognac
juice of 2 oranges

Place butter in saucepan. Add sugar and cook 2 minutes stirring constantly.

Add orange juice; stir.

Add cantaloup and Spanish melon; cook 2 to 3 minutes.

Mix cornstarch with cold water. Incorporate mixture with fruits; cook 1 minute.

Add cognac, flambé and serve.

Lemon Soufflé

Serves 4

125 ml (1/2 cup) milk
30 ml (2 tablespoons) sugar
30 ml (2 tablespoons) butter
30 ml (2 tablespoons) flour
30 ml (2 tablespoons) chopped lemon zest
3 egg yolks
3 egg whites
juice 2 lemons
pinch salt

Preheat oven to 190°C (375°F).

Well butter 1 L (4 cup) soufflé dish. Sprinkle with icing sugar.

Heat milk in saucepan and add sugar. Scald and set aside.

Melt butter in double boiler. Add flour and salt; mix and cook 2 minutes.

Add milk and cook 15 minutes. Mix well. Add lemon zest and juice; stir.

Remove from heat and add egg yolks, one at a time. Mix well.

Beat egg whites until stiff and fold into mixture.

Pour mixture into soufflé dish and sprinkle with icing sugar. Cook 20 to 25 minutes in oven.

Serve with rum sauce.

Rum Custard Cream

750 ml (3 cups) milk
7 eggs
250 ml (1 cup) sugar
30 ml (2 tablespoons) sifted cornstarch
50 ml (1/4 cup) rum
50 ml (1/4 cup) 35% cream

Bring milk to boil in saucepan over medium heat. Set aside.

Place eggs in stainless steel bowl. Add sugar and cornstarch; mix well with whisk.

Mix in rum and hot milk. Pour mixture into saucepan and cook over low heat. Continue cooking until mixture adheres to a spoon.

Pass through sieve and incorporate cream. Cool.

Serve over hot puddings.

Rum Sauce

125 ml (1/2 cup) 10% cream
125 ml (1/2 cup) milk
3 egg yolks
50 ml (1/4 cup) sugar
50 ml (1/4 cup) rum

Place cream and milk in small saucepan; scald.

Place egg yolks and sugar in small double-boiler. Mix well with electric beater.

Add cream mixture and stir. Continue cooking until sauce thickens.

Remove from heat and mix in rum. Cool before serving.

300 ml (1¹/₄ cups) water
125 ml (¹/₂ cup) sugar
30 ml (2 tablespoons) corn flour
15 ml (1 tablespoon) butter
4 egg yolks beaten
4 egg whites
150 g (¹/₃ cup) sugar
15 ml (1 tablespoon) icing sugar
juice 2 lemons
rind of 1 lemon

Preheat oven to 150°C (300°F).

Pour water into saucepan. Add 125 ml (¹/₂ cup) sugar; bring to boil. Mix in corn flour and cook for 1 minute.

Add lemon juice and rind; mix well.

Add butter and egg yolks; stir.

Pour mixture into pie plate and cook in oven at 150° C (300°F) for 10 minutes.

Whisk egg whites to stiff peaks. Add 75 ml (¹/₃ cup) sugar and mix very quickly.

Spread meringue on top of lemon mixture and dredge with icing sugar.

Bake in oven at 200°C (400°F) for 6 to 7 minutes.

Enjoy!

English Cream à la Moderne

Serves 4

2 whole eggs
3 egg yolks
125 ml (¹/₂ cup) sugar
625 ml (2¹/₂ cups) milk
5 ml (1 teaspoon) vanilla

In bowl, mix whole eggs, egg yolks and sugar with whisk.

Pour milk into saucepan and bring to boiling point. DO NOT BOIL. Pour milk into egg mixture, mix and transfer into double–boiler.

Add vanilla; cook stirring constantly, until mixture thickens. Remove and cool.

Pour English cream into glass serving dishes. Garnish with grapes rolled in sugar and sliced orange.

Lemon Meringue Pie

Serves 4 to 6

Line pie plate with commercial dough and let stand for 35 minutes before cooking to prevent shrinkage. Place one sheet of greaseproof paper on top of dough and fill with raw dry beans. Bake at 220°C (425°F) for 15 minutes. Remove beans and set aside.

Caramel Custard

Serves 4 to 6

Caramel:

175 ml (³/₄ cup) sugar

Place sugar in saucepan. Cook over medium heat, stirring constantly until sugar becomes golden colour.

Remove from heat and pour into custard dishes to cover bottom. Set aside.

Custard:

375 ml (1¹/₂ cups) milk
250 ml (1 cup) light cream
4 eggs
5 ml (1 teaspoon) vanilla extract
50 ml (¹/₄ cup) sugar
pinch salt

Preheat oven to 180°C (350°F).

Pour milk into saucepan and heat until scalding. Add cream and simmer several minutes.

Place eggs in mixing bowl. Add vanilla, sugar, and salt; mix well.

Incorporate milk mixture and stir.

Fill roasting pan with 4 cm (1½ inches) hot water. Set custard dishes in pan and fill with custard mixture.

Bake 40 to 45 minutes in oven.

When cooked, remove and cool. Unmold and serve.

Orange Bread Cake

375 ml (1½ cups) sifted flour
5 ml (1 teaspoon) baking powder
2 ml (½ teaspoon) salt

250 ml (1 cup) sugar
125 ml (½ cup) soft butter
15 ml (1 tablespoon) orange juice
2 eggs
125 ml (½ cup) milk
zest 1 orange, chopped

Preheat oven to 180°C (350°F).

Butter and flour 23 cm × 13 cm (9 in × 5 in), 8 cm (3 in) deep loaf pan; set aside.

Sift flour, baking powder, and salt together in large bowl. Set aside.

Blend sugar with butter in small bowl; incorporate to flour mixture.

Mix in orange juice. Add eggs, milk, and orange zest; mix until well blended.

Pour batter into loaf pan. Bake 1 hour in oven.

Cool and serve with tea.

The Nisutlin River, Yukon.

Orange Biscuits

250 ml (1 cup) unsalted soft butter
375 ml (1¹/₂ cups) sugar
1 egg
15 ml (1 tablespoon) water
15 ml (1 tablespoon) orange essence
625 ml (2¹/₂ cups) all-purpose flour
15 ml (1 tablespoon) baking powder
125 ml (¹/₂ cup) grated coconut
pinch salt
whole almonds for garnish

Preheat oven to 180°C (350°F).

Place butter and sugar in mixing bowl; cream. Add egg, water, and orange essence. Mix with electric mixer 3 minutes.

Sift flour, baking powder, and salt together in small bowl.

Incorporate sifted flour to egg mixture. Blend well and add coconut. Mix well.

Form dough into small balls and place on floured cookie sheet. Using the back of spoon, press cookies slightly. Set almonds on top.

Cook 12 to 15 minutes in oven. When cooked, remove and cool on rack.

Serve.

Baked Apples in White Wine

Serves 6

6 apples, cored
125 ml (¹/₂ cup) unsalted butter
250 ml (1 cup) golden raisins
250 ml (1 cup) brown sugar
15 ml (1 tablespoon) cinnamon
375 ml (1¹/₂ cups) dry white wine
25 ml (1¹/₂ tablespoons) cornstarch
45 ml (3 tablespoons) water
250 ml (1 cup) whipped 35% cream

Preheat oven to 180°C (350°F).

Using sharp knife, score around middle of apples. Set in roasting pan.

Fill apples with butter, raisins, and sugar. Sprinkle with cinnamon.

Pour wine into pan and cook 30 to 35 minutes in oven.

When cooked, remove and transfer apples to service platter.

Pour sauce into small saucepan. Mix cornstarch with water; incorporate to sauce. Cook 1 minute.

Pour sauce over apples and top with whipped cream.

Nut Brittle

Serves 6

375 g (³/₄ pound) sugar
30 ml (2 tablespoons) maple syrup
170 g (6 ounces) roasted almonds
pinch salt

Place sugar in heavy saucepan. Heat and stir constantly. Cook until sugar becomes a thin syrup.

Add maple syrup and continue cooking 30 seconds. Stir slightly and add salt.

Remove saucepan from heat and add almonds. Mix until well coated then spread mixture on oiled cookie sheet.

Cool, break in pieces and serve.

Strawberry and Yogurt Tartlets

Serves 4

Filling:

30 ml (2 tablespoons) water
45 ml (3 tablespoons) sugar
15 ml (1 tablespoon) grenadine
250 g (¹/₂ pound) strawberries, washed and hulled
250 ml (1 cup) plain yogurt
4 cooked tart shells

Place water, sugar, and grenadine in saucepan over high heat. Bring to boil.

Add strawberries and continue cooking 2 minutes over high heat.

Spoon yogurt into bottom of tart shells.

Using slotted spoon, remove strawberries and set over yogurt. Continue cooking syrup in saucepan until it thickens.

Dab strawberries with syrup and cool before serving.

Sweet dough:
750 ml (3 cups) sifted all–purpose flour
1 ml (¼ teaspoon) salt
125 ml (½ cup) fine sugar
300 ml (1¼ cup) cold unsalted butter
2 beaten eggs
50 ml (¼ cup) 35% cream

Preheat oven to 200°C (400°F).

Place flour, salt, and sugar in bowl and mix well.

Make well in middle of flour and add butter, eggs, and cream. Blend with pastry cutter. Knead dough 2 minutes, then lightly dust with flour.

Wrap dough in pastry cloth and refrigerate 1 hour.

Roll out half of dough and line 4 tart shells. Reserve remaining dough for other uses. Bake 15 minutes in oven.

Orange Surprise

Serves 4

4 large oranges
250 ml (1 cup) fruit salad, drained or fresh fruits
30 ml (2 tablespoons) Cointreau
2 egg whites
125 ml (½ cup) sugar
lemon zest for garnish

Preheat oven to 200°C (400°F).

Slice top from oranges and scoop out flesh with a spoon.

Place fruit salad inside orange shell and top with Cointreau. Refrigerate.

Place egg whites and sugar in double–boiler and mix with an electric beater at medium speed until mixture holds its shape. Then place mixture in pastry bag fitted with star nozzle. Fill orange shells.

Place 2 to 3 minutes in oven.

Garnish with lemon zest. Serve.

Canadian Cataloguing in Publication Data

Martin, Pol, 1929–
    Canada the scenic land cookbook

    Includes index.
    ISBN 0-920620-80-9

    1. Cookery, Canadian.   I. Title.
TX715.M37   1986   641.5   C86-091360-0

PHOTOGRAPHIC CREDITS

Page	
1	Bob Herger
2–3	J. A. Kraulis
4–5	Bob Herger
6–7	Warren Gordon
8–9	Michael Burch
10–11	Bob Herger
12–13	J. A. Kraulis
14–15	Warren Gordon
16–17	J. Vogt
22	J. A. Kraulis
23–24	Jurgen Vogt
32	J. A. Kraulis
33	Jurgen Vogt
34	John Burridge
40–41	Cosmo Condina
43	Cosmo Condina
47	Cosmo Condina
48–49	J. A. Kraulis
52	Cosmo Condina
62	J. A. Kraulis
64–65	Richard Wright
72–73	Michael Burch
75	Derek and Jane Abson
82–83	Bob Herger
86	Jurgen Vogt
88–89	Jurgen Vogt
98	Bob Herger

Page	
103	J. G. Brouwer
104	J. A. Kraulis
105	Rick Marotz
106–107	Richard Wright
112	Cameron Young
114	Pat Morrow
118–119	Gunter Marx
120–121	John Burridge
126	Cosmo Condina
135	Marin Petkov
136–137	Jurgen Vogt
142	J. A. Kraulis
143	Cameron Young
146–147	Marin Petkov
158–159	Patrick McGinley
160–161	Gunter Marx
166	Derek and Jane Abson
168–169	Derek and Jane Abson
174–175	Roger Laurilla
176–177	Cosmo Condina
184–185	Pat Morrow
189	Bob Herger
192–193	Fred Chapman
200–201	Cosmo Condina
203	Michael Burch
208–209	John Burridge
212–213	Jurgen Vogt

INDEX

Acorn Squash, Baked   46
Alberta Rib Roast   81
Almond Cookies   78
Alsatian Tart   202
Appetizers — **See** LIGHT PARTY FOODS
Apple and Celery Soup   125
Apple Pie   63
Apple Sauce   56
Apple Sauce Dessert   115
Après-ski Chili   183
Arctic Char, Grilled   43
Avocado Dip   157
Avocado Salad   188

Bacon and Corn Quiche   53
Baked Alaska   156
Baked Apples in White Wine   210
Baked Beans, French Canadian Style   26
Bamboo Shoots in Soya Sauce   131
Bannock, Savoury   112
Barbecued Apple Surprise   172
Barbecued Red Snapper   171
Barbecued Steaks   170
Barbecued T-Bone Steaks Western Style   70
B.B.Q. Pork Chops with Orange Sauce   163
B.B.Q. Short Loin Ribs   171
B.C. Clam Chowder   94
Beef — **See** MEAT
Beef à la Mode   26
Beef and Barley Soup   27
Beef Bourguignon   33
Beef Stewed with Apples   45
Berry Sauce   109
Berry Soup   115
BEVERAGES
    Canadian Coffee   157
    Champagne Punch   156
    Indian Beverage   115
    Mulled Burgundy Wine   190
    Rum Punch   156
    Spirited Coffee   191
Blueberry Pancakes   110
Blue Cheese Dressing   54
Boiled Beef Brisket   179
Boston Lettuce, with Thousand Island Dressing   60
Bouillabaisse Port-Cartier Style   35
Bread and Butter Pudding   61
Broccoli alla Romana   123
Brome Lake Duck   27
Buffalo — **See** GAME
Butter Tarts   38

Cabbage — **See** VEGETABLES
Cabbage Salad   71
Caesar Salad   32
CAKES
    Christmas   180
    Cointreau Marble   202
    Gingerbread   80
    Orange Bread   207
    Walnut Apple   80
Calf Liver and Bananas   172
Calgary Stampede Chili   71
Canadian Coffee   157
CANDY
    Honey Candy   77

Nut Brittle   210
Tia Maria Chocolate Treats   203
Cantaloup and Spanish Melon Flambé   204
Caramel Custard   206
Carbonnade of Beef   189
Carp — **See** FISH
CASSEROLES
    Baked Beans, French Canadian Style   26
    Chicken   182
    Ham   31
    Moussaka   134
Champagne Punch   156
Charcoal Porterhouse Steaks   165
Cheese Cake with Pastry   63
Cheese Crêpes   199
Cheese Fondue   155
Cheese Tarts   152
Cherries Jubilee   155
Cherry Flan   202
Cherry Tomato and Egg Canapés   150
Chicken — **See** POULTRY
Chicken and Oyster Pot Pie   51
Chicken Casserole   182
Chicken Curry Crêpe   149
Chicken Liver Pâté   53
Chicken Pie Niçoise   123
Chicken Salad   151
Chili, Après-ski   183
Chili Burgers   164
Chili, Calgary Stampede   71
Chili Dip   139
Chinese Cabbage, Braised   127
Chocolate Fondue   153
Chocolate Mousse   61
Chocolate Squares   197
Christmas Cake   180
Clam and Spinach Canapés   157
Clam Chowder   52
Club Steaks with Gherkin Sauce   81
Cod — **See** FISH
Cod Tongue Delight   36
Coho Salmon, Baked   92
Cointreau Marble Cake   202
COOKIES AND SQUARES
    Almond Cookies   78
    Chocolate Squares   197
    Date Squares   197
    Doris Biscuits   203
    Orange Biscuits   210
    Traditional Sugar Cookies   79
Coquille St-Jacques, Maritime Style   99
Corn Oysters   46
Crab and Rice Salad   144
Crab with Wood Sorrel   110
Crabmeat Coquille   91
Cranberry Sauce   59
Cream of Pumpkin Soup   51
Cream of Shrimp   100
CRÊPES
    Cheese   199
    Chicken Curry   149
    Crêpe Batter   151
    Crêpe Loaf   67
    Ham and Mushroom   150
    Normande   131

Suzette   195
    with Bananas   195
Cumberland Sauce   54
Curried Apple and Potato Soup   141
Curried Lobster   143

Dango Meatballs   138
Date Squares   197
Deluxe Hamburger   173
Deluxe Italian Cheeseburgers   165
DESSERTS — **See also** CAKES, COOKIES and SQUARES, CRÊPES, PIES
    Apple Sauce   56
    Apple Sauce Dessert   115
    Baked Alaska   156
    Baked Apples in White Wine   210
    Barbecued Apple Surprise   172
    Bread and Butter Pudding   61
    Cantaloup and Spanish Melon Flambé   204
    Caramel Custard   206
    Cheese Cake with Pastry   63
    Cherries Jubilee   155
    Cherry Flan   202
    Chocolate Fondue   153
    Chocolate Mousse   61
    English Cream à la Moderne   206
    English Pudding   179
    English Trifle   198
    Frozen Eggnog   199
    Lemon Soufflé   204
    Omelet Soufflé   198
    Orange Surprise   211
    Paris-Brest   196
    Pastry Cream   197
    Pumpkin with Maple Syrup   110
    Saskatoon Berry Torte   77
    Strawberries Romanoff   129
    Strawberry Cheesecake   195
Devil Sauce   95
Doris Biscuits   203
Doughnuts, Delicious   39
Duck — **See** POULTRY
Duck, Wild — **See** GAME
Duckling Breast with Green Peppercorn Sauce   187
Dungeness Crab Salad   97

Egg Sauce   93
Eggs Surprise   87
Eggplant and Zucchini, Baked   134
Eggplant Salad   135
English Cream à la Moderne   206
English Pudding   179
English Trifle   198

Famous Scotch Broth   45
Famous Western Chuck Stew   68
Fiddlehead Soup   30
Filet Mignon with Liver Pâté   139

FISH
    Carp
        Braised in Beer   92
        Poached   102
    Char, Grilled Arctic   43
    Cod
        Baked   38
        Cod Tongue Delight   36
        Filet Platter   86
        Pacific Cod Fish with Anchovies   96
        Poached Pacific Cod with Egg Sauce   93
        Salted Boiled Codfish with Egg Sauce   46
    Haddock Filets Flamande   102
    Halibut
        Broiled Halibut Steak   36
        Broiled Halibut Steak with Oysters and Mussels   35
        Pacific Halibut with Garlic Sauce   87
    Mackerel
        Filet, Sautéed with Peppers   100
        Filets Rosalie   104
        Sautéed Filet, with Gooseberries   102
    Perch Filets Stuffed with Shrimp and Clams   94
    Pike
        Baked Stuffed   50
        Filets Bordelaise   98
        Mousse   85
        Stuffed   70
    Red Mullet, Devil Sauce   95
    Red Snapper, Barbecued   171
    Rockfish, Silvergrey, Deep Fried Filets   93
    Salmon
        Baked Coho   92
        Gaspé   36
        Paupiettes of Salmon Stuffed with Pike Mousse   105
        Poached Salmon Steaks   94
        Poached, with Fine Herbs   101
        Salmon Steaks Broiled over Coals   116
        Spicy Grilled Salmon Steaks   172
    Shad
        Filets Florentine   105
        Filets Maître d'Hotel   93
    Skate with Capers   85
    Smelts, Deep Fried Ontario   44
    Sole
        Filets with Garlic and Tequila Carrots   123
        Lemon   100
        Terrine of Sole   50
    Trout
        à l'Estrie   38
        Broiled   104
        Fried   109
        Grilled, with Fennel   170

Stuffed Sea Trout   95
Whiting, Broiled   45
French-Canadian
    Crêtons   27
Fricassée, Grandmother
    Style   29
Frog's Legs à l'ail   90
Frozen Eggnog   199

GAME
    Buffalo
        Baked Buffalo
            Steak   77
        Ribs   76
    Duck, Wild Stuffed   111
    Goose, Roast Wild   116
    Moose
        and Fish Stew   116
        Shoulder Roast   115
        Steak   116
    Pheasant, Roast   191
    Quail
        with Grapes   181
        with Vegetables and
            Wine   188
    Rabbit
        (Prairie), Stew   71
        Stew   113
        with Maple Syrup   22
    Venison
        Roast   113
        Steaks   163
        Steaks with Marinated
            Onions   167
Garlic Bread with Feta
    Cheese   128
Garlic Honey Chicken   170
Gaspé Salmon   36
German Mashed
    Potatoes   140
Gingerbread   80
Goose, Wild — See GAME
Goulash, Hungarian
    Style   144
Grand-pères   23
Greek Lemon Soup   143
Green Pepper Rings   153
Green Salad with Mustard
    Vinaigrette   163

Haddock Filets
    Flamande   102
Halibut — See FISH
Ham — See MEAT — Pork
Ham and Mushroom
    Crêpes   150
Ham Casserole   31
Hambourg Steak   142
Hawaiian Curried
    Chicken   133
Hollandaise Sauce   86
Honey Candies   77
Hors d'oeuvres — See LIGHT
    PARTY FOODS
Horseradish Sauce   56
Horseradish Sauce   166

Indian Beverage   115
Indian Seafood, Modern
    Style   109

Japanese Mayonnaise   132
Japanese Yakitori
    Chicken   130

Kartoshnich (Potato
    Cake)   69
Ketchup, French Style   23
Kulich   75

Lac St. Jean Tourtière   34
Lamb — See MEAT

Lamb and White Bean
    Stew   76
Lamb Kebabs   171
Leek Soup au Gratin   187
Leeks Vinaigrette   20
Lemon Chiffon Pie   63
Lemon Meringue Pie   206
Lemon Pie   39
Lemon Sole   100
Lemon Soufflé   204
LIGHT PARTY FOODS
    Avocado Dip   157
    Cheese Fondue   155
    Cheese Tarts   152
    Cherry Tomato and Egg
        Canapés   150
    Chicken Liver Pâté   53
    Chili Dip   139
    Clam and Spinach
        Canapés   157
    Cocktail Meat Balls   154
    Crabmeat Coquille   91
    Green Pepper Rings   153
    Liver Pâté Puffs   151
        Pâté   21
    Saturna Island Shrimp
        Pâté   102
    Shrimp Stuffed Eggs   85
    Stuffed Mushroom
        Caps   150
Linguine à la Carbonara   138
Liver Pâté Puffs   151
Lobster — See SHELLFISH
London Broil with Horseradish
    Sauce   166

Macaroni Salad   149
Mackerel — See FISH
Manitoba Borsch   78
Maple-Glazed Baked
    Ham   23
Maple Syrup Pie   38
Marinated Lamb Shish
    Kebabs   167
MEAT — See also
CASSEROLES, MEAT
PIES, STEWS
    Beef
        à la mode   26
        B.B.Q. Short Loin
            Ribs   171
        Boiled Brisket   179
        Bourguignon   33
        Calf Liver and
            Bananas   172
        Carbonnade of
            Beef   189
        Chili Burgers   164
        Deluxe Hamburger   173
        Deluxe Italian
            Cheeseburgers   165
        Filet Mignon with Liver
            Pâté   139
        Fricassée, Grandmother
            Style   29
        London Broil with
            Horseradish
                Sauce   166
        Meatballs
            à la
                Bourguignonne   183
            Dango   138
        New York Cut
            Tyrolienne   186
        Roast
            Alberta Rib   81
            Beef, Horseradish
                Sauce   56
            Pot   19
            Pot   45
            Pot   69

Sour
    Schmurrbraten   130
Steak
    Barbecued   170
    Barbecued T-Bone,
        Western Style   70
    Charcoal
        Porterhouse   165
    Club, with Gherkin
        Sauce   81
    Hambourg   142
    Pepper, with
        Brandy   165
    Tartare   140
    Stewed with Apples   45
Veal
    Italienne   129
    Marengo   19
    Scallopini
        Marsala   141
Lamb
    Kebabs   171
    Marinated Shish
        Kebabs   167
    Roast Leg of Lamb with
        Garlic   32
    Roast Leg of Lamb with
        Rosemary   74
Pork
    alla Oneglia   134
    B.B.Q. Chops with Orange
        Sauce   163
    Chops, Braised, with
        Apples   33
    French Canadian
        Crêtons   27
    Ham
        Baked, with
            Cumberland
                Sauce   54
        Braised, with Madeira
            Wine   179
        Casserole   31
        Maple-Glazed
            Baked   23
        Roast Loin   43
        Sweet and Sour   144
    Tenderloin Barbecued
        Style   164
    Tenderloin à l'orange   190
    Ukrainian Braised   76
    Vietnamese   128
Meat and Cucumber
    Soup   74
Meatball Soup   127
Meatballs à la
    Bourguignonne   183
Meat Broth, Ukrainian
    Style   79
MEAT PIES
    Chicken and Oyster Pot
        Pie   51
    Chicken Pie Niçoise   123
    Lac St. Jean Tourtière   34
    Meat Pie   20
    Steak and Kidney Pie   52
Mexican Fruit Salad   127
Montreal Bouillabaisse   126
Montreal Vegetable Soup   29
Moose — See GAME
Mornay Sauce   90
Moussaka   134
Mulled Burgundy Wine   190
Mussels — See SHELLFISH
Mustard Vinaigrette   144
Mustard Vinaigrette   163

Nantua Sauce   92
New York Cut
    Tyrolienne   186
Nut Brittle   210

Omelet Souffle   198
Onion Soup au Gratin   30
Open Shrimp Sandwich   154
Orange Biscuits   210
Orange Bread Cake   207
Orange Surprise   211
Oxtail Soup   61
Oysters — See SHELLFISH

Pacific Cod, Poached, with Egg
    Sauce   93
Pacific Cod Fish with
    Anchovies   96
Pacific Halibut with Garlic
    Sauce   87
Pancakes, Blueberry   110
Pancakes, Potato   138
Paris-Brest   196
PASTA
    Linguine à la
        Carbonara   138
    Spaghetti with Shrimp
        Sauce   188
    Stuffed Cannelloni for
        Four   181
Pastry Cream   197
Pastry Dough for Quiche and
    Pie   53
Pâté — See LIGHT PARTY
    FOODS
Paupiettes of Salmon Stuffed
    with Pike Mousse   105
Pea Soup   29
Pepper Salad   130
Pepper Steak with
    Brandy   165
Perch Filets Stuffed with Shrimp
    and Clams   94
Pheasant — See GAME
Pickelsteiner Stew   142
PIES AND TARTS
    Alsatian Tart   202
    Apple   63
    Butter Tarts   38
    Lemon   39
    Lemon Chiffon   63
    Lemon Meringue   206
    Maple Syrup   38
    Pastry Dough For Quiche
        and Pie   53
    Pineapple Tart   199
    Saskatoon Berry   74
    Strawberry and Yogurt
        Tartlets   210
Pies, Meat — See MEAT PIES
Pike — See FISH
Pineapple Tart   199
Poached Chicken Breast   60
Pork — See MEAT
Pot Roasts — See MEAT —
    Beef
Potato Cake   69
Potato Pancakes   138
Potato Salad   26
Potato Soup   114
Potatoes — See VEGETABLES
Potted Shrimp   47
POULTRY
    Chicken
        au Gratin   133
        Fricassée   57
        Garlic Honey   170
        Hawaiian Curried   133
        Japanese Yakitori   130
        on Skewers   167
        Poached Breast   60
        Poached in White
            Wine   182
        Sauté, European
            Style   79
        Sautéed in Red
            Wine   34

Sweet Chicken Legs 19
Wings 152
with Sour Cream 78
with Sweet Pepper 58
Zesty B.B.Q.
Wings 165
Duck
Brome Lake 27
Duckling Breast with
Green Peppercorn
Sauce 187
Roast, with Apples 68
Roast, with Honey 62
Rock Cornish Hens, Garden
Style 180
Turkey
Breast, with Mushroom
Stuffing 190
Roast 186
Roast, Stuffed, with
Cranberry Sauce 59
Vol-au-vent 154
Prairie Rabbit Stew 71
Puff Dough 154
Pumpkin with Maple
Syrup 110

Quail with Grapes 181
Quails with Vegetables and
Wine 188
Quiche and Pie, Pastry Dough
for 53
Quiche, Bacon and Corn 53
Quiche Lorraine 125

Rabbit — See GAME
Ragoût de Boulettes 34
Raspberry Jam 19
Ratatouille 139
Red Mullet, Devil Sauce 95
Rice Croquettes 46
Roasts — See MEAT
Rock Cornish Hens, Garden
Style 180
Rockfish, Deep-Fried Silvergrey
Filets 93
Romaine Salad, with Blue
Cheese Dressing 54
Roquefort Salad 31
Rum Custard Cream 204
Rum Punch 156
Rum Sauce 204

St. Basil's Bread 67
SALADS
Avocado 188
Boston Lettuce, with
Thousand Island
Dressing 60
Cabbage 71
Caesar 32
Chicken 151
Crab and Rice 144
Dungeness Crab 97
Eggplant 135
Green, with Mustard
Vinaigrette 163
Macaroni 149
Mexican Fruit 127
Pepper 130
Potato 26
Romaine, with Blue Cheese
Dressing 54
Roquefort 31
Shrimp and
Mushroom 85
Spinach 54
Super Chef's 124
Ukrainian 81

SALAD DRESSINGS
Blue Cheese 54
Leeks Vinaigrette 20
Mustard Vinaigrette 144
Mustard Vinaigrette 163
Sour Cream 124
Thousand Island 60
Tomato 188
Salmon — See FISH
Salted Boiled Codfish with Egg
Sauce 46
Saskatoon Berry Pie 74
Saskatoon Berry Torte 77
Saturna Island Shrimp
Pâté 102
SAUCES
Savoury
Cumberland 54
Devil 95
Egg 93
Hollandaise 86
Horseradish 56
Horseradish 166
Japanese
Mayonnaise 132
Mornay 90
Nantua 92
Sweet and Sour
Barbecue 164
Tartar Sauce 93
Tempura 132
Turkey Gravy 186
White Fish 92
Sweet
Apple 56
Berry 109
Cranberry 59
Rum 204
Rum Custard
Cream 204
Sauerkraut Garnie 132
Sauté Chicken, European
Style 79
Savoury Bannock 112
Scalloped Potatoes 53
Scalloped Tomatoes 59
Scallopini Marsala 141
Seasoned Potatoes with
Cream 77
Shad — See FISH
SHELLFISH — See also
CRÊPES, LIGHT PARTY
FOODS, SALADS, SOUPS
Clams, Stuffed 97
Coquille St-Jacques,
Maritime Style 99
Crab
Crabmeat Coquille 91
Stuffed Dungeness 90
with Wood Sorrel 110
Indian Seafood, Modern
Style 109
Lobster
Boiled Live 96
Broiled 36
Cheese Sauce 101
Curried 143
Flambéed 99
Pekin 129
Mussels
Huron Style 113
Marinière 87
with Tomatoes 37
Oysters
Broiled 47
Florentine 90
Stewed 50
Shrimp
Cream of 100

in Black Bean
Sauce 124
Marinara 125
Newburg 98
Open Shrimp
Sandwich 154
Potted 47
Sweet and Sour 131
Tempura Fried 132
Teriyaki Style 153
Shrimp — See SHELLFISH
Shrimp and Mushroom
Salad 85
Shrimp Stuffed Eggs 85
Skate with Capers 85
Smelts, Deep Fried
Ontario 44
Snails à la Chablisienne 141
Sole Filets with Garlic and
Tequila Carrots 123
Soufflé Czecho-Slovak
Style 69
SOUPS
Apple and Celery 125
Beef and Barley 27
Berry 115
Bouillabaisse Port-Cartier
Style 35
Clam Chowder 52
Clam Chowder, B.C. 94
Cream of Pumpkin 51
Curried Apple and
Potato 141
Famous Scotch Broth 45
Fiddlehead 30
Greek Lemon 143
Leek, Au Gratin 187
Manitoba Borsch 78
Meat and Cucumber 74
Meat Broth, Ukrainian
Style 79
Meatball 127
Montreal Bouillabaisse 126
Montreal Vegetable 29
Onion, au Gratin 30
Oxtail 61
Pea 29
Potato 114
Squash 112
Tomato 31
Tomato and Dill 44
Sour Cream Dressing 124
Sour Schmurrbraten 130
Spaghetti with Shrimp
Sauce 188
Spinach Salad 54
Spirited Coffee 191
Squash Soup 112
Steak — See MEAT
Steak and Kidney Pie 52
Stewed Oysters 50
STEWS
Famous Western
Chuck 68
Goulash, Hungarian
Style 144
Huron Style 114
Lamb and White Bean 76
Moose and Fish 116
Pickelsteiner 142
Prairie Rabbit 71
Rabbit 113
Ragoût de Boulettes 34
Strawberries Romanoff 129
Strawberry and Yogurt
Tartlets 210
Strawberry Cheesecake 195
Stuffed Cannelloni for
Four 181

Stuffed Clams 97
Stuffed Dungeness Crab 90
Stuffed Mushroom Caps 150
Stuffed Pike 70
Stuffed Sea Trout 95
Succotash 111
Super Chef's Salad 124
Sweet and Sour Barbecue
Sauce 164
Sweet and Sour Pork 144
Sweet and Sour Shrimp 131
Sweet Chicken Legs 19

Tartar Sauce 93
Tarts — See PIES
Tempura Fried Shrimp 132
Tempura Sauce 132
Terrine of Sole 50
Thousand Island
Dressing 60
Tia Maria Chocolate
Treats 203
Tomato and Dill Soup 44
Tomato Dressing 188
Tomato Soup 31
Traditional Sugar
Cookies 79
Trout — See FISH
Turkey — See POULTRY
Turkey Apple Stuffing 182
Turkey Gravy 186

Ukrainian Braised Pork 76
Ukrainian Salad 81

Veal — See MEAT — Beef
VEGETABLES — See also
SALADS, SOUPS
Bamboo Shoots in Soya
Sauce 131
Baked Beans, French
Canadian Style 26
Broccoli alla Romana 123
Cabbage
Baked 43
Braised Chinese 127
Corn Oysters 46
Eggplant and Zucchini,
Baked 134
Potatoes
German Mashed 140
in Foil 170
Kartoshnich (Potato
Cake) 69
Pancakes 138
Scalloped 53
Seasoned, with
Cream 77
Ratatouille 139
Sauerkraut Garnie 132
Squash, Baked Acorn 46
Succotash 111
Tomatoes, Scalloped 59
Venison — See GAME
Vietnamese Pork 128

Walnut Apple Cake 80
White Fish Sauce 92
Whiting, Broiled 45
Wild Stuffed Duck 111
Wild Rice 109
Wild Rice with Tomatoes 111
Wild Rice with
Vegetables 68

Yorkshire Pudding 59

Zesty B.B.Q. Chicken
Wings 165

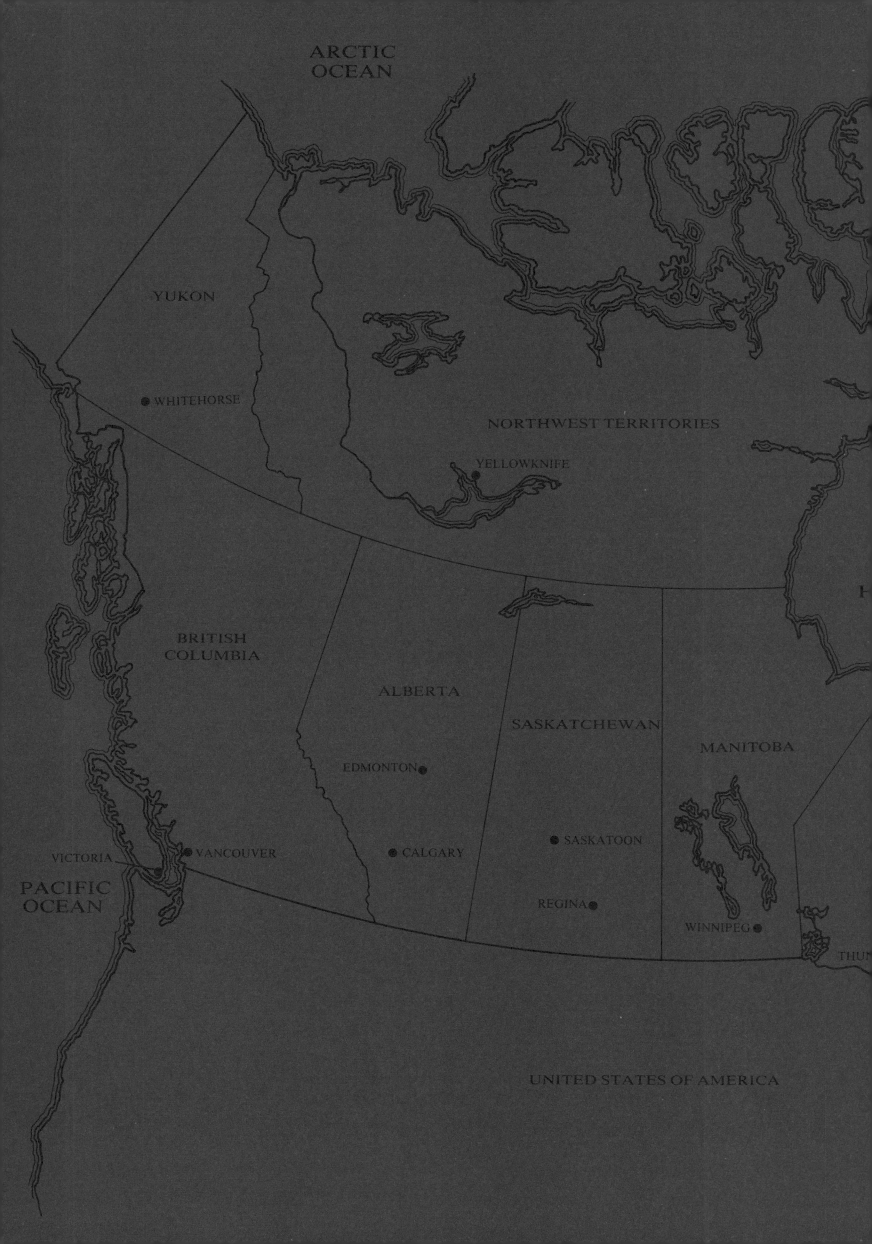